# Test for Motorcyclists

# Theory Test for Motorcyclists

## The **official revision questions** and **answers** for **learner riders**

Published by AA Publishing (a trading name of AA Media Limited, whose registered office is Fanum House, Basing View, Basingstoke, Hampshire RG21 4EA; registered number 06112600).

ISBN: 978-0-7495-7123-8

Visit AA Publishing at theAA.com/shop

Colour separation by Wellcom, London
Printed and bound by Leo Paper Products, China

Cover images
Front cover: © fckncg/Alamy
Back cover: © Oleksiy Maksymenko/Alamy

A04714

# Contents

# Learning to Ride

You want to pass your bike test and take advantage of the freedom and mobility that riding a motorcycle can give you. The following three things will help you achieve your goal – getting your licence.

- Acquire knowledge of the rules through your instructor and by carefully studying The Highway Code. A key element is to test and reinforce your knowledge.
- Take the right attitude. Be careful, courteous and considerate to all other road users.
- Learn and understand the skills of riding a motorcycle by taking lessons from a fully qualified motorcycle instructor.

This book has been designed to help you become a careful and safe motorcycle rider and take the first step towards achieving your goal – preparing for your Theory Test.

## Six essential steps to getting your motorcycle licence

### 1 Get your provisional licence

If you haven't got a driving licence already, you will need a provisional licence to undertake motorcycle-riding instruction and ride on the road. You can apply for a provisional licence by post by using application forms D1 available from the Post Office. The provisional licence is issued in the form of a two-part document: a photo card and paper counterpart. To legally begin learning to ride, at the appropriate date, you must be in possession of the correct licence documents. Take care when completing all the forms. Many licences cannot be issued for the required date because of errors or omissions on the application forms. You will have to provide proof of identity such as a UK passport; make sure you have all the documents needed. You can also apply for your provisional licence online at www.direct.gov.uk/motoring. For more information about applying for a provisional licence contact the Driver Vehicle Licensing Agency (DVLA).

**Post:** Drivers Customer Services (DCS) Correspondence Team, DVLA, Longview Road, Swansea SA6 7JL
**Tel:** 0870 240 0009
**Minicom:** 01792 782 787
**Fax:** 01792 783 071
**Online:** www.direct.gov.uk/motoring

### 2 Learn The Highway Code

The Highway Code is essential reading for all road users not just those learning to ride. It sets out all the rules for safe motorcycle riding, as well as the rules for other road users such as car drivers and pedestrians. When you have learned the rules you will be able to answer most of the questions in the Theory Test.

### 3 Take the Theory Test

The motorcycle test is in four parts: Compulsory Basic Training (CBT), the Theory Test (multiple-choice questions, case studies and hazard perception clips) and the Practical Tests (Module 1 Off Road and Module 2 On Road). Once you have a valid provisional or driving licence you may take your CBT and Theory Test at any time, but you must pass both tests before you are allowed to apply for Module 1 of the Practical Test. Once you have passed this test you can apply to take Module 2 of the Practical Test.

You can book your Theory Test by post, telephone or online. To book your test you will need your provisional licence number and a credit or debit card. You will be given a test date immediately. To book your test by post you will need to fill in an application form, available from Theory Test centres or your motorcycle instructor or by calling the booking number below. Forms need to be sent to the address on the application form with a cheque, postal order, credit or debit card details. You should receive a test date within 10 days.

Tel: 0300 200 1122
Welsh speakers: 0300 200 1133
Minicom: 0300 200 1166
Fax: 0300 200 1177
Online: www.direct.gov.uk/theorytest

**Useful Tip**
The majority of training schools require that you pass the Theory Test prior to taking practical training.

**Don't forget**
You'll need to take the following original documents with you to the Theory Test centre or you won't be allowed to take your Theory Test and will lose your exam fee.
**You will need either your**
• signed photo card licence and paper counterpart or
• signed provisional licence and passport

## 4 Compulsory Basic Training (CBT)

You cannot take your Practical Test until you have completed your Compulsory Basic Training (CBT). You can only use a training centre that has been approved by the Driving Standards Agency (DSA). Find approved CBT courses in your local area by contacting the DSA (www.direct.gov.uk/motoring), your local Road Safety Officer or motorcycle dealer.

CBT is a one-day training course that includes classroom and riding skills. The CBT, once successfully completed, provides the rider with a Certificate. This is valid for two years and in conjunction with the provisional motorcycle licence entitles the rider to ride up to a 125cc machine (50cc for 16 year olds) with 'L' plates. The rider, however, cannot carry a pillion passenger or use motorways.

## 5 Take the Practical Test

Once you have passed CBT and the Theory Test, and with your instructor's guidance based on your progress, you can plan ahead for a suitable test date for Module 1 and then Module 2 of the Practical Test.

The majority of motorcycle riders learn the necessary riding skills quite quickly and most training courses are between 3 to 5 days, depending on the rider's ability. Ensure the full official syllabus is covered and, as your skills develop, get as much practice as possible. (See page 8 or visit www.direct.gov.uk/motoring for minimum test vehicle requirements to make sure that you take your Practical Test [Modules 1 and 2] on the size of motorcycle that you intend to ride.)

You can book your Practical Test online or by phone at any time between 8am and 6pm Monday to Friday. You can pay for your test using a credit or debit card (the person who books the test must be the cardholder). If you need to, you can change your Practical Test appointment by phone or online.

**Tel:** 0300 200 1122
**Welsh speakers:** 0300 200 1133
**Minicom:** 0300 200 1144
**Online:** www.direct.gov.uk/motoring

Make sure you have the following details to hand when booking your Practical Test:
- Theory Test pass certificate number
- driver number shown on your licence
- your preferred date
- unacceptable days or periods
- if you can accept a test at short notice
- disability or any special circumstances
- your credit/debit card details.

## 6 Apply for your full driver's licence

After you have passed your Practical Test your examiner will send your provisional or driving licence and test certificate to the DVLA and you will receive your licence by post within four weeks of passing Module 2 of your Practical Test. When you receive your licence, it is important that you check that the correct motorcycle category has been added on the reverse of your photo card licence.

Once you have taken and passed your Practical Test, you will receive one of four types of licence, depending on your age and the size of motorcycle that you used for your Practical Test (Modules 1 and 2).

**Category P (minimum age 16)**
This category is for mopeds with an engine size of up to 50cc and a maximum speed of up to 50km per hour.

**Category A1 (age 17 and over)**
If you pass the Practical Test on a category A1 'light motorcycle' (75–125cc), you can ride a motorcycle up to 125cc with a maximum output of 14.6bhp without 'L' plates.

**Category A – Standard Motorcycle**
If you are under the age of 21, then the largest size motorcycle you can take your test on is a 125cc. If you pass the Practical Test on a category A 'standard motorcycle' (121–125cc), you can ride any motorcycle but the power output must be restricted to a maximum output of 33.3bhp. After two years the restriction is automatically lifted and you can ride any motorcycle with any power output.

**Category A – Larger Motorcycle**
If you are over 21, you can train and take your Practical Test on a larger motorcycle, usually 500–650cc (power output minimum of 46.6bhp), and have a full licence for any motorcycle.

# About the
# Theory Test

# Revising for the Theory Test

The Theory Test is all about making you a safer rider and it is a good idea to prepare for the Theory Test at the same time as you develop your skills on the road. By preparing for both the Theory and Practical tests at the same time, you will reinforce your knowledge and understanding of all aspects of riding and improve your chances of passing both tests first time.

## How to use this book

This book is designed to help you prepare for the multiple-choice questions part of the Theory Test and contains all the official revision questions from the DSA. From January 2012 the test will consist of 50 unseen Theory Test questions based on the topics shown here (see pages 18–228). The real test questions will no longer be published and so this book will help you revise for the test.

To help you study for the test, the questions are arranged into the Theory Test topics, such as Safety Margins and Hazard Awareness. Each topic has its own colour band to help you find your way through the book.

Start your revision by picking a topic; you don't have to study the topics in order. Study each question carefully to make sure you understand what it is asking you and how many answers you need to mark. Look carefully at any diagram or photograph before reading the explanatory information and deciding on your answer(s).

All the correct answers are given in the back of this book (see pages 236–240). You'll also find a short glossary near the back of this book (pages 229–235), which explains some of the more difficult words and terms used in the Theory Test.

## Remember

- Learning the Highway Code and getting some on-road riding experience are the best way to prepare for your Theory Test.
- Don't attempt too many questions at once.
- Don't try to learn the questions and answers by heart; the real test questions are not available for you to practice and are different from the revision questions given in this book.

Questions marked **NI** are **not** found in Theory Tests in Northern Ireland.

**1** Each question tells you how many boxes to tick to answer the question.

**29** Mark *three* answers
**As you approach this bridge you should**

**3** Look carefully at any photograph, symbol or diagram given within the question.

☐ **A** move into the middle of the road to get a better view
☐ **B** slow down
☐ **C** get over the bridge as quickly as possible
☐ **D** consider using your horn
☐ **E** find another route
☐ **F** beware of pedestrians

**2** Read through all the possible answers.

This sign gives you a warning. The brow of the hill prevents you seeing oncoming traffic so you must be cautious. The bridge is narrow and there may not be enough room for you to pass an oncoming vehicle at this point. There is no footpath, so pedestrians may be walking in the road. Consider the hidden hazards and be ready to react if necessary.

**4** Each question is accompanied by an explanation that will help you understand the theory behind the question and what answer may be appropriate. Make sure you read through this text before answering the question. Please note that this text will not appear in your live Theory Test.

# What to Expect in the Theory Test

The Theory Test consists of two parts: 50 multiple-choice questions and hazard perception. You have to pass both parts in order to pass your Theory Test. You will receive your test scores at the end of the test. Even if you only failed on one part of the Theory Test, you still have to take both parts again next time.

## Multiple-choice questions

You will have 57 minutes to complete the question part of the test using a touch-screen and all the questions are multiple-choice. The 50 questions appear on the screen one at a time and you can return to any of the questions within the 57 minutes to re-check or change your answers. You have to score a minimum of 43 out of 50 to pass. The Government may change the pass mark from time to time. Your driving school or the DSA will be able to tell you if there has been a change.

Each question has four, five or six possible answers. You must mark the boxes with the correct answer(s). Each question tells you how many answers to mark. Don't worry about accidentally missing marking an answer because you'll be reminded that you haven't ticked enough boxes before moving on to the next question.

Study each question carefully and look carefully at any diagram, drawing or photograph. Before you look at the answers given, decide what you think the correct answer(s) might be. Read through the options and then select the answer(s) that matches the one you had decided on. If you follow this system, you will avoid being confused by answers that appear to be similar.

You can answer the questions in any order you choose by moving forwards and backwards through the questions. You can also change your answer(s) if necessary and flag questions you're unsure about, then go back to them later in the test. Your remaining time is shown on the screen.

## Case study questions

Typically, five of the 50 questions will take the form of a case study. All five questions will be based on a single driving situation and appear one at time.

Case studies are designed to test that you not only know your car theory but also that you understand how to apply your knowledge when faced with a given driving situation.

The case study in your Theory Test could be based on any driving scenario and ask questions from a range of topics in the DSA's database of questions.

The following sample case study demonstrates how the case study questions may appear in your live test, so you'll know what to expect.

## CASE STUDY 1

You need to visit a relative in a hospital some distance from where you live. The journey will take you on various roads including both A-roads and motorways.

As you start your journey it begins to rain and continues to get heavier as you ride.

You have not ridden to the hospital before but you have planned your route before leaving and feel confident about the journey.

1. You are following a vehicle on a wet road. You should leave a time gap of at least

**Mark one answer**

☐ one second

☐ two seconds

☐ three seconds

☐ four seconds

Back   Flag   Review   Next

---

## CASE STUDY 1

You need to visit a relative in a hospital some distance from where you live. The journey will take you on various roads including both A-roads and motorways.

As you start your journey it begins to rain and continues to get heavier as you ride.

You have not ridden to the hospital before but you have planned your route before leaving and feel confident about the journey.

2. What does this sign mean?

**Mark one answer**

☐ you have priority

☐ no motor vehicles

☐ two-way traffic

☐ no overtaking

Back   Flag   Review   Next

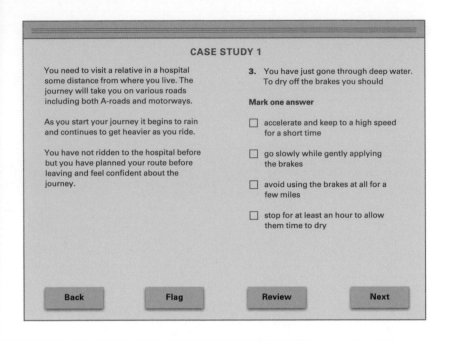

**CASE STUDY 1**

You need to visit a relative in a hospital some distance from where you live. The journey will take you on various roads including both A-roads and motorways.

As you start your journey it begins to rain and continues to get heavier as you ride.

You have not ridden to the hospital before but you have planned your route before leaving and feel confident about the journey.

**3.** You have just gone through deep water. To dry off the brakes you should

**Mark one answer**

☐ accelerate and keep to a high speed for a short time

☐ go slowly while gently applying the brakes

☐ avoid using the brakes at all for a few miles

☐ stop for at least an hour to allow them time to dry

Back    Flag    Review    Next

**CASE STUDY 1**

You need to visit a relative in a hospital some distance from where you live. The journey will take you on various roads including both A-roads and motorways.

As you start your journey it begins to rain and continues to get heavier as you ride.

You have not ridden to the hospital before but you have planned your route before leaving and feel confident about the journey.

**4.** A bus has stopped at a bus stop ahead of you. Its right-hand indicator is flashing. You should

**Mark one answer**

☐ flash your headlights and slow down

☐ slow down and give way if it is safe to do so

☐ sound your horn and keep going

☐ slow down and then sound your horn

Back    Flag    Review    Next

### CASE STUDY 1

You need to visit a relative in a hospital some distance from where you live. The journey will take you on various roads including both A-roads and motorways.

As you start your journey it begins to rain and continues to get heavier as you ride.

You have not ridden to the hospital before but you have planned your route before leaving and feel confident about the journey.

5. Where you see street lights but no speed limit signs the limit is usually

**Mark one answer**

☐ 30mph

☐ 40mph

☐ 50mph

☐ 60mph

| Back | Flag | Review | Next |

**Answers to sample case study questions: 1 D  2 D  3 B  4 B  5 A**

## Hazard perception

The video clips element of the Theory Test is known as hazard perception. Its aim is to find out how good you are at noticing hazards developing on the road ahead. The test will also show how much you know about the risks to you as a rider and the risks to other road users.

Who do you think have the most accidents – new or experienced riders? New riders have just been trained, so they should remember how to ride safely, but in fact they have the most accidents.

Proper training can help you to recognize more of the hazards that you will meet when riding and to spot those hazards earlier, so you are less likely to have an accident.

## What is a hazard?

A hazard is anything that might cause you to change speed or direction when riding. The hazard perception element of the Theory Test is about spotting developing hazards. This is one of the key skills of good riding and is also called anticipation. Anticipating hazards, such as car doors opening or children running into the road, means looking out for them in advance and taking the appropriate action.

As you get more experience you will start to learn about the times and places where you are most likely to meet hazards. An example of this is the rush hour. You know people take more risks when they are in a hurry. So you have to be prepared for bad driving.

You won't be able to practise with the real video clips used in the test, of course, but books and practice videos are available.

## What to expect in the hazard perception test

After answering the multiple-choice questions, you will be given a short break before you begin the hazard perception part of the test. The hazard perception test lasts for about 20 minutes. Before you start you will be given some instructions explaining how the test works; you'll also get a chance to practise with the computer and mouse before you start. This is to make sure that you know what to expect on the test and that you know what you have to do.

Next you will see 14 film clips of real street scenes with traffic such as cars, pedestrians, cyclists, etc. The scenes are shot from the point of view of a rider. You have to notice potential hazards that are developing on the road ahead – that is, problems that could lead to an incident. As soon as you notice a hazard developing, click the mouse. You will have plenty of time to see the hazard – but the sooner you notice it, the more marks you score.

Each clip has at least one hazard in it – some clips may have more than one hazard. You have to score a minimum of 44 out of 75 to pass, but the pass mark may change so check with your instructor or the DSA before sitting your test.

## Further information

For more practical information on learning to ride including CBT, the Theory and Practical tests visit www.direct.gov.uk/motoring.

Note that the computer has checks built in to show anyone trying to cheat – for example someone who keeps clicking the mouse all the time. Be aware that, unlike the Theory Test questions, you will not have an opportunity to go back to an earlier clip and change your response, so you need to concentrate throughout the test.

*Above: Click the mouse when you spot potential hazards – the pedestrian crossing the side road and the cyclist approaching a parked vehicle (ringed in yellow). Click again as the hazard develops when the cyclist (ringed in red) moves out to overtake the parked vehicle.*

# Theory Test Revision Questions

**1** Mark *one* answer

**You are about to turn right. What should you do just before you turn?**

☐ **A** Give the correct signal
☐ **B** Take a 'lifesaver' glance over your shoulder
☐ **C** Select the correct gear
☐ **D** Get in position ready for the turn

When you are turning right, plan your approach to the junction. Signal and select the correct gear in good time. Just before you turn, take a 'lifesaver' glance for a final check behind and to the side of you.

**2** Mark *one* answer

**What is the 'lifesaver' when riding a motorcycle?**

☐ **A** A certificate every motorcyclist must have
☐ **B** A final, rearward glance before changing direction
☐ **C** A part of the motorcycle tool kit
☐ **D** A mirror fitted to check blind spots

This action makes you aware of what's happening behind and alongside you. The 'lifesaver' glance should be timed so that you still have time to react if it isn't safe to perform the manoeuvre.

**3** Mark *one* answer

**You see road signs showing a sharp bend ahead. What should you do?**

☐ **A** Continue at the same speed
☐ **B** Slow down as you go around the bend
☐ **C** Slow down as you come out of the bend
☐ **D** Slow down before the bend

Always look for any advance warning of hazards, such as road signs and hazard warning lines. Use this information to plan ahead and to help you avoid the need for late, harsh braking. Your motorcycle should be upright and moving in a straight line when you brake. This will help you to keep maximum control when dealing with the hazard.

**4** Mark *one* answer

**You are riding at night and are dazzled by the headlights of an oncoming car. You should**

☐ **A** slow down or stop
☐ **B** close your eyes
☐ **C** flash your headlight
☐ **D** turn your head away

If you are dazzled by lights when riding, slow down or stop until your eyes have adjusted. Taking a hand off the handlebars to adjust your visor while riding could lead to loss of control. A dirty or scratched visor could cause dazzle and impair vision further.

**5** Mark *one* answer

**When riding, your shoulders obstruct the view in your mirrors. To overcome this you should**

☐ **A** indicate earlier than normal
☐ **B** fit smaller mirrors
☐ **C** extend the mirror arms
☐ **D** brake earlier than normal

It's essential that you have a clear view all around. Adjust your mirrors to give you the best view of the road behind. If your elbows obscure the view try fitting mirrors with longer stems.

**6** Mark *one* answer

**On a motorcycle you should only use a mobile telephone when you**

☐ **A** have a pillion passenger to help
☐ **B** have parked in a safe place
☐ **C** have a motorcycle with automatic gears
☐ **D** are travelling on a quiet road

It's important that you're in full control at all times. Even using a hands-free kit can distract your attention from the road. Don't take the risk. If you need to use a mobile phone stop at a safe and convenient place.

**7** Mark *one* answer

**You are riding at night. You have your headlight on main beam. Another vehicle is overtaking you. When should you dip your headlight?**

☐ **A** When the other vehicle signals to overtake
☐ **B** As soon as the other vehicle moves out to overtake
☐ **C** As soon as the other vehicle passes you
☐ **D** After the other vehicle pulls in front of you

At night you should dip your headlight to avoid dazzling oncoming drivers or those ahead of you. If you're being overtaken, dip your headlight as the other vehicle comes past. When you switch to dipped beam your view of the road ahead will be reduced, so look ahead for hazards on your side of the road before you do so.

**8** Mark *one* answer

**To move off safely from a parked position you should**

☐ **A** signal if other drivers will need to slow down
☐ **B** leave your motorcycle on its stand until the road is clear
☐ **C** give an arm signal as well as using your indicators
☐ **D** look over your shoulder for a final check

Before you move off from the side of the road on a motorcycle you must take a final look around over your shoulder. There may be another road user who is not visible in your mirrors.

**9** Mark *one* answer

**Riding a motorcycle when you are cold could cause you to**

☐ **A** be more alert
☐ **B** be more relaxed
☐ **C** react more quickly
☐ **D** lose concentration

It can be difficult to keep warm when riding a motorcycle. Although it isn't cheap, proper motorcycle clothing will help to keep you warm and is essential. It also helps to protect you if you fall off or are involved in a crash.

**10** Mark *one* answer

**You are riding at night and are dazzled by the lights of an approaching vehicle. What should you do?**

☐ **A** Switch off your headlight
☐ **B** Switch to main beam
☐ **C** Slow down and stop
☐ **D** Flash your headlight

If your view of the road ahead is restricted because you are being dazzled by approaching headlights, slow down and if you need to, pull over and stop.

**11** Mark *one* answer

**You should always check the 'blind areas' before**

☐ **A** moving off
☐ **B** slowing down
☐ **C** changing gear
☐ **D** giving a signal

These are the areas behind and to either side of you which are not covered by your mirrors. You should always check these areas before moving off or changing direction.

**12** Mark *one* answer

**The 'blind area' should be checked before**

☐ **A** giving a signal
☐ **B** applying the brakes
☐ **C** changing direction
☐ **D** giving an arm signal

The areas not covered by your mirrors are called blind spots. They should always be checked before changing direction. This check is so important that it is called the 'lifesaver'.

**13** Mark *one* answer

**It is vital to check the 'blind area' before**

☐ **A** changing gear
☐ **B** giving signals
☐ **C** slowing down
☐ **D** changing lanes

Other vehicles may be hidden in the blind spots that are not covered by your mirrors. Always make sure it is safe before changing lanes by taking a 'lifesaver' check.

**14** Mark *one* answer

**Why can it be helpful to have mirrors fitted on each side of your motorcycle?**

☐ **A** To judge the gap when filtering in traffic

☐ **B** To give protection when riding in poor weather

☐ **C** To make your motorcycle appear larger to other drivers

☐ **D** To give you the best view of the road behind

When riding on the road you need to know as much about following traffic as you can. A mirror fitted on each side of your motorcycle will help give you the best view of the road behind.

**15** Mark *one* answer

**In motorcycling, the term 'lifesaver' refers to**

☐ **A** a final rearward glance

☐ **B** an approved safety helmet

☐ **C** a reflective jacket

☐ **D** the two-second rule

Mirrors on motorcycles don't always give a clear view behind. There will be times when you need to look round to see the full picture.

**16** Mark *one* answer

**You are about to emerge from a junction. Your pillion passenger tells you it's clear. When should you rely on their judgement?**

☐ **A** Never, you should always look for yourself

☐ **B** When the roads are very busy

☐ **C** When the roads are very quiet

☐ **D** Only when they are a qualified rider

Your passenger may be inexperienced in judging traffic situations, have a poor view and not have seen a potential hazard. You are responsible for your own safety and your passenger. Always make your own checks to be sure it is safe to pull out.

**17** Mark *one* answer

**You are about to emerge from a junction. Your pillion passenger tells you it's safe to go. What should you do?**

☐ **A** Go, if you are sure they can see clearly

☐ **B** Check for yourself before pulling out

☐ **C** Take their advice and ride on

☐ **D** Ask them to check again before you go

You must rely on your own judgement when making decisions. Only you know your own capabilities and the performance of your machine.

**18** Mark *one* answer
**What must you do before stopping normally?**

☐ **A** Put both feet down
☐ **B** Select first gear
☐ **C** Use your mirrors
☐ **D** Move into neutral

Check your mirrors before slowing down or stopping as there could be vehicles close behind you. If necessary, look behind before stopping.

---

**19** Mark *two* answers
**You want to change lanes in busy, moving traffic. Why could looking over your shoulder help?**

☐ **A** Mirrors may not cover blind spots
☐ **B** To avoid having to give a signal
☐ **C** So traffic ahead will make room for you
☐ **D** So your balance will not be affected
☐ **E** Drivers behind you would be warned

Before changing lanes make sure there's a safe gap to move into. Looking over your shoulder allows you to check the area not covered by your mirrors, where a vehicle could be hidden from view. It also warns following drivers that you want to change lanes.

**20** Mark *one* answer
**You have been waiting for some time to make a right turn into a side road. What should you do just before you make the turn?**

☐ **A** Move close to the kerb
☐ **B** Select a higher gear
☐ **C** Make a 'lifesaver' check
☐ **D** Wave to the oncoming traffic

Remember your 'lifesaver' glance before you start to turn. If you've been waiting for some time and a queue has built up behind you, a vehicle further back may try to overtake. It is especially important to look out for other motorcycles in this situation which may be approaching at speed.

---

**21** Mark *one* answer
**You are turning right onto a dual carriageway. What should you do before emerging?**

☐ **A** Stop, and then select a very low gear
☐ **B** Position in the left gutter of the side road
☐ **C** Check that the central reservation is wide enough
☐ **D** Check there is enough room for vehicles behind you

Before emerging right onto a dual carriageway make sure that the central reservation is wide enough to protect your vehicle. If it's not, you should treat it as one road and check that it's clear in both directions before pulling out. Otherwise, you could obstruct part of the carriageway and cause a hazard, both for yourself and other road users.

**22** Mark *one* answer
**When riding a different motorcycle you should**

- ☐ **A** ask someone to ride with you for the first time
- ☐ **B** ride as soon as possible as all controls and switches are the same
- ☐ **C** leave your gloves behind so switches can be operated more easily
- ☐ **D** be sure you know where all controls and switches are

Before you ride any motorcycle make sure you're familiar with the layout of all the controls and switches. While control layouts are generally similar, there may be differences in their feel and method of operation.

**23** Mark *one* answer
**You are turning right at a large roundabout. Before you leave the roundabout you should**

- ☐ **A** take a 'lifesaver' glance over your left shoulder
- ☐ **B** give way to all traffic from the right
- ☐ **C** put on your right indicator
- ☐ **D** cancel the left indicator

You need to be aware of what's happening behind and alongside you. Looking left, just before you move across gives you time to react if it isn't safe to make the manoeuvre.

**24** Mark *one* answer
**You are turning right at a large roundabout. Before you cross a lane to reach your exit you should**

- ☐ **A** take a 'lifesaver' glance over your right shoulder
- ☐ **B** put on your right indicator
- ☐ **C** take a 'lifesaver' glance over your left shoulder
- ☐ **D** cancel the left indicator

On busy roundabouts traffic may be moving very quickly and changing lanes suddenly. You need to be aware of what's happening all around you. Before crossing lanes to the left make sure you take a 'lifesaver' glance to the left. This gives you time to react if it's not safe to make the manoeuvre.

**25** Mark *one* answer
**You are positioned to turn right on a multi-lane roundabout. What should you do before moving to a lane on your left?**

- ☐ **A** Take a 'lifesaver' glance over your right shoulder
- ☐ **B** Cancel the left signal
- ☐ **C** Signal to the right
- ☐ **D** Take a 'lifesaver' glance over your left shoulder

Beware of traffic changing lanes quickly and at the last moment on these roundabouts. Be aware of all signs and road markings so that you can position correctly in good time. Your life could depend on you knowing where other vehicles are.

## 26 Mark *one* answer

**You are turning right on a multi-lane roundabout. When should you take a 'lifesaver' glance over your left shoulder?**

☐ **A** After moving into the left lane
☐ **B** After leaving the roundabout
☐ **C** Before signalling to the right
☐ **D** Before moving into the left lane

The 'lifesaver' is essential to motorcyclists and is exactly what it says. It could save your life. It's purpose is to check the blind spot that is not covered by your mirrors. Understand and learn how and when you should use it.

## 27 Mark *one* answer

**You are on a motorway. You see an incident on the other side of the road. Your lane is clear. You should**

☐ **A** assist the emergency services
☐ **B** stop, and cross the road to help
☐ **C** concentrate on what is happening ahead
☐ **D** place a warning triangle in the road

Always concentrate on the road ahead. Try not to be distracted by an incident on the other side of the road. Many motorway collisions occur due to traffic slowing down. This is because drivers are looking at something on the other side of the road.

## 28 Mark *one* answer

**Before you make a U-turn in the road, you should**

☐ **A** give an arm signal as well as using your indicators
☐ **B** signal so that other drivers can slow down for you
☐ **C** look over your shoulder for a final check
☐ **D** select a higher gear than normal

If you want to make a U-turn, slow down and ensure that the road is clear in both directions. Make sure that the road is wide enough to carry out the manoeuvre safely.

## 29 Mark *three* answers

**As you approach this bridge you should**

☐ **A** move into the middle of the road to get a better view
☐ **B** slow down
☐ **C** get over the bridge as quickly as possible
☐ **D** consider using your horn
☐ **E** find another route
☐ **F** beware of pedestrians

This sign gives you a warning. The brow of the hill prevents you seeing oncoming traffic so you must be cautious. The bridge is narrow and there may not be enough room for you to pass an oncoming vehicle at this point. There is no footpath, so pedestrians may be walking in the road. Consider the hidden hazards and be ready to react if necessary.

## 30 Mark *one* answer
**In which of these situations should you avoid overtaking?**

☐ **A** Just after a bend
☐ **B** In a one-way street
☐ **C** On a 30mph road
☐ **D** Approaching a dip in the road

As you begin to think about overtaking, ask yourself if it's really necessary. If you can't see well ahead stay back and wait for a safer place to pull out.

## 31 Mark *one* answer
**This road marking warns**

☐ **A** drivers to use the hard shoulder
☐ **B** overtaking drivers there is a bend to the left
☐ **C** overtaking drivers to move back to the left
☐ **D** drivers that it is safe to overtake

You should plan your overtaking to take into account any hazards ahead. In this picture the marking indicates that you are approaching a junction. You will not have time to overtake and move back into the left safely.

## 32 Mark *one* answer
**Your mobile phone rings while you are travelling. You should**

☐ **A** stop immediately
☐ **B** answer it immediately
☐ **C** pull up in a suitable place
☐ **D** pull up at the nearest kerb

The safest option is to switch off your mobile phone before you set off, and use a message service. Even hands-free systems are likely to distract your attention. Don't endanger other road users. If you need to make a call, pull up in a safe place when you can, you may need to go some distance before you can find one. It's illegal to use a hand-held mobile or similar device when driving or riding, except in a genuine emergency.

## 33 Mark *one* answer
**Why are these yellow lines painted across the road?**

☐ **A** To help you choose the correct lane
☐ **B** To help you keep the correct separation distance
☐ **C** To make you aware of your speed
☐ **D** To tell you the distance to the roundabout

These lines are often found on the approach to a roundabout or a dangerous junction. They give you extra warning to adjust your speed. Look well ahead and do this in good time.

**34** Mark *one* answer

**You are approaching traffic lights that have been on green for some time. You should**

- ☐ **A** accelerate hard
- ☐ **B** maintain your speed
- ☐ **C** be ready to stop
- ☐ **D** brake hard

The longer traffic lights have been on green, the greater the chance of them changing. Always allow for this on approach and be prepared to stop.

**35** Mark *one* answer

**Which of the following should you do before stopping?**

- ☐ **A** Sound the horn
- ☐ **B** Use the mirrors
- ☐ **C** Select a higher gear
- ☐ **D** Flash your headlights

Before pulling up check the mirrors to see what is happening behind you. Also assess what is ahead and make sure you give the correct signal if it helps other road users.

**36** Mark *one* answer

**When following a large vehicle you should keep well back because this**

- ☐ **A** allows you to corner more quickly
- ☐ **B** helps the large vehicle to stop more easily
- ☐ **C** allows the driver to see you in the mirrors
- ☐ **D** helps you to keep out of the wind

If you're following a large vehicle but are so close to it that you can't see the exterior mirrors, the driver can't see you.

Keeping well back will also allow you to see the road ahead by looking past either side of the large vehicle.

**37** Mark *one* answer

**When you see a hazard ahead you should use the mirrors. Why is this?**

- ☐ **A** Because you will need to accelerate out of danger
- ☐ **B** To assess how your actions will affect following traffic
- ☐ **C** Because you will need to brake sharply to a stop
- ☐ **D** To check what is happening on the road ahead

You should be constantly scanning the road for clues about what is going to happen next. Check your mirrors regularly, particularly as soon as you spot a hazard. What is happening behind may affect your response to hazards ahead.

**38** Mark *one* answer

**You are waiting to turn right at the end of a road. Your view is obstructed by parked vehicles. What should you do?**

- ☐ **A** Stop and then move forward slowly and carefully for a proper view
- ☐ **B** Move quickly to where you can see so you only block traffic from one direction
- ☐ **C** Wait for a pedestrian to let you know when it is safe for you to emerge
- ☐ **D** Turn your vehicle around immediately and find another junction to use

At junctions your view is often restricted by buildings, trees or parked cars. You need to be able to see in order to judge a safe gap. Edge forward slowly and keep looking all the time. Don't cause other road users to change speed or direction as you emerge.

## 39 Mark *one* answer
**You are riding towards a zebra crossing. Pedestrians are waiting to cross. You should**

- ☐ **A** give way to the elderly and infirm only
- ☐ **B** slow down and prepare to stop
- ☐ **C** use your headlight to indicate they can cross
- ☐ **D** wave at them to cross the road

Look for people waiting to cross and be ready to slow down or stop. Some pedestrians may be hesitant. Children can be unpredictable and may hesitate or run out unexpectedly.

## 40 Mark *one* answer
**You are riding a motorcycle and following a large vehicle at 40mph. You should position yourself**

- ☐ **A** close behind to make it easier to overtake the vehicle
- ☐ **B** to the left of the road to make it easier to be seen
- ☐ **C** close behind the vehicle to keep out of the wind
- ☐ **D** well back so that you can see past the vehicle

You need to be able to see well down the road and be ready for any hazards. Staying too close to the vehicle will reduce your view of the road ahead and the driver of the vehicle in front may not be able to see you either. Without a safe separation gap you do not have the time and space necessary to react to any hazards.

## 41 Mark *one* answer
**You are riding on a country road. Two horses with riders are in the distance. You should**

- ☐ **A** continue at your normal speed
- ☐ **B** change down the gears quickly
- ☐ **C** slow down and be ready to stop
- ☐ **D** flash your headlight to warn them

Animals are easily frightened by moving motor vehicles. If you're approaching horses keep your speed down and watch to see if the rider has any difficulty keeping control. Always be ready to stop if necessary.

## 42 Mark *one* answer
**You are approaching a red light at a puffin crossing. Pedestrians are on the crossing. The red light will stay on until**

- ☐ **A** you start to edge forward on to the crossing
- ☐ **B** the pedestrians have reached a safe position
- ☐ **C** the pedestrians are clear of the front of your motorcycle
- ☐ **D** a driver from the opposite direction reaches the crossing

The electronic device will automatically detect when the pedestrians have reached a safe position. Don't proceed until the green light shows it is safe to do so.

**43** Mark *one* answer

**You are riding a slow-moving scooter on a narrow winding road. You should**

☐ **A** keep well out to stop vehicles overtaking dangerously
☐ **B** wave vehicles behind you to pass, if you think they can overtake quickly
☐ **C** pull in safely when you can, to let vehicles behind you overtake
☐ **D** give a left signal when it is safe for vehicles to overtake you

Try not to hold up a queue of traffic. This might lead to other road users becoming impatient and attempting dangerous manoeuvres.

If you're riding a slow-moving scooter or small motorcycle on a narrow road and a queue of traffic has built up behind you, look out for a safe place to pull in.

**44** Mark *two* answers

**When riding a motorcycle your normal road position should allow**

☐ **A** other vehicles to overtake on your left
☐ **B** the driver ahead to see you in their mirrors
☐ **C** you to prevent vehicles behind from overtaking
☐ **D** you to be seen by traffic that is emerging from junctions ahead
☐ **E** you to ride within half a metre (1 foot 8 inches) of the kerb

Aim to ride in the middle of your lane. Avoid riding in the gutter or in the centre of the road, where you might obstruct overtaking traffic or put yourself in danger from oncoming traffic. Riding in this position could also encourage other traffic to overtake you on the left.

**45** Mark *one* answer

**Young, inexperienced and newly qualified motorcyclists can often be involved in crashes. This is due to**

☐ **A** being too cautious at junctions
☐ **B** riding in the middle of their lane
☐ **C** showing off and being competitive
☐ **D** wearing full weather protection

Over-confidence, lack of experience and poor judgement can lead to disaster. No matter what anyone says, don't do anything that could endanger lives. It's not worth the risk.

**46** Mark *one* answer

**At a pelican crossing the flashing amber light means you MUST**

☐ **A** stop and wait for the green light
☐ **B** stop and wait for the red light
☐ **C** give way to pedestrians waiting to cross
☐ **D** give way to pedestrians already on the crossing

Pelican crossings are signal-controlled crossings operated by pedestrians. Push-button controls change the signals. Pelican crossings have no red-and-amber stage before green. Instead, they have a flashing amber light, which means you MUST give way to pedestrians already on the crossing, but if it is clear, you may continue.

**47** Mark *one* answer
**You should never wave people across at pedestrian crossings because**

☐ **A** there may be another vehicle coming
☐ **B** they may not be looking
☐ **C** it is safer for you to carry on
☐ **D** they may not be ready to cross

If people are waiting to use a pedestrian crossing, slow down and be prepared to stop. Don't wave them across the road since another driver may not have seen them, not have seen your signal and may not be able to stop safely.

**48** Mark *one* answer
**'Tailgating' means**

☐ **A** using the rear door of a hatchback car
☐ **B** reversing into a parking space
☐ **C** following another vehicle too closely
☐ **D** driving with rear fog lights on

'Tailgating' is used to describe this dangerous practice, often seen in fast-moving traffic and on motorways. Following the vehicle in front too closely is dangerous because it
• restricts your view of the road ahead
• leaves you no safety margin if the vehicle in front slows down or stops suddenly.

**49** Mark *one* answer
**Following this vehicle too closely is unwise because**

☐ **A** your brakes will overheat
☐ **B** your view ahead is increased
☐ **C** your engine will overheat
☐ **D** your view ahead is reduced

Staying back will increase your view of the road ahead. This will help you to see any hazards that might occur and allow you more time to react.

**50** Mark *one* answer
**You are following a vehicle on a wet road. You should leave a time gap of at least**

☐ **A** one second
☐ **B** two seconds
☐ **C** three seconds
☐ **D** four seconds

Wet roads will reduce your tyres' grip on the road. The safe separation gap of at least two seconds in dry conditions should be doubled in wet weather.

**51** Mark *one* answer

**A long, heavily-laden lorry is taking a long time to overtake you. What should you do?**

☐ **A** Speed up      ☐ **B** Slow down
☐ **C** Hold your speed  ☐ **D** Change direction

A long lorry with a heavy load will need more time to pass you than a car, especially on an uphill stretch of road. Slow down and allow the lorry to pass.

---

**52** Mark *three* answers

**Which of the following vehicles will use blue flashing beacons?**

☐ **A** Motorway maintenance
☐ **B** Bomb disposal
☐ **C** Blood transfusion
☐ **D** Police patrol
☐ **E** Breakdown recovery

When you see emergency vehicles with blue flashing beacons, move out of the way as soon as it is safe to do so.

---

**53** Mark *three* answers

**Which THREE of these emergency services might have blue flashing beacons?**

☐ **A** Coastguard
☐ **B** Bomb disposal
☐ **C** Gritting lorries
☐ **D** Animal ambulances
☐ **E** Mountain rescue
☐ **F** Doctors' cars

When attending an emergency these vehicles will be travelling at speed. You should help their progress by pulling over and allowing them to pass. Do so safely. Don't stop suddenly or in a dangerous position.

**54** Mark *one* answer

**When being followed by an ambulance showing a flashing blue beacon you should**

☐ **A** pull over as soon as safely possible to let it pass
☐ **B** accelerate hard to get away from it
☐ **C** maintain your speed and course
☐ **D** brake harshly and immediately stop in the road

Pull over in a place where the ambulance can pass safely. Check that there are no bollards or obstructions in the road that will prevent it from doing so.

---

**55** Mark *one* answer

**What type of emergency vehicle is fitted with a green flashing beacon?**

☐ **A** Fire engine
☐ **B** Road gritter
☐ **C** Ambulance
☐ **D** Doctor's car

A green flashing beacon on a vehicle means the driver or passenger is a doctor on an emergency call. Give way to them if it's safe to do so. Be aware that the vehicle may be travelling quickly or may stop in a hurry.

## 56 Mark *one* answer
**A flashing green beacon on a vehicle means**

☐ **A** police on non-urgent duties
☐ **B** doctor on an emergency call
☐ **C** road safety patrol operating
☐ **D** gritting in progress

If you see a vehicle with a flashing green beacon approaching, allow it to pass when you can do so safely. Be aware that someone's life could depend on the driver making good progress through traffic.

## 57 Mark *one* answer
**Diamond-shaped signs give instructions to**

☐ **A** tram drivers
☐ **B** bus drivers
☐ **C** lorry drivers
☐ **D** taxi drivers

These signs only apply to trams. They are directed at tram drivers but you should know their meaning so that you're aware of the priorities and are able to anticipate the actions of the driver.

## 58 Mark *one* answer
**On a road where trams operate, which of these vehicles will be most at risk from the tram rails?**

☐ **A** Cars   ☐ **B** Cycles
☐ **C** Buses   ☐ **D** Lorries

The narrow wheels of a bicycle can become stuck in the tram rails, causing the cyclist to stop suddenly, wobble or even lose balance altogether. The tram lines are also slippery which could cause a cyclist to slide or fall off.

## 59 Mark *one* answer
**What should you use your horn for?**

☐ **A** To alert others to your presence
☐ **B** To allow you right of way
☐ **C** To greet other road users
☐ **D** To signal your annoyance

Your horn must not be used between 11.30pm and 7am in a built-up area or when you are stationary, unless a moving vehicle poses a danger. Its function is to alert other road users to your presence.

## 60 Mark *one* answer
**You are in a one-way street and want to turn right. You should position yourself**

☐ **A** in the right-hand lane
☐ **B** in the left-hand lane
☐ **C** in either lane, depending on the traffic
☐ **D** just left of the centre line

If you're travelling in a one-way street and wish to turn right you should take up a position in the right-hand lane. This will enable other road users not wishing to turn to proceed on the left. Indicate your intention and take up your position in good time.

**61** Mark *one* answer

**You wish to turn right ahead. Why should you take up the correct position in good time?**

☐ **A** To allow other drivers to pull out in front of you

☐ **B** To give a better view into the road that you're joining

☐ **C** To help other road users know what you intend to do

☐ **D** To allow drivers to pass you on the right

If you wish to turn right into a side road take up your position in good time. Move to the centre of the road when it's safe to do so. This will allow vehicles to pass you on the left. Early planning will show other traffic what you intend to do.

**62** Mark *one* answer

**At which type of crossing are cyclists allowed to ride across with pedestrians?**

☐ **A** Toucan

☐ **B** Puffin

☐ **C** Pelican

☐ **D** Zebra

A toucan crossing is designed to allow pedestrians and cyclists to cross at the same time. Look out for cyclists approaching the crossing at speed.

**63** Mark *one* answer

**You are travelling at the legal speed limit. A vehicle comes up quickly behind, flashing its headlights. You should**

☐ **A** accelerate to make a gap behind you

☐ **B** touch the brakes sharply to show your brake lights

☐ **C** maintain your speed to prevent the vehicle from overtaking

☐ **D** allow the vehicle to overtake

Don't enforce the speed limit by blocking another vehicle's progress. This will only lead to the other driver becoming more frustrated. Allow the other vehicle to pass when you can do so safely.

**64** Mark *one* answer

**You should ONLY flash your headlights to other road users**

☐ **A** to show that you are giving way

☐ **B** to show that you are about to turn

☐ **C** to tell them that you have right of way

☐ **D** to let them know that you are there

You should only flash your headlights to warn others of your presence. Don't use them to greet others, show impatience or give priority to other road users. They could misunderstand your signal.

**65** Mark *one* answer

**You are approaching unmarked crossroads. How should you deal with this type of junction?**

- ☐ **A** Accelerate and keep to the middle
- ☐ **B** Slow down and keep to the right
- ☐ **C** Accelerate looking to the left
- ☐ **D** Slow down and look both ways

Be extra-cautious, especially when your view is restricted by hedges, bushes, walls and large vehicles etc. In the summer months these junctions can become more difficult to deal with when growing foliage may obscure your view.

**66** Mark *one* answer

**You are approaching a pelican crossing. The amber light is flashing. You must**

- ☐ **A** give way to pedestrians who are crossing
- ☐ **B** encourage pedestrians to cross
- ☐ **C** not move until the green light appears
- ☐ **D** stop even if the crossing is clear

While the pedestrians are crossing don't encourage them to cross by waving or flashing your headlights: other road users may misunderstand your signal. Don't harass them by creeping forward or revving your engine.

**67** Mark *one* answer

**The conditions are good and dry. You could use the 'two-second rule'**

- ☐ **A** before restarting the engine after it has stalled
- ☐ **B** to keep a safe gap from the vehicle in front
- ☐ **C** before using the 'Mirror-Signal-Manoeuvre' routine
- ☐ **D** when emerging on wet roads

To measure this, choose a fixed reference point such as a bridge, sign or tree. When the vehicle ahead passes the object, say to yourself 'Only a fool breaks the two-second rule.' If you reach the object before you finish saying this, you're TOO CLOSE.

**68** Mark *one* answer

**At a puffin crossing, which colour follows the green signal?**

- ☐ **A** Steady red
- ☐ **B** Flashing amber
- ☐ **C** Steady amber
- ☐ **D** Flashing green

Puffin crossings have infra-red sensors which detect when pedestrians are crossing and hold the red traffic signal until the crossing is clear. The use of a sensor means there is no flashing amber phase as there is with a pelican crossing.

## 69 Mark *one* answer

**You are in a line of traffic. The driver behind you is following very closely. What action should you take?**

- ☐ **A** Ignore the following driver and continue to travel within the speed limit
- ☐ **B** Slow down, gradually increasing the gap between you and the vehicle in front
- ☐ **C** Signal left and wave the following driver past
- ☐ **D** Move over to a position just left of the centre line of the road

It can be worrying to see that the car behind is following you too closely. Give yourself a greater safety margin by easing back from the vehicle in front.

## 70 Mark *one* answer

**A vehicle has a flashing green beacon. What does this mean?**

- ☐ **A** A doctor is answering an emergency call
- ☐ **B** The vehicle is slow-moving
- ☐ **C** It is a motorway police patrol vehicle
- ☐ **D** The vehicle is carrying hazardous chemicals

A doctor attending an emergency may show a green flashing beacon on their vehicle. Give way to them when you can do so safely as they will need to reach their destination quickly. Be aware that they might pull over suddenly.

## 71 Mark *one* answer

**A bus has stopped at a bus stop ahead of you. Its right-hand indicator is flashing. You should**

- ☐ **A** flash your headlights and slow down
- ☐ **B** slow down and give way if it is safe to do so
- ☐ **C** sound your horn and keep going
- ☐ **D** slow down and then sound your horn

Give way to buses whenever you can do so safely, especially when they signal to pull away from bus stops. Look out for people leaving the bus and crossing the road.

**72** Mark *one* answer

**A loose drive chain on a motorcycle could cause**

☐ **A** the front wheel to wobble
☐ **B** the ignition to cut out
☐ **C** the brakes to fail
☐ **D** the rear wheel to lock

Drive chains are subject to wear and require frequent adjustment to maintain the correct tension. Allowing the drive chain to run dry will greatly increase the rate of wear, so it is important to keep it lubricated. If the chain becomes worn or slack it can jump off the sprocket and lock the rear wheel.

**73** Mark *one* answer

**What is the most important reason why you should keep your motorcycle regularly maintained?**

☐ **A** To accelerate faster than other traffic
☐ **B** So the motorcycle can carry panniers
☐ **C** To keep the machine roadworthy
☐ **D** So the motorcycle can carry a passenger

Whenever you use any motorcycle on the road it must be in a roadworthy condition. Regular maintenance should identify any faults at an early stage and help prevent more serious problems.

**74** Mark *one* answer

**How should you ride a motorcycle when NEW tyres have just been fitted?**

☐ **A** Carefully, until the shiny surface is worn off
☐ **B** By braking hard especially into bends
☐ **C** Through normal riding with higher air pressures
☐ **D** By riding at faster than normal speeds

New tyres have a shiny finish which needs to wear off before the tyre will give the best grip. Take extra care if the road surface is wet or slippery.

**75** Mark *one* answer

**When riding and wearing brightly coloured clothing you will**

☐ **A** dazzle other motorists on the road
☐ **B** be seen more easily by other motorists
☐ **C** create a hazard by distracting other drivers
☐ **D** be able to ride on unlit roads at night with sidelights

For your own safety you need other road users to see you easily. Wearing brightly coloured or fluorescent clothing will help you to achieve this during daylight. At night, wearing clothing that includes reflective material is the best way of helping others to see you.

## 76 Mark *one* answer
**You are riding a motorcycle in very hot weather. You should**

- ☐ **A** ride with your visor fully open
- ☐ **B** continue to wear protective clothing
- ☐ **C** wear trainers instead of boots
- ☐ **D** slacken your helmet strap

Always wear your protective clothing, whatever the weather.

In very hot weather it's tempting to ride in light summer clothes. Don't take the risk. If you fall from your motorcycle you'll have no protection from the hard road surface.

## 77 Mark *one* answer
**Why should you wear fluorescent clothing when riding in daylight?**

- ☐ **A** It reduces wind resistance
- ☐ **B** It prevents injury if you come off the machine
- ☐ **C** It helps other road users to see you
- ☐ **D** It keeps you cool in hot weather

Motorcycles are smaller and therefore harder to see than most other vehicles on the road. You need to make yourself as visible as possible to other road users. Fluorescent and reflective clothing will help achieve this. You must be visible from all sides.

## 78 Mark *one* answer
**Why should riders wear reflective clothing?**

- ☐ **A** To protect them from the cold
- ☐ **B** To protect them from direct sunlight
- ☐ **C** To be seen better in daylight
- ☐ **D** To be seen better at night

Fluorescent clothing will help others to see you during the day. At night, however, you should wear clothing that reflects the light. This allows other road users to see you more easily in their headlights. Ask your local motorcycle dealer about fluorescent and reflective clothing.

## 79 Mark *one* answer
**Which of the following fairings would give you the best weather protection?**

- ☐ **A** Handlebar
- ☐ **B** Sports
- ☐ **C** Touring
- ☐ **D** Windscreen

Fairings give protection to the hands, legs and feet. They also make riding more comfortable by keeping you out of the wind.

## 80 Mark *one* answer
**Your visor becomes badly scratched. You should**

- ☐ **A** polish it with a fine abrasive
- ☐ **B** replace it
- ☐ **C** wash it in soapy water
- ☐ **D** clean it with petrol

Your visor protects your eyes from wind, rain, insects and road dirt. It's therefore important to keep it clean and in good repair. A badly scratched visor can, obscure your view and cause dazzle from lights of oncoming vehicles.

**81** Mark *one* answer

**The legal minimum depth of tread for motorcycle tyres is**

☐ **A** 1mm
☐ **B** 1.6mm
☐ **C** 2.5mm
☐ **D** 4mm

The entire original tread should be continuous. Don't ride a motorcycle with worn tyres. Your tyres are your only contact with the road so it's very important that you ensure they are in good condition.

**82** Mark *three* answers

**Which of the following makes it easier for motorcyclists to be seen?**

☐ **A** Using a dipped headlight
☐ **B** Wearing a fluorescent jacket
☐ **C** Wearing a white helmet
☐ **D** Wearing a grey helmet
☐ **E** Wearing black leathers
☐ **F** Using a tinted visor

Many incidents and collisions involving motorcyclists occur because another road user didn't see them. Do what you can to make yourself more visible to others. Be aware that you are vulnerable and ride defensively.

**83** Mark *one* answer

**Your oil light comes on as you are riding. You should**

☐ **A** go to a dealer for an oil change
☐ **B** go to the nearest garage for their advice
☐ **C** ride slowly for a few miles to see if the light goes out
☐ **D** stop as quickly as possible and try to find the cause

If the oil pressure warning light comes on when the engine is running you may have a serious problem. Pull over as soon as you can, stop the engine and investigate the cause.

**84** Mark *two* answers

**Motorcycle tyres MUST**

☐ **A** have the same tread pattern
☐ **B** be correctly inflated
☐ **C** be the same size, front and rear
☐ **D** both be the same make
☐ **E** have sufficient tread depth

Your safety and that of others may depend on the condition of your tyres. Before you ride you must check they are correctly inflated and have sufficient tread depth. Make sure these checks become part of a routine.

## 85 Mark *one* answer

**Riding your motorcycle with a slack or worn drive chain may cause**

- ☐ **A** an engine misfire
- ☐ **B** early tyre wear
- ☐ **C** increased emissions
- ☐ **D** a locked wheel

Check your drive chain regularly; adjust and lubricate it if necessary. It needs to be adjusted until the free play is as specified in the vehicle handbook.

## 86 Mark *one* answer

**You forget to switch the choke off after the engine warms up. This could**

- ☐ **A** flatten the battery
- ☐ **B** reduce braking distances
- ☐ **C** use less fuel
- ☐ **D** cause much more engine wear

Leaving the choke on for too long will cause unnecessary engine wear and waste fuel.

## 87 Mark *one* answer

**When riding your motorcycle a tyre bursts. What should you do?**

- ☐ **A** Slow gently to a stop
- ☐ **B** Brake firmly to a stop
- ☐ **C** Change to a high gear
- ☐ **D** Lower the side stand

If a tyre bursts, close the throttle smoothly and slow gently to a stop, holding the handlebars firmly to help you keep a straight course.

## 88 Mark *one* answer

**A motorcycle engine that is properly maintained will**

- ☐ **A** use much more fuel
- ☐ **B** have lower exhaust emissions
- ☐ **C** increase your insurance premiums
- ☐ **D** not need to have an MOT

A badly maintained engine can emit more exhaust fumes than one that is correctly serviced. This can be damaging to the environment and also cost you more in fuel.

## 89 Mark *one* answer
**What should you clean visors and goggles with?**

☐ **A** Petrol
☐ **B** White spirit
☐ **C** Antifreeze
☐ **D** Soapy water

It is very important to keep your visor or goggles clean. Clean them using warm soapy water. Do not use solvents or petrol.

## 90 Mark *one* answer
**You are riding on a quiet road. Your visor fogs up. What should you do?**

☐ **A** Continue at a reduced speed
☐ **B** Stop as soon as possible and wipe it
☐ **C** Build up speed to increase air flow
☐ **D** Close the helmet air vents

In cold and wet weather your visor may fog up. If this happens when you are riding choose somewhere safe to stop, and wipe it clean with a damp cloth. Special anti-fog products are available at motorcycle dealers.

## 91 Mark *one* answer
**You are riding in hot weather. What is the safest type of footwear?**

☐ **A** Sandals
☐ **B** Trainers
☐ **C** Shoes
☐ **D** Boots

It is important to wear good boots when you ride a motorcycle. Boots protect your feet and shins from knocks, and give some protection in a crash. They also help keep you warm and dry in cold or wet weather.

## 92 Mark *one* answer
**Which of the following should not be used to fasten your safety helmet?**

☐ **A** Double D ring fastening
☐ **B** Velcro tab
☐ **C** Quick release fastening
☐ **D** Bar and buckle

Some helmet straps have a velcro tab in addition to the main fastening, which is intended to secure the strap so that it does not flap in the wind. It should NOT be used on its own to fasten the helmet.

**93** Mark *one* answer

**After warming up the engine you leave the choke ON. What will this do?**

☐ **A** Discharge the battery
☐ **B** Use more fuel
☐ **C** Improve handling
☐ **D** Use less fuel

Leaving the choke on for too long could waste fuel and cause unnecessary pollution.

---

**94** Mark *two* answers

**You want to ride your motorcycle in the dark. What could you wear to be seen more easily?**

☐ **A** A black leather jacket
☐ **B** Reflective clothing
☐ **C** A white helmet
☐ **D** A red helmet

When riding in the dark you will be easier to see if you wear reflective clothing and a white helmet. A light-coloured helmet contrasts starkly with the surrounding darkness, while reflective clothing reflects the light from other vehicles and makes the rider much more visible.

**95** Mark *one* answer

**Your motorcycle has a catalytic converter. Its purpose is to reduce**

☐ **A** exhaust noise
☐ **B** fuel consumption
☐ **C** exhaust emissions
☐ **D** engine noise

Catalytic converters reduce the toxic and polluting gases given out by the engine. Never use leaded or lead replacement petrol in a vehicle with a catalytic converter, as even one tankful can permanently damage the system.

---

**96** Mark *one* answer

**Refitting which of the following will disturb your wheel alignment?**

☐ **A** front wheel    ☐ **B** front brakes
☐ **C** rear brakes    ☐ **D** rear wheel

When refitting the rear wheel or adjusting the drive chain it is possible to disturb the wheel alignment. Incorrect alignment can cause instability, especially when cornering, and increased tyre wear.

---

**97** Mark *one* answer

**After refitting your rear wheel what should you check?**

☐ **A** Your steering damper
☐ **B** Your side stand
☐ **C** Your wheel alignment
☐ **D** Your suspension preload

After refitting the rear wheel or adjusting the drive chain you should check your wheel alignment. Incorrect alignment will result in excessive tyre wear and poor road holding.

## 98 Mark *one* answer
**You are checking your direction indicators. How often per second must they flash?**

☐ **A** Between 1 and 2 times
☐ **B** Between 3 and 4 times
☐ **C** Between 5 and 6 times
☐ **D** Between 7 and 8 times

You should check that all your lights work properly before every journey. Make sure that any signals you give can be clearly seen.

If you're not sure whether your signals can be seen you can use arm signals as well to make your intentions clear. Only do this if you're going slowly.

## 99 Mark *one* answer
**After adjusting the final drive chain what should you check?**

☐ **A** The rear wheel alignment
☐ **B** The suspension adjustment
☐ **C** The rear shock absorber
☐ **D** The front suspension forks

Always check the rear wheel alignment after adjusting the chain tension. Marks on the chain adjuster may be provided to make this easy. Incorrect alignment can cause instability and increased tyre wear.

## 100 Mark *one* answer
**Your steering feels wobbly. Which of these is a likely cause?**

☐ **A** Tyre pressure is too high
☐ **B** Incorrectly adjusted brakes
☐ **C** Worn steering head bearings
☐ **D** A broken clutch cable

Worn bearings in the steering head can make your motorcycle very difficult to control. They should be checked for wear and correct adjustment.

## 101 Mark *one* answer
**You see oil on your front forks. Should you be concerned about this?**

☐ **A** No, unless the amount of oil increases
☐ **B** No, lubrication here is perfectly normal
☐ **C** Yes, it is illegal to ride with an oil leak
☐ **D** Yes, oil could drip onto your tyre

Oil leaking from your forks could get on to your tyre or brake disc. This could result in your tyre losing grip, or your brakes being less effective. A loss of front fork oil will also affect handling and stability.

**102** Mark *one* answer

**You have a faulty oil seal on a shock absorber. Why is this a serious problem?**

☐ **A** It will cause excessive chain wear
☐ **B** Dripping oil could reduce the grip of your tyre
☐ **C** Your motorcycle will be harder to ride uphill
☐ **D** Your motorcycle will not accelerate so quickly

Leaking oil could affect the grip of your tyres and also the effectiveness of your brakes. This could result in a loss of control, putting you and other road users in danger.

**103** Mark *one* answer

**Oil is leaking from your forks. Why should you NOT ride a motorcycle in this condition?**

☐ **A** Your brakes could be affected by dripping oil
☐ **B** Your steering is likely to seize up
☐ **C** The forks will quickly begin to rust
☐ **D** The motorcycle will become too noisy

Oil dripping from forks and shock absorbers is dangerous if it gets onto brakes and tyres. Replace faulty oil seals immediately.

**104** Mark *one* answer

**You have adjusted your drive chain. If this is not done properly, what problem could it cause?**

☐ **A** Inaccurate speedometer reading
☐ **B** Loss of braking power
☐ **C** Incorrect rear wheel alignment
☐ **D** Excessive fuel consumption

After carrying out drive chain adjustment, you should always check the rear wheel alignment. Many motorcycles have alignment guides stamped onto the frame to help you do this correctly.

**105** Mark *one* answer

**You have adjusted your drive chain. Why is it also important to check rear wheel alignment?**

☐ **A** Your tyre may be more likely to puncture
☐ **B** Fuel consumption could be greatly increased
☐ **C** You may not be able to reach top speed
☐ **D** Your motorcycle could be unstable on bends

Rear wheel alignment can be disturbed by adjustments to the drive chain. It's very important to make sure that the wheel is still properly aligned after doing this.

## 106 Mark *one* answer

**There is a cut in the sidewall of one of your tyres. What should you do about this?**

- ☐ **A** Replace the tyre before riding the motorcycle
- ☐ **B** Check regularly to see if it gets any worse
- ☐ **C** Repair the puncture before riding the motorcycle
- ☐ **D** Reduce pressure in the tyre before you ride

A cut in the sidewall can be very dangerous. The tyre is in danger of blowing out if you ride the motorcycle in this condition.

## 107 Mark *one* answer

**You need to put air into your tyres. How would you find out the correct pressure to use?**

- ☐ **A** It will be shown on the tyre wall
- ☐ **B** It will be stamped on the wheel
- ☐ **C** By checking the vehicle owner's manual
- ☐ **D** By checking the registration document

Tyre pressures should be checked regularly. Use your vehicle manual to find advice on the correct pressures to use.

## 108 Mark *one* answer

**You can prevent a cable operated clutch from becoming stiff by keeping the cable**

- ☐ **A** tight
- ☐ **B** dry
- ☐ **C** slack
- ☐ **D** oiled

Keeping the cable oiled will help it to move smoothly through its outer casing. This will extend the life of the cable and assist your control of the motorcycle.

## 109 Mark *one* answer

**When adusting your chain it is important for the wheels to be aligned accurately. Incorrect wheel alignment can cause**

- ☐ **A** a serious loss of power
- ☐ **B** reduced braking performance
- ☐ **C** increased tyre wear
- ☐ **D** reduced ground clearance

If a motorcycle's wheels are incorrectly aligned tyres may wear unevenly and the motorcycle can become unstable, especially when cornering.

## 110 Mark *one* answer

**What problem can incorrectly aligned wheels cause?**

- ☐ **A** Faulty headlight adjustment
- ☐ **B** Reduced braking performance
- ☐ **C** Better ground clearance
- ☐ **D** Instability when cornering

Wheels should be aligned accurately after refitting your rear wheel. Incorrect wheel alignment can cause uneven tyre wear and poor handling. Most motorcycles have wheel alignment guides stamped onto the swinging arm.

**111** Mark *one* answer
**What is most likely to be affected by incorrect wheel alignment?**

☐ **A** Braking performance
☐ **B** Stability
☐ **C** Acceleration
☐ **D** Suspension preload

It is important that your wheels are aligned accurately. It will be necessary to do this after removing your rear wheel or adjusting the chain. Incorrect alignment can cause instability, especially when cornering. It can also increase tyre wear.

**112** Mark *one* answer
**Why should you wear specialist motorcycle clothing when riding?**

☐ **A** Because the law requires you to do so
☐ **B** Because it looks better than ordinary clothing
☐ **C** Because it gives best protection from the weather
☐ **D** Because it will reduce your insurance

If you become cold and wet when riding, this can have a serious effect on your concentration and control of your motorcycle.

Proper riding gear can help shield you from the weather, as well as giving protection in the event of a crash.

**113** Mark *one* answer
**When leaving your motorcycle parked, you should always**

☐ **A** remove the battery lead
☐ **B** pull it onto the kerb
☐ **C** use the steering lock
☐ **D** leave the parking light on

When leaving your motorcycle you should always use the steering lock. You should also consider using additional locking devices such as a U-lock, disc lock or chain. If possible fasten it to an immovable post or another motorcycle.

**114** Mark *one* answer
**You are parking your motorcycle. Chaining it to an immovable object will**

☐ **A** be against the law
☐ **B** give extra security
☐ **C** be likely to cause damage
☐ **D** leave the motorcycle unstable

Theft of motorcycles is a very common crime. If you can, secure your vehicle to a lamp post or other such object, to help reduce the chances of it being stolen.

## 115 Mark *one* answer

**You are parking your motorcycle and sidecar on a hill. What is the best way to stop it rolling away?**

- ☐ **A** Leave it in neutral
- ☐ **B** Put the rear wheel on the pavement
- ☐ **C** Leave it in a low gear
- ☐ **D** Park very close to another vehicle

To make sure a sidecar outfit doesn't roll away when parking you should leave it in a low gear, and wedge it against the kerb or place a block behind the wheel.

## 116 Mark *one* answer

**An engine cut-out switch should be used to**

- ☐ **A** reduce speed in an emergency
- ☐ **B** prevent the motorcycle being stolen
- ☐ **C** stop the engine normally
- ☐ **D** stop the engine in an emergency

If you are involved in a collision or crash, using the engine cut-out switch will help to reduce any fire hazard. When stopping the engine normally, use the ignition switch.

## 117 Mark *one* answer

**You enter a road where there are road humps. What should you do?**

- ☐ **A** Maintain a reduced speed throughout
- ☐ **B** Accelerate quickly between each one
- ☐ **C** Always keep to the maximum legal speed
- ☐ **D** Ride slowly at school times only

The humps are there for a reason; to reduce the speed of the traffic. Don't accelerate harshly between them, as this means you will only have to brake sharply to negotiate the next hump.

Harsh braking and acceleration uses more fuel as well as causing wear and tear to your vehicle.

## 118 Mark *one* answer

**When should you especially check the engine oil level?**

- ☐ **A** Before a long journey
- ☐ **B** When the engine is hot
- ☐ **C** Early in the morning
- ☐ **D** Every 6,000 miles

As well as the oil you will also need to check other items. These include, fuel, water and tyres.

## 119 Mark *one* answer

**You service your own motorcycle. How should you get rid of the old engine oil?**

- ☐ **A** Take it to a local authority site
- ☐ **B** Pour it down a drain
- ☐ **C** Tip it into a hole in the ground
- ☐ **D** Put it into your dustbin

Never pour the oil down any drain. The oil is highly pollutant and could harm wildlife. Confine it in a container and dispose of it properly at an authorised site.

**120** Mark *one* answer
**What safeguard could you take against fire risk to your motorcycle?**

☐ **A** Keep water levels above maximum
☐ **B** Check out any strong smell of petrol
☐ **C** Avoid riding with a full tank of petrol
☐ **D** Use unleaded petrol

The fuel in your motorcycle can be a dangerous fire hazard. DON'T use a naked flame if you can smell fuel, or smoke when refuelling.

**121** Mark *one* answer
**Which of the following would NOT make you more visible in daylight?**

☐ **A** Wearing a black helmet
☐ **B** Wearing a white helmet
☐ **C** Switching on your dipped headlight
☐ **D** Wearing a fluorescent jacket

Wearing bright or fluorescent clothes will help other road users to see you. Wearing a white or brightly coloured helmet can also make you more visible.

**122** Mark *one* answer
**It would be illegal to ride with a helmet on when**

☐ **A** the helmet is not fastened correctly
☐ **B** the helmet is more than four years old
☐ **C** you have borrowed someone else's helmet
☐ **D** the helmet does not have chin protection

A helmet that is incorrectly fastened or not fastened at all is likely to come off in a crash. It will provide little or no protection. By law, you must wear a helmet when riding on the road and it must be correctly fastened (members of the Sikh religion who wear a turban are exempt).

**123** Mark *three* answers
**When may you have to increase the tyre pressures on your motorcycle?**

☐ **A** When carrying a passenger
☐ **B** After a long journey
☐ **C** When carrying a load
☐ **D** When riding at high speeds
☐ **E** When riding in hot weather

Read the manufacturer's handbook to see if they recommend increasing tyre pressures under certain conditions.

**124** Mark *two* answers
**Which TWO of these items on a motorcycle MUST be kept clean?**

☐ **A** Number plate    ☐ **B** Wheels
☐ **C** Engine          ☐ **D** Fairing
☐ **E** Headlight

Maintenance is a vital part of road safety. Lights, indicators, reflectors and number plates MUST be kept clean and clear.

## 125 Mark *one* answer

**You should use the engine cut-out switch on your motorcycle to**

- ☐ **A** save wear and tear on the battery
- ☐ **B** stop the engine for a short time
- ☐ **C** stop the engine in an emergency
- ☐ **D** save wear and tear on the ignition

Only use the engine cut-out switch in an emergency. When stopping the engine normally, use the ignition switch. This will remind you to take your keys with you when parking. It could also prevent starting problems if you forget you've left the cut-out switch in the 'off' position. When returning to your motorcycle make sure someone has not done this as a trick.

## 126 Mark *one* answer

**You have adjusted the tension on your drive chain. You should check the**

- ☐ **A** rear wheel alignment
- ☐ **B** tyre pressures
- ☐ **C** valve clearances
- ☐ **D** sidelights

Drive chains wear and need frequent adjustment and lubrication. If the drive chain is worn or slack it can jump off the sprocket and lock the rear wheel. When you have adjusted the chain tension, you need to check the rear wheel alignment. Marks by the chain adjusters may be provided to make this easier.

## 127 Mark *one* answer

**A friend offers you a second-hand safety helmet for you to use. Why may this be a bad idea?**

- ☐ **A** It may be damaged
- ☐ **B** You will be breaking the law
- ☐ **C** You will affect your insurance cover
- ☐ **D** It may be a full-face type

A second-hand helmet may look in good condition but it could have received damage that is not visible externally. A damaged helmet could be unreliable in a crash. Don't take the risk.

## 128 Mark *four* answers

**You are riding a motorcycle of more than 50cc. Which FOUR would make a tyre illegal?**

- ☐ **A** Tread less than 1.6mm deep
- ☐ **B** Tread less than 1mm deep
- ☐ **C** A large bulge in the wall
- ☐ **D** A recut tread
- ☐ **E** Exposed ply or cord
- ☐ **F** A stone wedged in the tread

When checking tyres make sure there are no bulges or cuts in the side walls. Always buy your tyres from a reputable dealer to ensure quality and value for money.

**129** Mark *two* answers
**You should maintain cable operated brakes**

☐ **A** by regular adjustment when necessary
☐ **B** at normal service times only
☐ **C** yearly, before taking the motorcycle for its MOT
☐ **D** by oiling cables and pivots regularly

Keeping your brakes in good working order is vital for safety. Cables will stretch with use and need checking and adjusting regularly. They will also need lubricating to prevent friction and wear of the cables and pivots.

**130** Mark *two* answers
**A properly serviced motorcycle will give**

☐ **A** lower insurance premiums
☐ **B** a refund on your road tax
☐ **C** better fuel economy
☐ **D** cleaner exhaust emissions

When you purchase your motorcycle, check at what intervals you should have it serviced. This can vary depending on model or manufacturer. Use the service manual and keep it up to date.

**131** Mark *one* answer
**A loosely adjusted drive chain could**

☐ **A** lock the rear wheel
☐ **B** make wheels wobble
☐ **C** cause a braking fault
☐ **D** affect your headlight beam

A motorcycle chain will stretch as it wears. It needs frequent checking, and adjustment if necessary, to keep the tension correct. In extreme cases a loose chain can jump off the sprocket and become wedged in the rear wheel. This could cause serious loss of control and result in a crash.

**132** Mark *one* answer
**Your motorcycle is NOT fitted with daytime running lights. When MUST you use a dipped headlight during the day?**

☐ **A** On country roads
☐ **B** In poor visibility
☐ **C** Along narrow streets
☐ **D** When parking

It's important that other road users can see you clearly at all times. It will help other road users to see you if you use a dipped headlight during the day. You MUST use a dipped headlight during the day if visibility is seriously reduced, that is, when you can't see for more than 100 metres (328 feet).

## 133 Mark *one* answer

**Tyre pressures should usually be increased on your motorcycle when**

- ☐ **A** riding on a wet road
- ☐ **B** carrying a pillion passenger
- ☐ **C** travelling on an uneven surface
- ☐ **D** riding on twisty roads

Sometimes manufacturers advise you to increase your tyre pressures for high-speed riding and when carrying extra weight. This information can be found in the handbook.

## 134 Mark *one* answer

**You have too much oil in your engine. What could this cause?**

- ☐ **A** Low oil pressure
- ☐ **B** Engine overheating
- ☐ **C** Chain wear
- ☐ **D** Oil leaks

Too much oil in the engine will create excess pressure and could damage engine seals and cause oil leaks. Any excess oil should be drained off.

## 135 Mark *one* answer

**You are leaving your motorcycle unattended on a road. When may you leave the engine running?**

- ☐ **A** When parking for less than five minutes
- ☐ **B** If the battery is flat
- ☐ **C** When in a 20mph zone
- ☐ **D** Not on any occasion

When you leave your motorcycle parked and unattended on a road, switch off the engine, use the steering lock and remove the ignition key. Also take any tank bags, panniers or loose luggage with you, set the alarm if it has one, and use an additional lock and chain or cable lock.

## 136 Mark *one* answer

**You are involved in a crash. To reduce the risk of fire what is the best thing to do?**

- ☐ **A** Keep the engine running
- ☐ **B** Open the choke
- ☐ **C** Turn the fuel tap to reserve
- ☐ **D** Use the engine cut-out switch

The engine cut-out switch is used to stop the engine in an emergency. In the event of a crash this may help to reduce any fire risk.

## 137 Mark *two* answers
**When riding at night you should**

☐ **A** ride with your headlight on
☐ **B** wear reflective clothing
☐ **C** wear a tinted visor
☐ **D** ride in the centre of the road
☐ **E** give arm signals

At night you should wear clothing that includes reflective material to help other road users see you. This could be a vest, tabard or reflective body strap. Use your headlight on dipped or main beam as appropriate without dazzling other road users.

## 138 Mark *two* answers
**Which TWO are badly affected if the tyres are under-inflated?**

☐ **A** Braking
☐ **B** Steering
☐ **C** Changing gear
☐ **D** Parking

Your tyres are your only contact with the road so it is very important to ensure that they are free from defects, have sufficient tread depth and are correctly inflated. Correct tyre pressures help reduce the risk of skidding and provide a safer and more comfortable drive or ride.

## 139 Mark *one* answer
**You must NOT sound your horn**

☐ **A** between 10pm and 6am in a built-up area
☐ **B** at any time in a built-up area
☐ **C** between 11.30pm and 7am in a built-up area
☐ **D** between 11.30pm and 6am on any road

Vehicles can be noisy. Every effort must be made to prevent excessive noise, especially in built-up areas at night. Don't
• rev the engine
• sound the horn unnecessarily.
It is illegal to sound your horn in a built-up area between 11.30pm and 7am, except when another vehicle poses a danger.

## 140 Mark *three* answers
**The pictured vehicle is 'environmentally friendly' because it**

☐ **A** reduces noise pollution
☐ **B** uses diesel fuel
☐ **C** uses electricity
☐ **D** uses unleaded fuel
☐ **E** reduces parking spaces
☐ **F** reduces town traffic

Trams are powered by electricity and therefore do not emit exhaust fumes. They are also much quieter than petrol or diesel engined vehicles and can carry a large number of passengers.

**141** Mark *one* answer
**Supertrams or Light Rapid Transit (LRT) systems are environmentally friendly because**

☐ **A** they use diesel power
☐ **B** they use quieter roads
☐ **C** they use electric power
☐ **D** they do not operate during rush hour

This means that they do not emit toxic fumes, which add to city pollution problems. They are also a lot quieter and smoother to ride on.

**142** Mark *one* answer
**'Red routes' in major cities have been introduced to**

☐ **A** raise the speed limits
☐ **B** help the traffic flow
☐ **C** provide better parking
☐ **D** allow lorries to load more freely

Traffic jams today are often caused by the volume of traffic. However, inconsiderate parking can lead to the closure of an inside lane or traffic having to wait for oncoming vehicles. Driving slowly in traffic increases fuel consumption and causes a build-up of exhaust fumes.

**143** Mark *one* answer
**Road humps, chicanes, and narrowings are**

☐ **A** always at major road works
☐ **B** used to increase traffic speed
☐ **C** at toll-bridge approaches only
☐ **D** traffic-calming measures

Traffic-calming measures help keep vehicle speeds low in congested areas where there are pedestrians and children. A pedestrian is much more likely to survive a collision with a vehicle travelling at 20mph than at 40mph.

**144** Mark *one* answer
**The purpose of a catalytic converter is to reduce**

☐ **A** fuel consumption
☐ **B** the risk of fire
☐ **C** toxic exhaust gases
☐ **D** engine wear

Catalytic converters are designed to reduce a large percentage of toxic emissions. They work more efficiently when the engine has reached its normal working temperature.

**145** Mark *one* answer
**Catalytic converters are fitted to make the**

☐ **A** engine produce more power
☐ **B** exhaust system easier to replace
☐ **C** engine run quietly
☐ **D** exhaust fumes cleaner

Harmful gases in the exhaust system pollute the atmosphere. These gases are reduced by up to 90% if a catalytic converter is fitted. Cleaner air benefits everyone, especially people who live or work near congested roads.

**146** Mark *one* answer
**It is essential that tyre pressures are checked regularly. When should this be done?**

☐ **A** After any lengthy journey
☐ **B** After travelling at high speed
☐ **C** When tyres are hot
☐ **D** When tyres are cold

When you check the tyre pressures do so when the tyres are cold. This will give you a more accurate reading. The heat generated from a long journey will raise the pressure inside the tyre.

**147** Mark *one* answer
**When should you NOT use your horn in a built-up area?**

☐ **A** Between 8pm and 8am
☐ **B** Between 9pm and dawn
☐ **C** Between dusk and 8am
☐ **D** Between 11.30pm and 7am

By law you must not sound your horn in a built-up area between 11.30pm and 7am. The exception to this is when another road user poses a danger.

**148** Mark *one* answer
**You will use more fuel if your tyres are**

☐ **A** under-inflated
☐ **B** of different makes
☐ **C** over-inflated
☐ **D** new and hardly used

Check your tyre pressures frequently – normally once a week. If pressures are lower than those recommended by the manufacturer, there will be more 'rolling resistance'. The engine will have to work harder to overcome this, leading to increased fuel consumption.

**149** Mark *two* answers
**How should you dispose of a used battery?**

☐ **A** Take it to a local authority site
☐ **B** Put it in the dustbin
☐ **C** Break it up into pieces
☐ **D** Leave it on waste land
☐ **E** Take it to a garage
☐ **F** Burn it on a fire

Batteries contain acid which is hazardous and must be disposed of safely.

**150** Mark *one* answer
**What is most likely to cause high fuel consumption?**

☐ **A** Poor steering control
☐ **B** Accelerating around bends
☐ **C** Staying in high gears
☐ **D** Harsh braking and accelerating

Accelerating and braking gently and smoothly will help to save fuel, reduce wear on your vehicle and is better for the environment.

**151** Mark *one* answer
**The fluid level in your battery is low. What should you top it up with?**

☐ **A** Battery acid
☐ **B** Distilled water
☐ **C** Engine oil
☐ **D** Engine coolant

Some modern batteries are maintenance-free. Check your vehicle handbook and, if necessary, make sure that the plates in each battery cell are covered.

---

**152** Mark *one* answer
**You are parked on the road at night. Where must you use parking lights?**

☐ **A** Where there are continuous white lines in the middle of the road
☐ **B** Where the speed limit exceeds 30mph
☐ **C** Where you are facing oncoming traffic
☐ **D** Where you are near a bus stop

When parking at night, park in the direction of the traffic. This will enable other road users to see the reflectors on the rear of your vehicle. Use your parking lights if the speed limit is over 30mph.

**153** Mark *three* answers
**Motor vehicles can harm the environment. This has resulted in**

☐ **A** air pollution
☐ **B** damage to buildings
☐ **C** less risk to health
☐ **D** improved public transport
☐ **E** less use of electrical vehicles
☐ **F** using up of natural resources

Exhaust emissions are harmful to health. Together with vibration from heavy traffic this can result in damage to buildings. Most petrol and diesel fuels come from a finite and non-renewable source. Anything you can do to reduce your use of these fuels will help the environment.

---

**154** Mark *three* answers
**Excessive or uneven tyre wear can be caused by faults in which THREE of the following?**

☐ **A** The gearbox
☐ **B** The braking system
☐ **C** The accelerator
☐ **D** The exhaust system
☐ **E** Wheel alignment
☐ **F** The suspension

Regular servicing will help to detect faults at an early stage and this will avoid the risk of minor faults becoming serious or even dangerous.

**155** Mark *one* answer
**You need to top up your battery.**
**What level should you fill to?**

☐ **A** The top of the battery
☐ **B** Half-way up the battery
☐ **C** Just below the cell plates
☐ **D** Just above the cell plates

Top up the battery with distilled water and make sure each cell plate is covered.

**156** Mark *one* answer
**You are parking on a two-way road at night. The speed limit is 40mph. You should park on the**

☐ **A** left with parking lights on
☐ **B** left with no lights on
☐ **C** right with parking lights on
☐ **D** right with dipped headlights on

At night all vehicles must display parking lights when parked on a road with a speed limit greater than 30mph. They should be close to the kerb, facing in the direction of the traffic flow and not within a distance as specified in The Highway Code.

**157** Mark *one* answer
**Before starting a journey it is wise to plan your route. How can you do this?**

☐ **A** Look at a map
☐ **B** Contact your local garage
☐ **C** Look in your vehicle handbook
☐ **D** Check your vehicle registration document

Planning your journey before you set out can help to make it much easier, more pleasant and may help to ease traffic congestion. Look at a map to help you to do this. You may need different scale maps depending on where and how far you're going. Printing or writing out the route can also help.

**158** Mark *one* answer    NI
**It can help to plan your route before starting a journey. You can do this by contacting**

☐ **A** your local filling station
☐ **B** a motoring organisation
☐ **C** the Driver Vehicle Licensing Agency
☐ **D** your vehicle manufacturer

Most motoring organisations will give you a detailed plan of your trip showing directions and distance. Some will also include advice on rest and fuel stops. The Highways Agency website will also give you information on roadworks and incidents and gives expected delay times.

## 159 Mark *one* answer
**How can you plan your route before starting a long journey?**

- ☐ **A** Check your vehicle's workshop manual
- ☐ **B** Ask your local garage
- ☐ **C** Use a route planner on the internet
- ☐ **D** Consult your travel agents

Various route planners are available on the internet. Most of them give you various options allowing you to choose the most direct, quickest or scenic route. They can also include rest and fuel stops and distances. Print them off and take them with you.

## 160 Mark *one* answer
**Planning your route before setting out can be helpful. How can you do this?**

- ☐ **A** Look in a motoring magazine
- ☐ **B** Only visit places you know
- ☐ **C** Try to travel at busy times
- ☐ **D** Print or write down the route

Print or write down your route before setting out. Some places are not well signed so using place names and road numbers may help you avoid problems en route. Try to get an idea of how far you're going before you leave. You can also use it to re-check the next stage at each rest stop.

## 161 Mark *one* answer
**Why is it a good idea to plan your journey to avoid busy times?**

- ☐ **A** You will have an easier journey
- ☐ **B** You will have a more stressful journey
- ☐ **C** Your journey time will be longer
- ☐ **D** It will cause more traffic congestion

No one likes to spend time in traffic queues. Try to avoid busy times related to school or work travel. As well as moving vehicles you should also consider congestion caused by parked cars, buses and coaches around schools.

## 162 Mark *one* answer
**Planning your journey to avoid busy times has a number of advantages.
One of these is**

- ☐ **A** your journey will take longer
- ☐ **B** you will have a more pleasant journey
- ☐ **C** you will cause more pollution
- ☐ **D** your stress level will be greater

Having a pleasant journey can have safety benefits. You will be less tired and stressed and this will allow you to concentrate more on your driving or riding.

**163** Mark *one* answer

**It is a good idea to plan your journey to avoid busy times. This is because**

☐ **A** your vehicle will use more fuel
☐ **B** you will see less road works
☐ **C** it will help to ease congestion
☐ **D** you will travel a much shorter distance

Avoiding busy times means that you are not adding needlessly to traffic congestion. Other advantages are that you will use less fuel and feel less stressed.

---

**164** Mark *one* answer

**By avoiding busy times when travelling**

☐ **A** you are more likely to be held up
☐ **B** your journey time will be longer
☐ **C** you will travel a much shorter distance
☐ **D** you are less likely to be delayed

If possible, avoid the early morning and, late afternoon and early evening 'rush hour'. Doing this should allow you to travel in a more relaxed frame of mind, concentrate solely on what you're doing and arrive at your destination feeling less stressed.

**165** Mark *one* answer

**It can help to plan your route before starting a journey. Why should you also plan an alternative route?**

☐ **A** Your original route may be blocked
☐ **B** Your maps may have different scales
☐ **C** You may find you have to pay a congestion charge
☐ **D** Because you may get held up by a tractor

It can be frustrating and worrying to find your planned route is blocked by roadworks or diversions. If you have planned an alternative you will feel less stressed and more able to concentrate fully on your driving or riding. If your original route is mostly on motorways it's a good idea to plan an alternative using non-motorway roads. Always carry a map with you just in case you need to refer to it.

---

**166** Mark *one* answer

**As well as planning your route before starting a journey, you should also plan an alternative route. Why is this?**

☐ **A** To let another driver overtake
☐ **B** Your first route may be blocked
☐ **C** To avoid a railway level crossing
☐ **D** In case you have to avoid emergency vehicles

It's a good idea to plan an alternative route in case your original route is blocked for any reason. You're less likely to feel worried and stressed if you've got an alternative in mind. This will enable you to concentrate fully on your driving or riding. Always carry a map that covers the area you will travel in.

**167** Mark *one* answer

**You are making an appointment and will have to travel a long distance. You should**

☐ **A** allow plenty of time for your journey
☐ **B** plan to go at busy times
☐ **C** avoid all national speed limit roads
☐ **D** prevent other drivers from overtaking

Always allow plenty of time for your journey in case of unforeseen problems. Anything can happen, punctures, breakdowns, road closures, diversions etc. You will feel less stressed and less inclined to take risks if you are not 'pushed for time'.

**168** Mark *one* answer

**Rapid acceleration and heavy braking can lead to**

☐ **A** reduced pollution
☐ **B** increased fuel consumption
☐ **C** reduced exhaust emissions
☐ **D** increased road safety

Using the controls smoothly can reduce fuel consumption by about 15% as well as reducing wear and tear on your vehicle. Plan ahead and anticipate changes of speed well in advance. This will reduce the need to accelerate rapidly or brake sharply.

**169** Mark *one* answer

**What percentage of all emissions does road transport account for?**

☐ **A** 10%
☐ **B** 20%
☐ **C** 30%
☐ **D** 40%

Transport is an essential part of modern life but it does have environmental effects. In heavily populated areas traffic is the biggest source of air pollution. Eco-safe driving and riding will reduce emissions and can make a surprising difference to local air quality.

**170** Mark *one* answer

**Which of these, if allowed to get low, could cause you to crash?**

☐ **A** Anti-freeze level
☐ **B** Brake fluid level
☐ **C** Battery water level
☐ **D** Radiator coolant level

You should carry out frequent checks on all fluid levels but particularly brake fluid. As the brake pads or shoes wear down the brake fluid level will drop. If it drops below the minimum mark on the fluid reservoir, air could enter the hydraulic system and lead to a loss of braking efficiency or complete brake failure.

**171** Mark *one* answer
**Your overall stopping distance will be longer when riding**

☐ **A** at night
☐ **B** in the fog
☐ **C** with a passenger
☐ **D** up a hill

When carrying a passenger on a motorcycle the overall weight will be much more than when riding alone. This additional weight will make it harder for you to stop quickly in an emergency.

**172** Mark *one* answer
**On a wet road what is the safest way to stop?**

☐ **A** Change gear without braking
☐ **B** Use the back brake only
☐ **C** Use the front brake only
☐ **D** Use both brakes

Motorcyclists need to take extra care when stopping on wet road surfaces. Plan well ahead so that you're able to brake in good time. You should ensure your motorcycle is upright and brake when travelling in a straight line.

**173** Mark *one* answer
**You are riding in heavy rain when your rear wheel skids as you accelerate. To get control again you must**

☐ **A** change down to a lower gear
☐ **B** ease off the throttle
☐ **C** brake to reduce speed
☐ **D** put your feet down

If you feel your back wheel beginning to skid as you pull away, ease off the throttle. This will give your rear tyre the chance to grip the road and stop the skid.

**174** Mark *one* answer
**It is snowing. Before starting your journey you should**

☐ **A** think if you need to ride at all
☐ **B** try to avoid taking a passenger
☐ **C** plan a route avoiding towns
☐ **D** take a hot drink before setting out

Do not ride in snowy or icy conditions unless your journey is essential. If you must go out, try and keep to main roads which are more likely to be treated and clear.

**175** Mark *one* answer
**Why should you ride with a dipped headlight on in the daytime?**

☐ **A** It helps other road users to see you
☐ **B** It means that you can ride faster
☐ **C** Other vehicles will get out of the way
☐ **D** So that it is already on when it gets dark

Make yourself as visible as possible, from the side as well as from the front and rear. Having your headlight on, even in good daylight, can help make you more conspicuous.

**176** Mark *one* answer
**Motorcyclists are only allowed to use high-intensity rear fog lights when**

☐ **A** a pillion passenger is being carried
☐ **B** they ride a large touring machine
☐ **C** visibility is 100 metres (328 feet) or less
☐ **D** they are riding on the road for the first time

If your motorcycle is fitted with high-intensity rear fog lights you must only use them when visibility is seriously reduced, that is, when you can see no further than 100 metres (328 feet). This rule also applies to all other motor vehicles using these lights.

**177** Mark *three* answers
**You MUST use your headlight**

☐ **A** when riding in a group
☐ **B** at night when street lighting is poor
☐ **C** when carrying a passenger
☐ **D** on motorways during darkness
☐ **E** at times of poor visibility
☐ **F** when parked on an unlit road

Your headlight helps you to see in the dark and helps other road users to see you. You must also use your headlight at any time when visibility is seriously reduced.

**178** Mark *one* answer
**You are riding in town at night. The roads are wet after rain. The reflections from wet surfaces will**

☐ **A** affect your stopping distance
☐ **B** affect your road holding
☐ **C** make it easy to see unlit objects
☐ **D** make it hard to see unlit objects

If you can't see clearly, slow down and stop. Make sure that your visor or goggles are clean. Be extra-cautious in these conditions and allow twice the normal separation distance.

**179** Mark *two* answers
**You are riding through a flood. Which TWO should you do?**

☐ **A** Keep in a high gear and stand up on the footrests
☐ **B** Keep the engine running fast to keep water out of the exhaust
☐ **C** Ride slowly and test your brakes when you are out of the water
☐ **D** Turn your headlight off to avoid any electrical damage

Take extra care when riding through flood water or fords. Ride through with high engine revs while partly slipping the clutch to prevent water entering the exhaust system. Try your brakes as soon as you are clear.

## 180 Mark *one* answer
**You have just ridden through a flood. When clear of the water you should test your**

- ☐ **A** starter motor
- ☐ **B** headlight
- ☐ **C** steering
- ☐ **D** brakes

If you have ridden through deep water your brakes may be less effective. If they have been affected, ride slowly while gently applying both brakes until normal braking is restored.

## 181 Mark *one* answer
**When going through flood water you should ride**

- ☐ **A** quickly in a high gear
- ☐ **B** slowly in a high gear
- ☐ **C** quickly in a low gear
- ☐ **D** slowly in a low gear

If you have to go through a flood, ride slowly in a low gear. Keep the engine running fast enough to keep water out of the exhaust. You may need to slip the clutch to do this.

## 182 Mark *one* answer
**When riding at night you should NOT**

- ☐ **A** switch on full beam headlights
- ☐ **B** overtake slower vehicles in front
- ☐ **C** use dipped beam headlights
- ☐ **D** use tinted glasses, lenses or visors

Do not use tinted glasses, lenses or visors at night because they reduce the amount of available light reaching your eyes. It's also important to keep your visor or goggles clean to give a clear view of the road at all times.

## 183 Mark *two* answers
**Which of the following should you do when riding in fog?**

- ☐ **A** Keep close to the vehicle in front
- ☐ **B** Use your dipped headlight
- ☐ **C** Ride close to the centre of the road
- ☐ **D** Keep your visor or goggles clear
- ☐ **E** Keep the vehicle in front in view

You must use your dipped headlight when visibility is seriously reduced. In fog a film of mist can form over the outside of your visor or goggles. This can further reduce your ability to see. Be aware of this hazard and keep your visor or goggles clear.

## 184 Mark *one* answer
**You are riding in heavy rain. Why should you try to avoid this marked area?**

- ☐ **A** It is illegal to ride over bus stops
- ☐ **B** The painted lines may be slippery
- ☐ **C** Cyclists may be using the bus stop
- ☐ **D** Only emergency vehicles may drive over bus stops

Painted lines and road markings can be very slippery, especially for motorcyclists. Try to avoid them if you can do so safely.

**185** Mark *one* answer
**When riding at night you should**

☐ **A** wear reflective clothing
☐ **B** wear a tinted visor
☐ **C** ride in the middle of the road
☐ **D** always give arm signals

You need to make yourself as visible as possible, from the front and rear and also from the side. Don't just rely on your headlight and tail light. Wear clothing that uses reflective material as this stands out in other vehicles' headlights.

**186** Mark *one* answer
**When riding in extremely cold conditions what can you do to keep warm?**

☐ **A** Stay close to the vehicles in front
☐ **B** Wear suitable clothing
☐ **C** Lie flat on the tank
☐ **D** Put one hand on the exhaust pipe

Motorcyclists are exposed to the elements and can become very cold when riding in wintry conditions. It's important to keep warm or your concentration could be affected. The only way to stay warm is to wear suitable clothing. If you do find yourself getting cold then stop at a suitable place to warm up.

**187** Mark *two* answers
**You are riding at night. To be seen more easily you should**

☐ **A** ride with your headlight on dipped beam
☐ **B** wear reflective clothing
☐ **C** keep the motorcycle clean
☐ **D** stay well out to the right
☐ **E** wear waterproof clothing

Reflective clothing works by reflecting light from the headlights of the other vehicles. This will make it easier for you to be seen.
Fluorescent clothing, although effective during the day, won't show up as well as reflective clothing at night.

**188** Mark *one* answer
**Your overall stopping distance will be much longer when riding**

☐ **A** in the rain
☐ **B** in fog
☐ **C** at night
☐ **D** in strong winds

Extra care should be taken in wet weather. Wet roads will affect the time it takes you to stop. Your stopping distance could be at least doubled.

**189** Mark *four* answers

**The road surface is very important to motorcyclists. Which FOUR of these are more likely to reduce the stability of your motorcycle?**

- ☐ **A** Potholes
- ☐ **B** Drain covers
- ☐ **C** Concrete
- ☐ **D** Oil patches
- ☐ **E** Tarmac
- ☐ **F** Loose gravel

Apart from the weather conditions, the road surface and any changes in it can affect the stability of your motorcycle. Be on the lookout for poor road surfaces and be aware of any traffic around you, in case you need to take avoiding action.

**190** Mark *two* answers

**You are riding in very hot weather. What are TWO effects that melting tar has on the control of your motorcycle?**

- ☐ **A** It can make the surface slippery
- ☐ **B** It can reduce tyre grip
- ☐ **C** It can reduce stopping distances
- ☐ **D** It can improve braking efficiency

If the tarmac road surface has softened in the heat, take extra care when braking and cornering. You should also look out for loose chippings where roads have been resurfaced. These will reduce your tyres' grip and can fly up, causing injury and damage.

**191** Mark *one* answer

**You are riding past queuing traffic. Why should you be more cautious when approaching this road marking?**

- ☐ **A** Lorries will be unloading here
- ☐ **B** School children will be crossing here
- ☐ **C** Pedestrians will be standing in the road
- ☐ **D** Traffic could be emerging and may not see you

When riding past queuing traffic look out for 'keep clear' road markings that will indicate a side road or entrance on the left. Vehicles may emerge between gaps in the traffic.

**192** Mark *one* answer

**What can cause your tyres to skid and lose their grip on the road surface?**

- ☐ **A** Giving hand signals
- ☐ **B** Riding one handed
- ☐ **C** Looking over your shoulder
- ☐ **D** Heavy braking

You can cause your motorcycle to skid by heavy or uncoordinated braking, as well as excessive acceleration, swerving or changing direction too sharply, and leaning over too far.

## 193 Mark *one* answer

**When riding in heavy rain a film of water can build up between your tyres and the road surface. This may result in loss of control. What can you do to avoid this happening?**

☐ **A** Keep your speed down
☐ **B** Increase your tyre pressures
☐ **C** Decrease your tyre pressures
☐ **D** Keep trying your brakes

There is a greater risk of aquaplaning when riding at speed. Keeping your speed down will help prevent aquaplaning.

If you can do so safely, try to avoid pools of water on the road.

## 194 Mark *one* answer

**When riding in heavy rain a film of water can build up between your tyres and the road. This is known as aquaplaning. What should you do to keep control?**

☐ **A** Use your rear brakes gently
☐ **B** Steer to the crown of the road
☐ **C** Ease off the throttle smoothly
☐ **D** Change up into a higher gear.

If your vehicle starts to aquaplane ease off the throttle smoothly. Do not brake or turn the steering until tyre grip has been restored.

## 195 Mark *one* answer

**After riding through deep water you notice your scooter brakes do not work properly. What would be the best way to dry them out?**

☐ **A** Ride slowly, braking lightly
☐ **B** Ride quickly, braking harshly
☐ **C** Stop and dry them with a cloth
☐ **D** Stop and wait for a few minutes

You can help to dry out brakes by riding slowly and applying light pressure to the brake pedal/lever. DO NOT ride at normal speeds until they are working normally again.

## 196 Mark *two* answers

**You have to ride in foggy weather. You should**

☐ **A** stay close to the centre of the road
☐ **B** switch only your sidelights on
☐ **C** switch on your dipped headlights
☐ **D** be aware of others not using their headlights
☐ **E** always ride in the gutter to see the kerb

Only travel in fog if your journey is absolutely necessary. Fog is often patchy and visibility can suddenly reduce without warning.

**197** Mark *one* answer

**Only a fool breaks the two-second rule refers to**

☐ **A** the time recommended when using the choke

☐ **B** the separation distance when riding in good conditions

☐ **C** restarting a stalled engine in busy traffic

☐ **D** the time you should keep your foot down at a junction

It is very important that you always leave a safe gap between yourself and any vehicle you're following. In good conditions you need to leave at least one metre for every mile per hour of your speed or a two-second time interval.

---

**198** Mark *one* answer

**At a mini-roundabout it is important that a motorcyclist should avoid**

☐ **A** turning right

☐ **B** using signals

☐ **C** taking 'lifesavers'

☐ **D** the painted area

Avoid riding over the painted area as these can become very slippery, especially when wet. Even on dry roads only a small part of the motorcycle's tyre makes contact with the road. Any reduction in grip can therefore affect the stability of your machine.

**199** Mark *two* answers

**You are riding on a motorway in a crosswind. You should take extra care when**

☐ **A** approaching service areas

☐ **B** overtaking a large vehicle

☐ **C** riding in slow-moving traffic

☐ **D** approaching an exit

☐ **E** riding in exposed places

Take extra care when overtaking large vehicles as they can cause air turbulence and buffeting. Beware of crosswinds when riding on exposed stretches of road, which can suddenly blow you off course. Bear in mind that strong winds can also affect the stability of other road users.

---

**200** Mark *one* answer

**Why should you try to avoid riding over this marked area?**

☐ **A** It is illegal to ride over bus stops

☐ **B** It will alter your machine's centre of gravity

☐ **C** Pedestrians may be waiting at the bus stop

☐ **D** A bus may have left patches of oil

Try to anticipate slippery road surfaces. Watch out for oil patches at places where vehicles stop for some time, such as bus stops, lay-bys and busy junctions.

**201** Mark *one* answer
**Your overall stopping distance comprises thinking and braking distance. You are on a good, dry road surface with good brakes and tyres. What is the typical BRAKING distance at 50mph?**

☐ **A** 14 metres (46 feet)
☐ **B** 24 metres (79 feet)
☐ **C** 38 metres (125 feet)
☐ **D** 55 metres (180 feet)

Different factors can affect how long it takes you to stop, such as weather and road conditions, vehicle condition and loading. You also need to add reaction time to this. The overall stopping distance at 50mph includes 15 metres thinking distance (the reaction time before braking starts) plus your braking distance of 38 metres', giving a typical overall stopping distance of 53 metres (175 feet) in good conditions.

**202** Mark *one* answer
**You are riding at speed through surface water. A thin film of water has built up between your tyres and the road surface. To keep control what should you do?**

☐ **A** Turn the steering quickly
☐ **B** Use the rear brake gently
☐ **C** Use both brakes gently
☐ **D** Ease off the throttle

Riding at speed where there is surface water can cause it to build up between your tyres and the road. This is known as aquaplaning and results in serious loss of steering and braking control, and can cause you to crash. The faster you are going, the more likely it is to happen. If it does, ease off the throttle smoothly.

**203** Mark *one* answer
**Braking distances on ice can be**

☐ **A** twice the normal distance
☐ **B** five times the normal distance
☐ **C** seven times the normal distance
☐ **D** ten times the normal distance

In icy and snowy weather, your stopping distance will increase by up to ten times compared to good, dry conditions.
Take extra care when braking, accelerating and steering, to cut down the risk of skidding.

**204** Mark *one* answer
**Freezing conditions will affect the distance it takes you to come to a stop. You should expect stopping distances to increase by up to**

☐ **A** two times
☐ **B** three times
☐ **C** five times
☐ **D** ten times

Your tyre grip is greatly reduced on icy roads and you need to allow up to ten times the normal stopping distance.

**205** Mark *one* answer
**In windy conditions you need to take extra care when**

☐ **A** using the brakes
☐ **B** making a hill start
☐ **C** turning into a narrow road
☐ **D** passing pedal cyclists

You should always give cyclists plenty of room when overtaking. When it's windy, a sudden gust could blow them off course.

## 206 Mark *one* answer

**When approaching a right-hand bend you should keep well to the left. Why is this?**

- ☐ **A** To improve your view of the road
- ☐ **B** To overcome the effect of the road's slope
- ☐ **C** To let faster traffic from behind overtake
- ☐ **D** To be positioned safely if you skid

Doing this will give you an earlier view around the bend and enable you to see any hazards sooner.

It also reduces the risk of collision with an oncoming vehicle that may have drifted over the centre line while taking the bend.

## 207 Mark *one* answer

**You have just gone through deep water. To dry off the brakes you should**

- ☐ **A** accelerate and keep to a high speed for a short time
- ☐ **B** go slowly while gently applying the brakes
- ☐ **C** avoid using the brakes at all for a few miles
- ☐ **D** stop for at least an hour to allow them time to dry

Water on the brakes will act as a lubricant, causing them to work less efficiently. Using the brakes lightly as you go along will dry them out.

## 208 Mark *two* answers

**In very hot weather the road surface can become soft. Which TWO of the following will be most affected?**

- ☐ **A** The suspension
- ☐ **B** The grip of the tyres
- ☐ **C** The braking
- ☐ **D** The exhaust

Only a small part of your tyres is in contact with the road. This is why you must consider the surface on which you're travelling, and alter your speed to suit the road conditions.

## 209 Mark *one* answer

**Where are you most likely to be affected by a side wind?**

- ☐ **A** On a narrow country lane
- ☐ **B** On an open stretch of road
- ☐ **C** On a busy stretch of road
- ☐ **D** On a long, straight road

In windy conditions, care must be taken on exposed roads. A strong gust of wind can blow you off course. Watch out for other road users who are particularly likely to be affected, such as cyclists, motorcyclists, high-sided lorries and vehicles towing trailers.

**210** Mark *one* answer
**In good conditions, what is the typical stopping distance at 70mph?**

☐ **A** 53 metres (175 feet)
☐ **B** 60 metres (197 feet)
☐ **C** 73 metres (240 feet)
☐ **D** 96 metres (315 feet)

Note that this is the typical stopping distance. It will take at least this distance to think, brake and stop in good conditions. In poor conditions it will take much longer.

**211** Mark *one* answer
**What is the shortest overall stopping distance on a dry road at 60mph?**

☐ **A** 53 metres (175 feet)
☐ **B** 58 metres (190 feet)
☐ **C** 73 metres (240 feet)
☐ **D** 96 metres (315 feet)

This distance is the equivalent of 18 car lengths. Try pacing out 73 metres and then look back. It's probably further than you think.

**212** Mark *one* answer
**You are following a vehicle at a safe distance on a wet road. Another driver overtakes you and pulls into the gap you have left. What should you do?**

☐ **A** Flash your headlights as a warning
☐ **B** Try to overtake safely as soon as you can
☐ **C** Drop back to regain a safe distance
☐ **D** Stay close to the other vehicle until it moves on

Wet weather will affect the time it takes for you to stop and can affect your control. Your speed should allow you to stop safely and in good time. If another vehicle pulls into the gap you've left, ease back until you've regained your stopping distance.

**213** Mark *one* answer
**You are travelling at 50mph on a good, dry road. What is your typical overall stopping distance?**

☐ **A** 36 metres (118 feet)
☐ **B** 53 metres (175 feet)
☐ **C** 75 metres (245 feet)
☐ **D** 96 metres (315 feet)

Even in good conditions it will usually take you further than you think to stop. Don't just learn the figures, make sure you understand how far the distance is.

# 214 Mark *one* answer
**You are on a good, dry, road surface. Your brakes and tyres are good. What is the typical overall stopping distance at 40mph?**

☐ **A** 23 metres (75 feet)
☐ **B** 36 metres (118 feet)
☐ **C** 53 metres (175 feet)
☐ **D** 96 metres (315 feet)

Stopping distances are affected by a number of variable factors. These include the type, model and condition of your vehicle, road and weather conditions, and your reaction time. Look well ahead for hazards and leave enough space between you and the vehicle in front. This should allow you to pull up safely if you have to, without braking sharply.

# 215 Mark *one* answer
**What should you do when overtaking a motorcyclist in strong winds?**

☐ **A** Pass close
☐ **B** Pass quickly
☐ **C** Pass wide
☐ **D** Pass immediately

In strong winds riders of two-wheeled vehicles are particularly vulnerable. When you overtake them allow plenty of room. Always check to the left as you pass.

# 216 Mark *one* answer
**You are overtaking a motorcyclist in strong winds. What should you do?**

☐ **A** Allow extra room
☐ **B** Give a thank you wave
☐ **C** Move back early
☐ **D** Sound your horn

It is easy for motorcyclists to be blown off course. Always give them plenty of room if you decide to overtake, especially in strong winds. Decide whether you need to overtake at all. Always check to the left as you pass.

# 217 Mark *one* answer
**Overall stopping distance is made up of thinking and braking distance. You are on a good, dry road surface with good brakes and tyres. What is the typical BRAKING distance from 50mph?**

☐ **A** 14 metres (46 feet)
☐ **B** 24 metres (80 feet)
☐ **C** 38 metres (125 feet)
☐ **D** 55 metres (180 feet)

Be aware this is just the braking distance. You need to add the thinking distance to this to give the OVERALL STOPPING DISTANCE. At 50mph the typical thinking distance will be 15 metres (50 feet), plus a braking distance of 38 metres (125 feet), giving an overall stopping distance of 53 metres (175 feet). The distance could be greater than this depending on your attention and response to any hazards. These figures are a general guide.

**218** Mark *one* answer

**In heavy motorway traffic the vehicle behind you is following too closely. How can you lower the risk of a collision?**

☐ **A** Increase your distance from the vehicle in front
☐ **B** Operate the brakes sharply
☐ **C** Switch on your hazard lights
☐ **D** Move onto the hard shoulder and stop

On busy roads traffic may still travel at high speeds despite being close together. Don't follow too closely to the vehicle in front. If a driver behind seems to be 'pushing' you, gradually increase your distance from the vehicle in front by slowing down gently. This will give you more space in front if you have to brake, and lessen the risk of a collision involving several vehicles.

**219** Mark *one* answer

**You are following other vehicles in fog. You have your lights on. What else can you do to reduce the chances of being in a collision?**

☐ **A** Keep close to the vehicle in front
☐ **B** Use your main beam instead of dipped headlights
☐ **C** Keep up with the faster vehicles
☐ **D** Reduce your speed and increase the gap in front

When it's foggy use dipped headlights. This will help you see and be seen by other road users. If visibility is seriously reduced consider using front and rear fog lights. Keep a sensible speed and don't follow the vehicle in front too closely. If the road is wet and slippery you'll need to allow twice the normal stopping distance.

**220** Mark *three* answers

**To avoid a collision when entering a contraflow system, you should**

☐ **A** reduce speed in good time
☐ **B** switch lanes at any time to make progress
☐ **C** choose an appropriate lane in good time
☐ **D** keep the correct separation distance
☐ **E** increase speed to pass through quickly
☐ **F** follow other motorists closely to avoid long queues

In a contraflow system you will be travelling close to oncoming traffic and sometimes in narrow lanes. You should obey the temporary speed limit signs, get into the correct lane at the proper time and keep a safe separation distance from the vehicle ahead. When traffic is at a very low speed, merging in turn is recommended if it's safe and appropriate.

**221** Mark *two* answers
**You get cold and wet when riding. Which TWO are likely to happen?**

☐ **A** You may lose concentration
☐ **B** You may slide off the seat
☐ **C** Your visor may freeze up
☐ **D** Your reaction times may be slower
☐ **E** Your helmet may loosen

When you're riding a motorcycle make sure you're wearing suitable clothing. If you become cold and uncomfortable this could cause you to lose concentration and could slow down your reaction time.

**222** Mark *one* answer
**You are riding up to a zebra crossing. You intend to stop for waiting pedestrians. How could you let them know you are stopping?**

☐ **A** By signalling with your left arm
☐ **B** By waving them across
☐ **C** By flashing your headlight
☐ **D** By signalling with your right arm

Giving the correct arm signal would indicate to approaching vehicles, as well as pedestrians, that you are stopping at the pedestrian crossing.

**223** Mark *one* answer
**You are about to ride home. You cannot find the glasses you need to wear. You should**

☐ **A** ride home slowly, keeping to quiet roads
☐ **B** borrow a friend's glasses and use those
☐ **C** ride home at night, so that the lights will help you
☐ **D** find a way of getting home without riding

Don't be tempted to ride if you've lost or forgotten your glasses. You must be able to see clearly when riding. If you can't you will be endangering yourself and other road users.

**224** Mark *three* answers
**Which THREE of these are likely effects of drinking alcohol?**

☐ **A** Reduced co-ordination
☐ **B** Increased confidence
☐ **C** Poor judgement
☐ **D** Increased concentration
☐ **E** Faster reactions
☐ **F** Colour blindness

Alcohol can increase confidence to a point where a rider's behaviour might become 'out of character'. Someone who normally behaves sensibly suddenly takes risks and could endanger themselves and others. Never drink and ride, or accept a ride from anyone who's been drinking.

**225** Mark *one* answer
**You find that you need glasses to read vehicle number plates at the required distance. When MUST you wear them?**

☐ **A** Only in bad weather conditions
☐ **B** At all times when riding
☐ **C** Only when you think it necessary
☐ **D** Only in bad light or at night time

Have your eyesight tested before you start your practical training. Then, throughout your riding life, have periodical checks to ensure that your eyesight hasn't deteriorated.

**226** Mark *three* answers
**Drinking any amount of alcohol is likely to**

☐ **A** slow down your reactions to hazards
☐ **B** increase the speed of your reactions
☐ **C** worsen your judgement of speed
☐ **D** improve your awareness of danger
☐ **E** give a false sense of confidence

Never drink if you are going to ride. It's always the safest option not to drink at all. Don't take risks, it's not worth it.

**227** Mark *one* answer
**Which of the following types of glasses should NOT be worn when riding at night?**

☐ **A** Half-moon
☐ **B** Round
☐ **C** Bi-focal
☐ **D** Tinted

If you are riding at night or in poor visibility, tinted lenses or a tinted visor will reduce the amount of available light reaching your eyes, making you less able to see clearly.

**228** Mark *one* answer
**For which of these may you use hazard warning lights?**

☐ **A** When riding on a motorway to warn traffic behind of a hazard ahead
☐ **B** When you are double parked on a two-way road
☐ **C** When your direction indicators are not working
☐ **D** When warning oncoming traffic that you intend to stop

Hazard warning lights are an important safety feature. Use them when riding on a motorway to warn following traffic of danger ahead. You should also use them if your motorcycle has broken down and is causing an obstruction.

**229** Mark *one* answer
**When riding how can you help to reduce the risk of hearing damage?**

☐ **A** Wearing goggles
☐ **B** Using ear plugs
☐ **C** Wearing a scarf
☐ **D** Keeping the visor up

Using ear plugs can help prevent hearing damage and fatigue caused by noise.

**230** Mark *one* answer

**When riding long distances at speed, noise can cause fatigue. What can you do to help reduce this?**

☐ **A** Vary your speed
☐ **B** Wear ear plugs
☐ **C** Use an open-face helmet
☐ **D** Ride in an upright position

Wearing ear plugs can help prevent hearing damage and also fatigue caused by noise.

**231** Mark *one* answer

**Why should you wear ear plugs when riding a motorcycle?**

☐ **A** To help to prevent ear damage
☐ **B** To make you less aware of traffic
☐ **C** To help to keep you warm
☐ **D** To make your helmet fit better

The use of ear plugs is recommended to reduce the effect of noise levels and protect your hearing.

**232** Mark *one* answer

**You are going out to a social event and alcohol will be available. You will be riding your motorcycle shortly afterwards. What is the safest thing to do?**

☐ **A** Stay just below the legal limit
☐ **B** Have soft drinks and alcohol in turn
☐ **C** Don't go beyond the legal limit
☐ **D** Stick to non-alcoholic drinks

The legal limit of alcohol is 80 milligrams per 100 millilitres of blood. However, drinking even the smallest amount of alcohol can affect your judgement and reactions. The safest and best option is to avoid any alcohol at all when riding or driving.

**233** Mark *one* answer

**You are convicted of riding after drinking too much alcohol. How could this affect your insurance?**

☐ **A** Your insurance may become invalid
☐ **B** The amount of excess you pay will be reduced
☐ **C** You will only be able to get third party cover
☐ **D** Cover will only be given for riding smaller motorcycles

Riding while under the influence of drink or drugs can invalidate your insurance. This also endangers yourself and others. It's not a risk worth taking.

**234** Mark *one* answer

**Why should you check over your shoulder before turning right into a side road?**

☐ **A** To make sure the side road is clear
☐ **B** To check for emerging traffic
☐ **C** To check for overtaking vehicles
☐ **D** To confirm your intention to turn

Take a last check over your shoulder before committing yourself to a manoeuvre. This is especially important when turning right, as other road users may not have seen your signal or may not understand your intentions.

**235** Mark *two* answers
**You are not sure if your cough medicine will affect you. What TWO things should you do?**

☐ **A** Ask your doctor
☐ **B** Check the medicine label
☐ **C** Ride if you feel alright
☐ **D** Ask a friend or relative for advice

If you're taking medicine or drugs prescribed by your doctor, check to ensure that they won't make you drowsy. If you forget to ask when you're at the surgery, check with your pharmacist.

**236** Mark *one* answer
**When should you use hazard warning lights?**

☐ **A** When you are double-parked on a two-way road
☐ **B** When your direction indicators are not working
☐ **C** When warning oncoming traffic that you intend to stop
☐ **D** When your motorcycle has broken down and is causing an obstruction

Hazard warning lights are an important safety feature and should be used if you have broken down and are causing an obstruction. Don't use them as an excuse to park illegally, such as when using a cash machine or post box. You may also use them on motorways to warn following traffic of danger ahead.

**237** Mark *one* answer
**It is a very hot day. What would you expect to find?**

☐ **A** Mud on the road
☐ **B** A soft road surface
☐ **C** Roadworks ahead
☐ **D** Banks of fog

In very hot weather the road surface can become soft and may melt. Take care when braking and cornering on soft tarmac, as this can lead to reduced grip and cause skidding.

**238** Mark *one* answer
**You see this road marking in between queuing traffic. What should you look out for?**

KEEP CLEAR

☐ **A** Overhanging trees
☐ **B** Roadworks
☐ **C** Traffic wardens
☐ **D** Traffic emerging

'Keep clear' markings should not be obstructed. They can be found in congested areas to help traffic waiting to emerge onto a busy road.

## 239 Mark *two* answers
**Where would you expect to see these markers?**

- ☐ **A** On a motorway sign
- ☐ **B** At the entrance to a narrow bridge
- ☐ **C** On a large goods vehicle
- ☐ **D** On a builder's skip placed on the road

These markers must be fitted to vehicles over 13 metres long, large goods vehicles, and rubbish skips placed in the road. They are reflective to make them easier to see in the dark.

## 240 Mark *one* answer
**What is the main hazard shown in this picture?**

- ☐ **A** Vehicles turning right
- ☐ **B** Vehicles doing U-turns
- ☐ **C** The cyclist crossing the road
- ☐ **D** Parked cars around the corner

Look at the picture carefully and try to imagine you're there. The cyclist in this picture appears to be trying to cross the road. You must be able to deal with the unexpected, especially when you're approaching a hazardous junction. Look well ahead to give yourself time to deal with any hazards.

## 241 Mark *one* answer
**Which road user has caused a hazard?**

- ☐ **A** The parked car (arrowed A)
- ☐ **B** The pedestrian waiting to cross (arrowed B)
- ☐ **C** The moving car (arrowed C)
- ☐ **D** The car turning (arrowed D)

The car arrowed A is parked within the area marked by zigzag lines at the pedestrian crossing. Parking here is illegal. It also

- blocks the view for pedestrians wishing to cross the road
- restricts the view of the crossing for approaching traffic.

**242** Mark *one* answer

**What should the driver of the car approaching the crossing do?**

- ☐ **A** Continue at the same speed
- ☐ **B** Sound the horn
- ☐ **C** Drive through quickly
- ☐ **D** Slow down and get ready to stop

Look well ahead to see if any hazards are developing. This will give you more time to deal with them in the correct way. The man in the picture is clearly intending to cross the road. You should be travelling at a speed that allows you to check your mirror, slow down and stop in good time. You shouldn't have to brake harshly.

**243** Mark *three* answers

**What THREE things should the driver of the grey car (arrowed) be especially aware of?**

- ☐ **A** Pedestrians stepping out between cars
- ☐ **B** Other cars behind the grey car
- ☐ **C** Doors opening on parked cars
- ☐ **D** The bumpy road surface
- ☐ **E** Cars leaving parking spaces
- ☐ **F** Empty parking spaces

You need to be aware that other road users may not have seen you. Always be on the lookout for hazards that may develop suddenly and need you to take avoiding action.

**244** Mark *one* answer

**You see this sign ahead. You should expect the road to**

- ☐ **A** go steeply uphill
- ☐ **B** go steeply downhill
- ☐ **C** bend sharply to the left
- ☐ **D** bend sharply to the right

Adjust your speed in good time and select the correct gear for your speed. Going too fast into the bend could cause you to lose control.

Braking late and harshly while changing direction reduces your vehicle's grip on the road, and is likely to cause a skid.

## 245 Mark *one* answer

**You are approaching this cyclist. You should**

☐ **A** overtake before the cyclist gets
to the junction
☐ **B** flash your headlights at the cyclist
☐ **C** slow down and allow the cyclist to turn
☐ **D** overtake the cyclist on the left-hand side

Keep well back and allow the cyclist room
to take up the correct position for the turn.
Don't get too close behind or try to squeeze
past.

## 246 Mark *one* answer

**Why must you take extra care when turning right at this junction?**

☐ **A** Road surface is poor
☐ **B** Footpaths are narrow
☐ **C** Road markings are faint
☐ **D** There is reduced visibility

You may have to pull forward slowly until
you can see up and down the road. Be aware
that the traffic approaching the junction
can't see you either. If you don't know that
it's clear, don't go.

## 247 Mark *one* answer

**When approaching this bridge you should give way to**

☐ **A** bicycles     ☐ **B** buses
☐ **C** motorcycles     ☐ **D** cars

A double-deck bus or high-sided lorry will
have to take up a position in the centre of
the road so that it can clear the bridge.
There is normally a sign to indicate this.
　Look well down the road, through the
bridge and be aware you may have to stop
and give way to an oncoming large vehicle.

## 248 Mark *one* answer

**What type of vehicle could you expect to meet in the middle of the road?**

☐ **A** Lorry     ☐ **B** Bicycle
☐ **C** Car     ☐ **D** Motorcycle

The highest point of the bridge is in the
centre so a large vehicle might have to move
to the centre of the road to allow it enough
room to pass under the bridge.

## 249 Mark *one* answer
### At this blind junction you must stop

- ☐ **A** behind the line, then edge forward to see clearly
- ☐ **B** beyond the line at a point where you can see clearly
- ☐ **C** only if there is traffic on the main road
- ☐ **D** only if you are turning to the right

The 'stop' sign has been put here because there is a poor view into the main road. You must stop because it will not be possible to assess the situation on the move, however slowly you are travelling.

## 250 Mark *one* answer
### A driver pulls out of a side road in front of you. You have to brake hard. You should

- ☐ **A** ignore the error and stay calm
- ☐ **B** flash your lights to show your annoyance
- ☐ **C** sound your horn to show your annoyance
- ☐ **D** overtake as soon as possible

Where there are a number of side roads, be alert. Be especially careful if there are a lot of parked vehicles because they can make it more difficult for drivers emerging to see you. Try to be tolerant if a vehicle does emerge and you have to brake quickly. Don't react aggressively.

## 251 Mark *one* answer
### An elderly person's driving ability could be affected because they may be unable to

- ☐ **A** obtain car insurance
- ☐ **B** understand road signs
- ☐ **C** react very quickly
- ☐ **D** give signals correctly

Be tolerant of older drivers. Poor eyesight and hearing could affect the speed with which they react to a hazard and may cause them to be hesitant.

## 252 Mark *one* answer
### You have just passed these warning lights. What hazard would you expect to see next?

- ☐ **A** A level crossing with no barrier
- ☐ **B** An ambulance station
- ☐ **C** A school crossing patrol
- ☐ **D** An opening bridge

These lights warn that children may be crossing the road to a nearby school. Slow down so that you're ready to stop if necessary.

**253** Mark *one* answer

**You are planning a long journey. Do you need to plan rest stops?**

- ☐ **A** Yes, you should plan to stop every half an hour
- ☐ **B** Yes, regular stops help concentration
- ☐ **C** No, you will be less tired if you get there as soon as possible
- ☐ **D** No, only fuel stops will be needed

Try to plan your journey so that you can take rest stops. It's recommended that you take a break of at least 15 minutes after every two hours of driving. This should help to maintain your concentration.

---

**254** Mark *one* answer

**A driver does something that upsets you. You should**

- ☐ **A** try not to react
- ☐ **B** let them know how you feel
- ☐ **C** flash your headlights several times
- ☐ **D** sound your horn

There are times when other road users make a misjudgement or mistake. When this happens try not to get annoyed and don't react by showing anger. Sounding your horn, flashing your headlights or shouting won't help the situation. Good anticipation will help to prevent these incidents becoming collisions.

**255** Mark *one* answer

**The red lights are flashing. What should you do when approaching this level crossing?**

- ☐ **A** Go through quickly
- ☐ **B** Go through carefully
- ☐ **C** Stop before the barrier
- ☐ **D** Switch on hazard warning lights

At level crossings the red lights flash before and when the barrier is down. At most crossings an amber light will precede the red lights. You must stop behind the white line unless you have already crossed it when the amber light comes on. NEVER zigzag around half-barriers.

---

**256** Mark *one* answer

**You are approaching crossroads. The traffic lights have failed. What should you do?**

- ☐ **A** Brake and stop only for large vehicles
- ☐ **B** Brake sharply to a stop before looking
- ☐ **C** Be prepared to brake sharply to a stop
- ☐ **D** Be prepared to stop for any traffic

When approaching a junction where the traffic lights have failed, you should proceed with caution. Treat the situation as an unmarked junction and be prepared to stop.

**257** Mark *one* answer

**What should the driver of the red car (arrowed) do?**

☐ **A** Wave the pedestrians who are waiting to cross

☐ **B** Wait for the pedestrian in the road to cross

☐ **C** Quickly drive behind the pedestrian in the road

☐ **D** Tell the pedestrian in the road she should not have crossed

Some people might take longer to cross the road. They may be older or have a disability. Be patient and don't hurry them by showing your impatience. They might have poor eyesight or not be able to hear traffic approaching. If pedestrians are standing at the side of the road, don't signal or wave them to cross. Other road users may not have seen your signal and this could lead the pedestrians into a hazardous situation.

**258** Mark *one* answer

**You are following a slower-moving vehicle on a narrow country road. There is a junction just ahead on the right. What should you do?**

☐ **A** Overtake after checking your mirrors and signalling

☐ **B** Stay behind until you are past the junction

☐ **C** Accelerate quickly to pass before the junction

☐ **D** Slow down and prepare to overtake on the left

You should never overtake as you approach a junction. If a vehicle emerged from the junction while you were overtaking, a dangerous situation could develop very quickly.

**259** Mark *one* answer

**What should you do as you approach this overhead bridge?**

☐ **A** Move out to the centre of the road before going through

☐ **B** Find another route, this is only for high vehicles

☐ **C** Be prepared to give way to large vehicles in the middle of the road

☐ **D** Move across to the right hand side before going through

Oncoming large vehicles may need to move to the middle of the road so that they can pass safely under the bridge. There will not be enough room for you to continue and you should be ready to stop and wait.

## 260 Mark *one* answer
**Why are mirrors often slightly curved (convex)?**

- ☐ **A** They give a wider field of vision
- ☐ **B** They totally cover blind spots
- ☐ **C** They make it easier to judge the speed of following traffic
- ☐ **D** They make following traffic look bigger

Although a convex mirror gives a wide view of the scene behind, you should be aware that it will not show you everything behind or to the side of the vehicle. Before you move off you will need to check over your shoulder to look for anything not visible in the mirrors.

## 261 Mark *one* answer
**You see this sign on the rear of a slow-moving lorry that you want to pass. It is travelling in the middle lane of a three-lane motorway. You should**

- ☐ **A** cautiously approach the lorry then pass on either side
- ☐ **B** follow the lorry until you can leave the motorway
- ☐ **C** wait on the hard shoulder until the lorry has stopped
- ☐ **D** approach with care and keep to the left of the lorry

This sign is found on slow-moving or stationary works vehicles. If you wish to overtake, do so on the left, as indicated. Be aware that there might be workmen in the area.

## 262 Mark *one* answer
**You think the driver of the vehicle in front has forgotten to cancel their right indicator. You should**

- ☐ **A** flash your lights to alert the driver
- ☐ **B** sound your horn before overtaking
- ☐ **C** overtake on the left if there is room
- ☐ **D** stay behind and not overtake

The driver may be unsure of the location of a junction and turn suddenly. Be cautious and don't attempt to overtake.

## 263 Mark *one* answer
**What is the main hazard the driver of the red car (arrowed) should be aware of?**

- ☐ **A** Glare from the sun may affect the driver's vision
- ☐ **B** The black car may stop suddenly
- ☐ **C** The bus may move out into the road
- ☐ **D** Oncoming vehicles will assume the driver is turning right

If you can do so safely give way to buses signalling to move off at bus stops. Try to anticipate the actions of other road users around you. The driver of the red car should be prepared for the bus pulling out. As you approach a bus stop look to see how many passengers are waiting to board. If the last one has just got on, the bus is likely to move off.

## 264 Mark *one* answer
**This yellow sign on a vehicle indicates this is**

- ☐ **A** a broken-down vehicle
- ☐ **B** a school bus
- ☐ **C** an ice cream van
- ☐ **D** a private ambulance

Buses which carry children to and from school may stop at places other than scheduled bus stops. Be aware that they might pull over at any time to allow children to get on or off. This will normally be when traffic is heavy during rush hour.

## 265 Mark *two* answers
**What TWO main hazards should you be aware of when going along this street?**

- ☐ **A** Glare from the sun
- ☐ **B** Car doors opening suddenly
- ☐ **C** Lack of road markings
- ☐ **D** The headlights on parked cars being switched on
- ☐ **E** Large goods vehicles
- ☐ **F** Children running out from between vehicles

On roads where there are many parked vehicles you should take extra care. You might not be able to see children between parked cars and they may run out into the road without looking.

People may open car doors without realising the hazard this can create. You will also need to look well down the road for oncoming traffic.

### 266 Mark *one* answer
**What is the main hazard you should be aware of when following this cyclist?**

- ☐ **A** The cyclist may move to the left and dismount
- ☐ **B** The cyclist may swerve out into the road
- ☐ **C** The contents of the cyclist's carrier may fall onto the road
- ☐ **D** The cyclist may wish to turn right at the end of the road

When following a cyclist be aware that they have to deal with the hazards around them. They may wobble or swerve to avoid a pothole in the road or see a potential hazard and change direction suddenly. Don't follow them too closely or rev your engine impatiently.

### 267 Mark *one* answer
**A driver's behaviour has upset you. It may help if you**

- ☐ **A** stop and take a break
- ☐ **B** shout abusive language
- ☐ **C** gesture to them with your hand
- ☐ **D** follow their car, flashing your headlights

Tiredness may make you more irritable than you would be normally. You might react differently to situations because of it. If you feel yourself becoming tense, take a break.

### 268 Mark *one* answer
**In areas where there are 'traffic-calming' measures you should**

- ☐ **A** travel at a reduced speed
- ☐ **B** always travel at the speed limit
- ☐ **C** position in the centre of the road
- ☐ **D** only slow down if pedestrians are near

Traffic-calming measures such as road humps, chicanes and narrowings are intended to slow you down. Maintain a reduced speed until you reach the end of these features. They are there to protect pedestrians. Kill your speed!

### 269 Mark *two* answers
**When approaching this hazard why should you slow down?**

- ☐ **A** Because of the bend
- ☐ **B** Because it's hard to see to the right
- ☐ **C** Because of approaching traffic
- ☐ **D** Because of animals crossing
- ☐ **E** Because of the level crossing

There are two hazards clearly signed in this picture. You should be preparing for the bend by slowing down and selecting the correct gear. You might also have to stop at the level crossing, so be alert and be prepared to stop if necessary.

## 270 Mark *one* answer
**Why are place names painted on the road surface?**

☐ **A** To restrict the flow of traffic
☐ **B** To warn you of oncoming traffic
☐ **C** To enable you to change lanes early
☐ **D** To prevent you changing lanes

The names of towns and cities may be painted on the road at busy junctions and complex road systems. Their purpose is to let you move into the correct lane in good time, allowing traffic to flow more freely.

## 271 Mark *one* answer
**Some two-way roads are divided into three lanes. Why are these particularly dangerous?**

☐ **A** Traffic in both directions can use the middle lane to overtake
☐ **B** Traffic can travel faster in poor weather conditions
☐ **C** Traffic can overtake on the left
☐ **D** Traffic uses the middle lane for emergencies only

If you intend to overtake you must consider that approaching traffic could be planning the same manoeuvre. When you have considered the situation and have decided it is safe, indicate your intentions early. This will show the approaching traffic that you intend to pull out.

## 272 Mark *one* answer
**You are on a dual carriageway. Ahead you see a vehicle with an amber flashing light. What could this be?**

☐ **A** An ambulance
☐ **B** A fire engine
☐ **C** A doctor on call
☐ **D** A disabled person's vehicle

An amber flashing light on a vehicle indicates that it is slow-moving. Battery powered vehicles used by disabled people are limited to 8mph. It's not advisable for them to be used on dual carriageways where the speed limit exceeds 50mph. If they are then an amber flashing light must be used.

## 273 Mark *one* answer
**What does this signal from a police officer mean to oncoming traffic?**

☐ **A** Go ahead
☐ **B** Stop
☐ **C** Turn left
☐ **D** Turn right

Police officers may need to direct traffic, for example, at a junction where the traffic lights have broken down. Check your copy of The Highway Code for the signals that they use.

## 274 Mark *two* answers

**Why should you be especially cautious when going past this stationary bus?**

- ☐ **A** There is traffic approaching in the distance
- ☐ **B** The driver may open the door
- ☐ **C** It may suddenly move off
- ☐ **D** People may cross the road in front of it
- ☐ **E** There are bicycles parked on the pavement

A stationary bus at a bus stop can hide pedestrians just in front of it who might be about to cross the road. Only go past at a speed that will enable you to stop safely if you need to.

## 275 Mark *three* answers

**Overtaking is a major cause of collisions. In which THREE of these situations should you NOT overtake?**

- ☐ **A** If you are turning left shortly afterwards
- ☐ **B** When you are in a one-way street
- ☐ **C** When you are approaching a junction
- ☐ **D** If you are travelling up a long hill
- ☐ **E** When your view ahead is blocked

You should not overtake unless it is really necessary. Arriving safely is more important than taking risks. Also look out for road signs and markings that show it is illegal or would be unsafe to overtake. In many cases overtaking is unlikely to significantly improve journey times.

## 276 Mark *three* answers

**Which THREE result from drinking alcohol?**

- ☐ **A** Less control
- ☐ **B** A false sense of confidence
- ☐ **C** Faster reactions
- ☐ **D** Poor judgement of speed
- ☐ **E** Greater awareness of danger

You must understand the serious dangers of mixing alcohol with driving or riding. Alcohol will severely reduce your ability to drive or ride safely. Just one drink could put you over the limit. Don't risk people's lives – DON'T DRINK AND DRIVE OR RIDE!

**277** Mark *one* answer

**You should not ride too closely behind a lorry because**

- ☐ **A** you will breathe in the lorry's exhaust fumes
- ☐ **B** wind from the lorry will slow you down
- ☐ **C** drivers behind you may not be able to see you
- ☐ **D** it will reduce your view ahead

If you're following too close behind a large vehicle your view beyond it will be restricted. Drop back. This will help you to see more of the road ahead. It will also help the driver of the large vehicle to see you in the mirror and gives you a safe separation distance in which to take avoiding action if a hazardous situation arises.

**278** Mark *three* answers

**You are riding on a country lane. You see cattle on the road. You should**

- ☐ **A** slow down
- ☐ **B** stop if necessary
- ☐ **C** give plenty of room
- ☐ **D** rev your engine
- ☐ **E** sound your horn
- ☐ **F** ride up close behind them

Try not to startle the animals. They can be easily frightened by noise or by traffic passing too closely.

**279** Mark *one* answer

**A learner driver has begun to emerge into your path from a side road on the left. You should**

- ☐ **A** be ready to slow down and stop
- ☐ **B** let them emerge then ride close behind
- ☐ **C** turn into the side road
- ☐ **D** brake hard, then wave them out

If you see another vehicle begin to emerge into your path you should ride defensively. Always be ready to slow down or stop if necessary.

**280** Mark *one* answer

**The vehicle ahead is being driven by a learner. You should**

- ☐ **A** keep calm and be patient
- ☐ **B** ride up close behind
- ☐ **C** put your headlight on full beam
- ☐ **D** sound your horn and overtake

Learners might take longer to react to traffic situations. Don't unnerve them by riding up close behind or showing signs of impatience.

## 281 Mark *one* answer

**You are riding in fast-flowing traffic. The vehicle behind is following too closely. You should**

- ☐ **A** slow down gradually to increase the gap in front of you
- ☐ **B** slow down as quickly as possible by braking
- ☐ **C** accelerate to get away from the vehicle behind you
- ☐ **D** apply the brakes sharply to warn the driver behind

It is dangerous for vehicles to travel too close together. Visibility is reduced and there is a higher risk of collision if a vehicle brakes suddenly to avoid a hazard. By increasing the separation distance between you and the vehicle in front, you have a greater safety margin. It also gives space for the vehicles behind to overtake you if they wish.

## 282 Mark *one* answer

**You are riding towards a zebra crossing. Waiting to cross is a person in a wheelchair. You should**

- ☐ **A** continue on your way
- ☐ **B** wave to the person to cross
- ☐ **C** wave to the person to wait
- ☐ **D** be prepared to stop

As you would with an able-bodied person, you should prepare to slow down and stop. Don't wave them across, as other traffic may not stop.

## 283 Mark *one* answer

**Why should you allow extra room when overtaking another motorcyclist on a windy day?**

- ☐ **A** The rider may turn off suddenly to get out of the wind
- ☐ **B** The rider may be blown across in front of you
- ☐ **C** The rider may stop suddenly
- ☐ **D** The rider may be travelling faster than normal

On a windy day, be aware that the blustery conditions might blow you or other motorcyclists out of position. Think about this before deciding to overtake.

## 284 Mark *two* answers

**You have stopped at a pelican crossing. A disabled person is crossing slowly in front of you. The lights have now changed to green. You should**

- ☐ **A** allow the person to cross
- ☐ **B** ride in front of the person
- ☐ **C** ride behind the person
- ☐ **D** sound your horn
- ☐ **E** be patient
- ☐ **F** edge forward slowly

At a pelican crossing the green light means you may proceed as long as the crossing is clear. If someone hasn't finished crossing, be patient and wait for them.

## 285 Mark *one* answer
**Where should you take particular care to look out for other motorcyclists and cyclists?**

☐ **A** On dual carriageways
☐ **B** At junctions
☐ **C** At zebra crossings
☐ **D** On one-way streets

Other motorcyclists and cyclists may be difficult to see on the road, particularly at junctions. If your view is blocked by other traffic you may not be able to see them approaching.

## 286 Mark *one* answer
**Why is it vital for a rider to make a 'lifesaver' check before turning right?**

☐ **A** To check for any overtaking traffic
☐ **B** To confirm that they are about to turn
☐ **C** To make sure the side road is clear
☐ **D** To check that the rear indicator is flashing

The 'lifesaver' glance makes you aware of what is happening behind and alongside you before altering your course. This glance must be timed so that you still have time to react if it isn't safe to carry out your manoeuvre.

## 287 Mark *two* answers
**You are about to overtake horse riders. Which TWO of the following could scare the horses?**

☐ **A** Sounding your horn
☐ **B** Giving arm signals
☐ **C** Riding slowly
☐ **D** Revving your engine

When passing horses allow them plenty of space and slow down. Animals can be frightened by sudden or loud noises, so don't sound your horn or rev the engine.

## 288 Mark *one* answer
**What is a main cause of road traffic incidents among young and new motorcyclists?**

☐ **A** Using borrowed equipment
☐ **B** Lack of experience and judgement
☐ **C** Riding in bad weather conditions
☐ **D** Riding on country roads

Young and inexperienced motorcyclists are far more likely to be involved in incidents than more experienced riders. Reasons for this include natural exuberance, showing off, competitive behaviour and over confidence. Don't overestimate your abilities and never ride too fast for the conditions.

**289** Mark *one* answer
**Which of the following is applicable to young motorcyclists?**

☐ **A** They are normally better than experienced riders
☐ **B** They are usually less likely to have a crash
☐ **C** They are often over-confident of their own ability
☐ **D** They are more likely to get cheaper insurance

Young and inexperienced motorcyclists often have more confidence than ability. It takes time to gain experience and become a good rider. Make sure you have the right attitude and put safety first.

**290** Mark *one* answer
**The road outside this school is marked with yellow zigzag lines. What do these lines mean?**

☐ **A** You may park on the lines when dropping off school children
☐ **B** You may park on the lines when picking up school children
☐ **C** You should not wait or park your motorcycle here
☐ **D** You must stay with your motorcycle if you park here

Parking here will block the view of the school gates, endangering the lives of children on their way to and from school.

**291** Mark *one* answer
**Which sign means that there may be people walking along the road?**

☐ **A**   ☐ **B**

☐ **C**   ☐ **D**

Always check the road signs. Triangular signs are warning signs and they'll keep you informed of hazards ahead and help you to anticipate any problems. There are a number of different signs showing pedestrians. Learn the meaning of each one.

## 292 Mark *one* answer

**You are turning left at a junction. Pedestrians have started to cross the road. You should**

- ☐ **A** go on, giving them plenty of room
- ☐ **B** stop and wave at them to cross
- ☐ **C** blow your horn and proceed
- ☐ **D** give way to them

If you're turning into a side road, pedestrians already crossing the road have priority and you should give way to them. Don't wave them across the road, sound your horn, flash your lights or give any other misleading signal. Other road users may misinterpret your signal and this may lead the pedestrians into a dangerous situation. If a pedestrian is slow or indecisive be patient and wait. Don't hurry them across by revving your engine.

## 293 Mark *one* answer

**You are turning left from a main road into a side road. People are already crossing the road into which you are turning. You should**

- ☐ **A** continue, as it is your right of way
- ☐ **B** signal to them to continue crossing
- ☐ **C** wait and allow them to cross
- ☐ **D** sound your horn to warn them of your presence

Always check the road into which you are turning. Approaching at the correct speed will allow you enough time to observe and react.

Give way to any pedestrians already crossing the road.

**294** Mark *one* answer

**You are at a road junction, turning into a minor road. There are pedestrians crossing the minor road. You should**

- ☐ **A** stop and wave the pedestrians across
- ☐ **B** sound your horn to let the pedestrians know that you are there
- ☐ **C** give way to the pedestrians who are already crossing
- ☐ **D** carry on; the pedestrians should give way to you

Always look into the road into which you are turning. If there are pedestrians crossing, give way to them, but don't wave or signal to them to cross. Signal your intention to turn as you approach.

**295** Mark *one* answer

**You are turning left into a side road. What hazards should you be especially aware of?**

- ☐ **A** One-way street
- ☐ **B** Pedestrians
- ☐ **C** Traffic congestion
- ☐ **D** Parked vehicles

Make sure that you have reduced your speed and are in the correct gear for the turn. Look into the road before you turn and always give way to any pedestrians who are crossing.

**296** Mark *one* answer

**You intend to turn right into a side road. Just before turning you should check for motorcyclists who might be**

- ☐ **A** overtaking on your left
- ☐ **B** following you closely
- ☐ **C** emerging from the side road
- ☐ **D** overtaking on your right

Never attempt to change direction to the right without first checking your right-hand mirror. A motorcyclist might not have seen your signal and could be hidden by the car behind you. This action should become a matter of routine.

**297** Mark *one* answer

**A toucan crossing is different from other crossings because**

- ☐ **A** moped riders can use it
- ☐ **B** it is controlled by a traffic warden
- ☐ **C** it is controlled by two flashing lights
- ☐ **D** cyclists can use it

Toucan crossings are shared by pedestrians and cyclists and they are shown the green light together. Cyclists are permitted to cycle across.

The signals are push-button operated and there is no flashing amber phase.

## 298 Mark *one* answer
**How will a school crossing patrol signal you to stop?**

☐ **A** By pointing to children on the opposite pavement
☐ **B** By displaying a red light
☐ **C** By displaying a stop sign
☐ **D** By giving you an arm signal

If a school crossing patrol steps out into the road with a stop sign you must stop. Don't wave anyone across the road and don't get impatient or rev your engine.

## 299 Mark *one* answer
**Where would you see this sign?**

☐ **A** In the window of a car taking children to school
☐ **B** At the side of the road
☐ **C** At playground areas
☐ **D** On the rear of a school bus or coach

Vehicles that are used to carry children to and from school will be travelling at busy times of the day. If you're following a vehicle with this sign be prepared for it to make frequent stops. It might pick up or set down passengers in places other than normal bus stops.

## 300 Mark *one* answer
**Which sign tells you that pedestrians may be walking in the road as there is no pavement?**

Give pedestrians who are walking at the side of the road plenty of room when you pass them. They may turn around when they hear your engine and unintentionally step into the path of your vehicle.

## 301 Mark *one* answer
**What does this sign mean?**

☐ **A** No route for pedestrians and cyclists
☐ **B** A route for pedestrians only
☐ **C** A route for cyclists only
☐ **D** A route for pedestrians and cyclists

This sign shows a shared route for pedestrians and cyclists: when it ends, the cyclists will be rejoining the main road.

## 302 Mark *one* answer
**You see a pedestrian with a white stick and red band. This means that the person is**

- ☐ **A** physically disabled
- ☐ **B** deaf only
- ☐ **C** blind only
- ☐ **D** deaf and blind

If someone is deaf as well as blind, they may be carrying a white stick with a red reflective band. You can't see if a pedestrian is deaf. Don't assume everyone can hear you approaching.

## 303 Mark *one* answer
**What action would you take when elderly people are crossing the road?**

- ☐ **A** Wave them across so they know that you have seen them
- ☐ **B** Be patient and allow them to cross in their own time
- ☐ **C** Rev the engine to let them know that you are waiting
- ☐ **D** Tap the horn in case they are hard of hearing

Be aware that older people might take a long time to cross the road. They might also be hard of hearing and not hear you approaching. Don't hurry older people across the road by getting too close to them or revving your engine.

## 304 Mark *one* answer
**You see two elderly pedestrians about to cross the road ahead. You should**

- ☐ **A** expect them to wait for you to pass
- ☐ **B** speed up to get past them quickly
- ☐ **C** stop and wave them across the road
- ☐ **D** be careful, they may misjudge your speed

Older people may have impaired hearing, vision, concentration and judgement. They may also walk slowly and so could take a long time to cross the road.

## 305 Mark *one* answer
**You are coming up to a roundabout. A cyclist is signalling to turn right. What should you do?**

- ☐ **A** Overtake on the right
- ☐ **B** Give a horn warning
- ☐ **C** Signal the cyclist to move across
- ☐ **D** Give the cyclist plenty of room

If you're following a cyclist who's signalling to turn right at a roundabout leave plenty of room. Give them space and time to get into the correct lane.

## 306 Mark *two* answers
**Which TWO should you allow extra room when overtaking?**

- ☐ **A** Motorcycles
- ☐ **B** Tractors
- ☐ **C** Bicycles
- ☐ **D** Road-sweeping vehicles

Don't pass riders too closely as this may cause them to lose balance. Always leave as much room as you would for a car, and don't cut in.

**307** Mark *one* answer
**Why should you look particularly for motorcyclists and cyclists at junctions?**

☐ **A** They may want to turn into the side road
☐ **B** They may slow down to let you turn
☐ **C** They are harder to see
☐ **D** They might not see you turn

Cyclists and motorcyclists are smaller than other vehicles and so are more difficult to see. They can easily become hidden from your view by cars parked near a junction.

**308** Mark *one* answer
**You are waiting to come out of a side road. Why should you watch carefully for motorcycles?**

☐ **A** Motorcycles are usually faster than cars
☐ **B** Police patrols often use motorcycles
☐ **C** Motorcycles are small and hard to see
☐ **D** Motorcycles have right of way

If you're waiting to emerge from a side road watch out for motorcycles: they're small and can be difficult to see. Be especially careful if there are parked vehicles restricting your view, there might be a motorcycle approaching.
IF YOU DON'T KNOW, DON'T GO.

**309** Mark *one* answer
**In daylight, an approaching motorcyclist is using a dipped headlight. Why?**

☐ **A** So that the rider can be seen more easily
☐ **B** To stop the battery overcharging
☐ **C** To improve the rider's vision
☐ **D** The rider is inviting you to proceed

A motorcycle can be lost from sight behind another vehicle. The use of the headlight helps to make it more conspicuous and therefore more easily seen.

**310** Mark *one* answer
**Motorcyclists should wear bright clothing mainly because**

☐ **A** they must do so by law
☐ **B** it helps keep them cool in summer
☐ **C** the colours are popular
☐ **D** drivers often do not see them

Motorcycles are small vehicles and can be difficult to see. If the rider wears bright clothing it can make it easier for other road users to see them approaching, especially at junctions.

## 311 Mark *one* answer

**There is a slow-moving motorcyclist ahead of you. You are unsure what the rider is going to do. You should**

☐ **A** pass on the left
☐ **B** pass on the right
☐ **C** stay behind
☐ **D** move closer

If a motorcyclist is travelling slowly it may be that they are looking for a turning or entrance. Be patient and stay behind them in case they need to make a sudden change of direction.

## 312 Mark *one* answer

**Motorcyclists will often look round over their right shoulder just before turning right. This is because**

☐ **A** they need to listen for following traffic
☐ **B** motorcycles do not have mirrors
☐ **C** looking around helps them balance as they turn
☐ **D** they need to check for traffic in their blind area

If you see a motorcyclist take a quick glance over their shoulder, this could mean they are about to change direction. Recognising a clue like this helps you to be prepared and take appropriate action, making you safer on the road.

## 313 Mark *three* answers

**At road junctions which of the following are most vulnerable?**

☐ **A** Cyclists
☐ **B** Motorcyclists
☐ **C** Pedestrians
☐ **D** Car drivers
☐ **E** Lorry drivers

Pedestrians and riders on two wheels can be harder to see than other road users. Make sure you keep a look-out for them, especially at junctions. Good effective observation, coupled with appropriate action, can save lives.

## 314 Mark *one* answer

**Motorcyclists are particularly vulnerable**

☐ **A** when moving off
☐ **B** on dual carriageways
☐ **C** when approaching junctions
☐ **D** on motorways

Another road user failing to see a motorcyclist is a major cause of collisions at junctions. Wherever streams of traffic join or cross there's the potential for this type of incident to occur.

**315** Mark *two* answers

**You are approaching a roundabout. There are horses just ahead of you. You should**

☐ **A** be prepared to stop
☐ **B** treat them like any other vehicle
☐ **C** give them plenty of room
☐ **D** accelerate past as quickly as possible
☐ **E** sound your horn as a warning

Horse riders often keep to the outside of the roundabout even if they are turning right. Give them plenty of room and remember that they may have to cross lanes of traffic.

**316** Mark *one* answer

**As you approach a pelican crossing the lights change to green. Elderly people are halfway across. You should**

☐ **A** wave them to cross as quickly as they can
☐ **B** rev your engine to make them hurry
☐ **C** flash your lights in case they have not heard you
☐ **D** wait because they will take longer to cross

Even if the lights turn to green, wait for them to clear the crossing. Allow them to cross the road in their own time, and don't try to hurry them by revving your engine.

**317** Mark *one* answer

**There are flashing amber lights under a school warning sign. What action should you take?**

☐ **A** Reduce speed until you are clear of the area
☐ **B** Keep up your speed and sound the horn
☐ **C** Increase your speed to clear the area quickly
☐ **D** Wait at the lights until they change to green

The flashing amber lights are switched on to warn you that children may be crossing near a school. Slow down and take extra care as you may have to stop.

**318** Mark *one* answer

**These road markings must be kept clear to allow**

☐ **A** school children to be dropped off
☐ **B** for teachers to park
☐ **C** school children to be picked up
☐ **D** a clear view of the crossing area

The markings are there to show that the area must be kept clear to allow an unrestricted view for
- approaching drivers and riders
- children wanting to cross the road.

## 319 Mark *one* answer
**Where would you see this sign?**

☐ **A** Near a school crossing
☐ **B** At a playground entrance
☐ **C** On a school bus
☐ **D** At a 'pedestrians only' area

Watch out for children crossing the road from the other side of the bus.

---

## 320 Mark *one* answer
**You are following two cyclists. They approach a roundabout in the left-hand lane. In which direction should you expect the cyclists to go?**

☐ **A** Left
☐ **B** Right
☐ **C** Any direction
☐ **D** Straight ahead

Cyclists approaching a roundabout in the left-hand lane may be turning right but may not have been able to get into the correct lane due to the heavy traffic. They may also feel safer keeping to the left all the way round the roundabout. Be aware of them and give them plenty of room.

## 321 Mark *one* answer
**You are travelling behind a moped. You want to turn left just ahead. You should**

☐ **A** overtake the moped before the junction
☐ **B** pull alongside the moped and stay level until just before the junction
☐ **C** sound your horn as a warning and pull in front of the moped
☐ **D** stay behind until the moped has passed the junction

Passing the moped and turning into the junction could mean that you cut across the front of the rider. This might force them to slow down, stop or even lose control. Slow down and stay behind the moped until it has passed the junction and you can then turn safely.

---

## 322 Mark *one* answer
**You see a horse rider as you approach a roundabout. They are signalling right but keeping well to the left. You should**

☐ **A** proceed as normal
☐ **B** keep close to them
☐ **C** cut in front of them
☐ **D** stay well back

Allow the horse rider to enter and exit the roundabout in their own time. They may feel safer keeping to the left all the way around the roundabout. Don't get up close behind or alongside them. This is very likely to upset the horse and create a dangerous situation.

**323** Mark *one* answer

**How would you react to drivers who appear to be inexperienced?**

☐ **A** Sound your horn to warn them of your presence

☐ **B** Be patient and prepare for them to react more slowly

☐ **C** Flash your headlights to indicate that it is safe for them to proceed

☐ **D** Overtake them as soon as possible

Learners might not have confidence when they first start to drive. Allow them plenty of room and don't react adversely to their hesitation. We all learn from experience, but new drivers will have had less practice in dealing with all the situations that might occur.

**324** Mark *one* answer

**You are following a learner driver who stalls at a junction. You should**

☐ **A** be patient as you expect them to make mistakes

☐ **B** stay very close behind and flash your headlights

☐ **C** start to rev your engine if they take too long to restart

☐ **D** immediately steer around them and drive on

Learning is a process of practice and experience. Try to understand this and tolerate those who are at the beginning of this process.

**325** Mark *one* answer

**You are on a country road. What should you expect to see coming towards you on YOUR side of the road?**

☐ **A** Motorcycles

☐ **B** Bicycles

☐ **C** Pedestrians

☐ **D** Horse riders

On a quiet country road always be aware that there may be a hazard just around the next bend, such as a slow-moving vehicle or pedestrians. Pedestrians are advised to walk on the right-hand side of the road if there is no pavement, so they may be walking towards you on your side of the road.

**326** Mark *one* answer

**You are turning left into a side road. Pedestrians are crossing the road near the junction. You must**

☐ **A** wave them on

☐ **B** sound your horn

☐ **C** switch on your hazard lights

☐ **D** wait for them to cross

Check that it's clear before you turn into a junction. If there are pedestrians crossing they have priority, so let them cross in their own time.

**327** Mark *one* answer
**You are following a car driven by an elderly driver. You should**

☐ **A** expect the driver to drive badly
☐ **B** flash your lights and overtake
☐ **C** be aware that the driver's reactions may not be as fast as yours
☐ **D** stay very close behind but be careful

You must show consideration to other road users. The reactions of older drivers may be slower and they might need more time to deal with a situation. Be tolerant and don't lose patience or show your annoyance.

**328** Mark *one* answer
**You are following a cyclist. You wish to turn left just ahead. You should**

☐ **A** overtake the cyclist before the junction
☐ **B** pull alongside the cyclist and stay level until after the junction
☐ **C** hold back until the cyclist has passed the junction
☐ **D** go around the cyclist on the junction

Make allowances for cyclists. Allow them plenty of room. Don't try to overtake and then immediately turn left. Be patient and stay behind them until they have passed the junction.

**329** Mark *one* answer
**A horse rider is in the left-hand lane approaching a roundabout. You should expect the rider to**

☐ **A** go in any direction
☐ **B** turn right
☐ **C** turn left
☐ **D** go ahead

Horses and their riders will move more slowly than other road users. They might not have time to cut across heavy traffic to take up positions in the offside lane. For this reason a horse and rider may approach a roundabout in the left-hand lane, even though they're turning right.

**330** Mark *one* answer
**Powered vehicles used by disabled people are small and hard to see. How do they give early warning when on a dual carriageway?**

☐ **A** They will have a flashing red light
☐ **B** They will have a flashing green light
☐ **C** They will have a flashing blue light
☐ **D** They will have a flashing amber light

Powered vehicles used by disabled people are small, low, hard to see and travel very slowly. On a dual carriageway a flashing amber light will warn other road users.

## 331 Mark *one* answer
**You should never attempt to overtake a cyclist**

- ☐ **A** just before you turn left
- ☐ **B** on a left-hand bend
- ☐ **C** on a one-way street
- ☐ **D** on a dual carriageway

If you want to turn left and there's a cyclist in front of you, hold back. Wait until the cyclist has passed the junction and then turn left behind them.

## 332 Mark *one* answer
**Ahead of you there is a moving vehicle with a flashing amber beacon. This means it is**

- ☐ **A** slow moving
- ☐ **B** broken down
- ☐ **C** a doctor's car
- ☐ **D** a school crossing patrol

As you approach the vehicle, assess the situation. Due to its slow progress you will need to judge whether it is safe to overtake.

## 333 Mark *one* answer
**What does this sign mean?**

- ☐ **A** Contraflow pedal cycle lane
- ☐ **B** With-flow pedal cycle lane
- ☐ **C** Pedal cycles and buses only
- ☐ **D** No pedal cycles or buses

The picture of a cycle will also usually be painted on the road, sometimes with a different coloured surface. Leave these clear for cyclists and don't pass too closely when you overtake.

## 334 Mark *one* answer
**You notice horse riders in front. What should you do FIRST?**

- ☐ **A** Pull out to the middle of the road
- ☐ **B** Slow down and be ready to stop
- ☐ **C** Accelerate around them
- ☐ **D** Signal right

Be particularly careful when approaching horse riders – slow down and be prepared to stop. Always pass wide and slowly and look out for signals given by horse riders. Horses are unpredictable: always treat them as potential hazards and take great care when passing them.

### 335 Mark *one* answer
**You must not stop on these road markings because you may obstruct**

- ☐ **A** children's view of the crossing area
- ☐ **B** teachers' access to the school
- ☐ **C** delivery vehicles' access to the school
- ☐ **D** emergency vehicles' access to the school

These markings are found on the road outside schools. DO NOT stop (even to set down or pick up children) or park on them. The markings are to make sure that drivers, riders, children and other pedestrians have a clear view.

### 336 Mark *one* answer
**The left-hand pavement is closed due to street repairs. What should you do?**

- ☐ **A** Watch out for pedestrians walking in the road
- ☐ **B** Use your right-hand mirror more often
- ☐ **C** Speed up to get past the roadworks quicker
- ☐ **D** Position close to the left-hand kerb

Where street repairs have closed off pavements, proceed carefully and slowly as pedestrians might have to walk in the road.

### 337 Mark *one* answer
**You are following a motorcyclist on an uneven road. You should**

- ☐ **A** allow less room so you can be seen in their mirrors
- ☐ **B** overtake immediately
- ☐ **C** allow extra room in case they swerve to avoid potholes
- ☐ **D** allow the same room as normal because road surfaces do not affect motorcyclists

Potholes and bumps in the road can unbalance a motorcyclist. For this reason the rider might swerve to avoid an uneven road surface. Watch out at places where this is likely to occur.

### 338 Mark *one* answer
**What does this sign tell you?**

- ☐ **A** No cycling
- ☐ **B** Cycle route ahead
- ☐ **C** Cycle parking only
- ☐ **D** End of cycle route

With people's concern today for the environment, cycle routes are being created in our towns and cities. These are usually defined by road markings and signs.

Respect the presence of cyclists on the road and give them plenty of room if you need to pass.

## 339 Mark *one* answer

**You are approaching this roundabout and see the cyclist signal right. Why is the cyclist keeping to the left?**

- ☐ **A** It is a quicker route for the cyclist
- ☐ **B** The cyclist is going to turn left instead
- ☐ **C** The cyclist thinks The Highway Code does not apply to bicycles
- ☐ **D** The cyclist is slower and more vulnerable

Cycling in today's heavy traffic can be hazardous. Some cyclists may not feel happy about crossing the path of traffic to take up a position in an outside lane. Be aware of this and understand that, although in the left-hand lane, the cyclist might be turning right.

## 340 Mark *one* answer

**You are approaching this crossing. You should**

- ☐ **A** prepare to slow down and stop
- ☐ **B** stop and wave the pedestrians across
- ☐ **C** speed up and pass by quickly
- ☐ **D** continue unless the pedestrians step out

Be courteous and prepare to stop. Do not wave people across as this could be dangerous if another vehicle is approaching the crossing.

## 341 Mark *one* answer

**You see a pedestrian with a dog. The dog has a yellow or burgundy coat. This especially warns you that the pedestrian is**

- ☐ **A** elderly
- ☐ **B** dog training
- ☐ **C** colour blind
- ☐ **D** deaf

Take extra care as the pedestrian may not be aware of vehicles approaching.

## 342 Mark *one* answer
**At toucan crossings**

☐ **A** you only stop if someone is waiting to cross
☐ **B** cyclists are not permitted
☐ **C** there is a continuously flashing amber beacon
☐ **D** pedestrians and cyclists may cross

There are some crossings where cycle routes lead the cyclists to cross at the same place as pedestrians. These are called toucan crossings. Always look out for cyclists, as they're likely to be approaching faster than pedestrians.

## 343 Mark *one* answer
**Some junctions controlled by traffic lights have a marked area between two stop lines. What is this for?**

☐ **A** To allow taxis to position in front of other traffic
☐ **B** To allow people with disabilities to cross the road
☐ **C** To allow cyclists and pedestrians to cross the road together
☐ **D** To allow cyclists to position in front of other traffic

These are known as advanced stop lines. When the lights are red (or about to become red) you should stop at the first white line. However if you have crossed that line as the lights change you must stop at the second line even if it means you are in the area reserved for cyclists.

## 344 Mark *one* answer
**At some traffic lights there are advance stop lines and a marked area. What are these for?**

☐ **A** To allow cyclists to position in front of other traffic
☐ **B** To let pedestrians cross when the lights change
☐ **C** To prevent traffic from jumping the lights
☐ **D** To let passengers get off a bus which is queuing

You should always stop at the first white line. Avoid going into the marked area which is reserved for cyclists only. However, if you have crossed the first white line at the time the signal changes to red you must stop at the second line even if you are in the marked area.

## 345 Mark *one* answer
**When you are overtaking a cyclist you should leave as much room as you would give to a car. What is the main reason for this?**

☐ **A** The cyclist might speed up
☐ **B** The cyclist might get off the bike
☐ **C** The cyclist might swerve
☐ **D** The cyclist might have to make a left turn

Before overtaking assess the situation. Look well ahead to see if the cyclist will need to change direction. Be especially aware of the cyclist approaching parked vehicles as they will need to alter course. Do not pass too closely or cut in sharply.

## 346 Mark *three* answers
**Which THREE should you do when passing sheep on a road?**

☐ **A** Allow plenty of room
☐ **B** Go very slowly
☐ **C** Pass quickly but quietly
☐ **D** Be ready to stop
☐ **E** Briefly sound your horn

Slow down and be ready to stop if you see animals in the road ahead. Animals are easily frightened by noise and vehicles passing too close to them. Stop if signalled to do so by the person in charge.

## 347 Mark *one* answer
**At night you see a pedestrian wearing reflective clothing and carrying a bright red light. What does this mean?**

☐ **A** You are approaching roadworks
☐ **B** You are approaching an organised walk
☐ **C** You are approaching a slow-moving vehicle
☐ **D** You are approaching a traffic danger spot

The people on the walk should be keeping to the left, but don't assume this. Pass slowly, make sure you have time to do so safely. Be aware that the pedestrians have their backs to you and may not know that you're there.

## 348 Mark *one* answer
**You have just passed your test. How can you reduce your risk of being involved in a collision?**

☐ **A** By always staying close to the vehicle in front
☐ **B** By never going over 40mph
☐ **C** By staying only in the left-hand lane on all roads
☐ **D** By taking further training

New drivers and riders are often involved in a collision or incident early in their driving career. Due to a lack of experience they may not react to hazards as quickly as more experienced road users. Approved training courses are offered by driver and rider training schools. The Pass Plus scheme has been created by DSA for new drivers who would like to improve their basic skills and safely widen their driving experience.

### 349 Mark *one* answer

**You are riding behind a long vehicle. There is a mini-roundabout ahead. The vehicle is signalling left, but positioned to the right. You should**

- ☐ **A** sound your horn
- ☐ **B** overtake on the left
- ☐ **C** keep well back
- ☐ **D** flash your headlights

The long vehicle needs more room than other vehicles in order to make the left turn. Don't overtake on the left – the driver will not expect you to be there and may not see you. Staying well back will also give you a better view around the vehicle.

### 350 Mark *two* answers

**Why should you be careful when riding on roads where electric trams operate?**

- ☐ **A** They cannot steer to avoid you
- ☐ **B** They move quickly and quietly
- ☐ **C** They are noisy and slow
- ☐ **D** They can steer to avoid you
- ☐ **E** They give off harmful exhaust fumes

Electric trams run on rails and cannot steer to avoid you. Keep a lookout for trams as they move very quietly and can appear suddenly.

### 351 Mark *one* answer

**You are about to overtake a slow-moving motorcyclist. Which one of these signs would make you take special care?**

☐ **A**     ☐ **B**

☐ **C**     ☐ **D**

In windy weather, watch out for motorcyclists and also cyclists as they can be blown sideways into your path. When you pass them, leave plenty of room and check their position in your mirror before pulling back in.

### 352 Mark *one* answer

**You are waiting to emerge left from a minor road. A large vehicle is approaching from the right. You have time to turn, but you should wait. Why?**

- ☐ **A** The large vehicle can easily hide an overtaking vehicle
- ☐ **B** The large vehicle can turn suddenly
- ☐ **C** The large vehicle is difficult to steer in a straight line
- ☐ **D** The large vehicle can easily hide vehicles from the left

Large vehicles can hide other vehicles that are overtaking, especially motorcycles which may be filtering past queuing traffic. You need to be aware of the possibility of hidden vehicles and not assume that it is safe to emerge.

**353** Mark *one* answer

**You are following a long vehicle. It approaches a crossroads and signals left, but moves out to the right. You should**

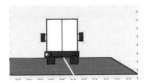

- ☐ **A** get closer in order to pass it quickly
- ☐ **B** stay well back and give it room
- ☐ **C** assume the signal is wrong and it is really turning right
- ☐ **D** overtake as it starts to slow down

A lorry may swing out to the right as it approaches a left turn. This is to allow the rear wheels to clear the kerb as it turns. Don't try to filter through if you see a gap on the nearside.

**354** Mark *one* answer

**You are following a long vehicle approaching a crossroads. The driver signals right but moves close to the left-hand kerb. What should you do?**

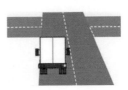

- ☐ **A** Warn the driver of the wrong signal
- ☐ **B** Wait behind the long vehicle
- ☐ **C** Report the driver to the police
- ☐ **D** Overtake on the right-hand side

When a long vehicle is going to turn right it may need to keep close to the left-hand kerb. This is to prevent the rear end of the trailer cutting the corner. You need to be aware of how long vehicles behave in such situations. Don't overtake the lorry because it could turn as you're alongside. Stay behind and wait for it to turn.

## 355 Mark *one* answer

**You are approaching a mini-roundabout. The long vehicle in front is signalling left but positioned over to the right. You should**

☐ **A** sound your horn
☐ **B** overtake on the left
☐ **C** follow the same course as the lorry
☐ **D** keep well back

At mini-roundabouts there isn't much room for a long vehicle to manoeuvre. It will have to swing out wide so that it can complete the turn safely. Keep well back and don't try to move up alongside it.

## 356 Mark *one* answer

**Before overtaking a large vehicle you should keep well back. Why is this?**

☐ **A** To give acceleration space to overtake quickly on blind bends
☐ **B** To get the best view of the road ahead
☐ **C** To leave a gap in case the vehicle stops and rolls back
☐ **D** To offer other drivers a safe gap if they want to overtake you

When following a large vehicle keep well back. If you're too close you won't be able to see the road ahead and the driver of the long vehicle might not be able to see you in their mirrors.

## 357 Mark *two* answers

**You are travelling behind a bus that pulls up at a bus stop. What should you do?**

☐ **A** Accelerate past the bus sounding your horn
☐ **B** Watch carefully for pedestrians
☐ **C** Be ready to give way to the bus
☐ **D** Pull in closely behind the bus

There might be pedestrians crossing from in front of the bus. Look out for them if you intend to pass. Consider staying back and waiting.

How many people are waiting to get on the bus? Check the queue if you can. The bus might move off straight away if there is no one waiting to get on.

If a bus is signalling to pull out, give it priority as long as it is safe to do so.

## 358 Mark *one* answer

**You are following a large lorry on a wet road. Spray makes it difficult to see. You should**

- ☐ **A** drop back until you can see better
- ☐ **B** put your headlights on full beam
- ☐ **C** keep close to the lorry, away from the spray
- ☐ **D** speed up and overtake quickly

Large vehicles may throw up a lot of spray when the roads are wet. This will make it difficult for you to see ahead. Dropping back further will

- move you out of the spray and allow you to see further
- increase your separation distance. It takes longer to stop when the roads are wet and you need to allow more room.

Don't

- follow the vehicle in front too closely
- overtake, unless you can see and are sure that the way ahead is clear.

## 359 Mark *one* answer

**You are following a large articulated vehicle. It is going to turn left into a narrow road. What action should you take?**

- ☐ **A** Move out and overtake on the right
- ☐ **B** Pass on the left as the vehicle moves out
- ☐ **C** Be prepared to stop behind
- ☐ **D** Overtake quickly before the lorry moves out

Lorries are larger and longer than other vehicles and this can affect their position when approaching junctions. When turning left they may move out to the right so that they don't cut in and mount the kerb with the rear wheels.

## 360 Mark *one* answer

**You keep well back while waiting to overtake a large vehicle. A car fills the gap. You should**

- ☐ **A** sound your horn
- ☐ **B** drop back further
- ☐ **C** flash your headlights
- ☐ **D** start to overtake

It's very frustrating when your separation distance is shortened by another vehicle. React positively, stay calm and drop further back.

## 361 Mark *one* answer

**You are following a long lorry. The driver signals to turn left into a narrow road. What should you do?**

☐ **A** Overtake on the left before the lorry reaches the junction

☐ **B** Overtake on the right as soon as the lorry slows down

☐ **C** Do not overtake unless you can see there is no oncoming traffic

☐ **D** Do not overtake, stay well back and be prepared to stop.

When turning into narrow roads articulated and long vehicles will need more room. Initially they will need to swing out in the opposite direction to which they intend to turn. They could mask another vehicle turning out of the same junction. DON'T be tempted to overtake them or pass on the inside.

## 362 Mark *one* answer

**When you approach a bus signalling to move off from a bus stop you should**

☐ **A** get past before it moves

☐ **B** allow it to pull away, if it is safe to do so

☐ **C** flash your headlights as you approach

☐ **D** signal left and wave the bus on

Try to give way to buses if you can do so safely, especially when they signal to pull away from bus stops. Look out for people who've stepped off the bus or are running to catch it, and may try to cross the road without looking. Don't try to accelerate past before it moves away or flash your lights as other road users may be misled by this signal.

## 363 Mark *one* answer

**You wish to overtake a long, slow-moving vehicle on a busy road. You should**

☐ **A** follow it closely and keep moving out to see the road ahead

☐ **B** flash your headlights for the oncoming traffic to give way

☐ **C** stay behind until the driver waves you past

☐ **D** keep well back until you can see that it is clear

If you want to overtake a long vehicle, stay well back so that you can get a better view of the road ahead. The closer you get the less you will be able to see of the road ahead. Be patient, overtaking calls for sound judgement. DON'T take a gamble, only overtake when you are certain that you can complete the manoeuvre safely.

## 364 Mark *one* answer
**Which of these is LEAST likely to be affected by crosswinds?**

☐ **A** Cyclists
☐ **B** Motorcyclists
☐ **C** High-sided vehicles
☐ **D** Cars

Although cars are the least likely to be affected, crosswinds can take anyone by surprise. This is most likely to happen after overtaking a large vehicle, when passing gaps between hedges or buildings, and on exposed sections of road.

## 365 Mark *one* answer
**What should you do as you approach this lorry?**

☐ **A** Slow down and be prepared to wait
☐ **B** Make the lorry wait for you
☐ **C** Flash your lights at the lorry
☐ **D** Move to the right-hand side of the road

When turning, long vehicles need much more room on the road than other vehicles. At junctions they may take up the whole of the road space, so be patient and allow them the room they need.

## 366 Mark *one* answer
**You are following a large vehicle approaching crossroads. The driver signals to turn left. What should you do?**

☐ **A** Overtake if you can leave plenty of room
☐ **B** Overtake only if there are no oncoming vehicles
☐ **C** Do not overtake until the vehicle begins to turn.
☐ **D** Do not overtake when at or approaching a junction.

Hold back and wait until the vehicle has turned before proceeding. Do not overtake because the vehicle turning left could hide a vehicle emerging from the same junction.

## 367 Mark *one* answer
**Powered vehicles, such as wheelchairs or scooters, used by disabled people have a maximum speed of**

☐ **A** 8mph
☐ **B** 12mph
☐ **C** 16mph
☐ **D** 20mph

These are small battery powered vehicles and include wheelchairs and mobility scooters. Some are designed for use on the pavement only and have an upper speed limit of 4mph (6km/h). Others can go on the road as well and have a speed limit of 8mph (12km/h). They are now very common and are generally used by the elderly, disabled or infirm. Take great care as they are extremely vulnerable because of their low speed and small size.

**368** Mark *one* answer

**Why is it more difficult to overtake a large vehicle than a car?**

☐ **A** It takes longer to pass one
☐ **B** They may suddenly pull up
☐ **C** Their brakes are not as good
☐ **D** They climb hills more slowly

Depending on relevant speed, it will usually take you longer to pass a lorry than other vehicles. Some hazards to watch for include oncoming traffic, junctions ahead, bends or dips which could restrict your view, and signs or road markings that prohibit overtaking. Make sure you can see that it's safe to complete the manoeuvre before you start to overtake.

**369** Mark *one* answer

**In front of you is a class 3 powered vehicle (powered wheelchair) driven by a disabled person. These vehicles have a maximum speed of**

☐ **A** 8mph (12km/h)
☐ **B** 18mph (29km/h)
☐ **C** 28mph (45km/h)
☐ **D** 38mph (61km/h)

These vehicles are battery powered and very vulnerable due to their slow speed, small size and low height. Some are designed for pavement and road use and have a maximum speed of 8mph (12km/h). Others are for pavement use only and are restricted to 4mph (6km/h). Take extra care and be patient if you are following one. Allow plenty of room when overtaking and do not go past unless you can do so safely.

## 370 Mark *two* answers
**As a safety measure before starting your engine, you should**

☐ **A** push the motorcycle forward to check the rear wheel turns freely
☐ **B** engage first gear and apply the rear brake
☐ **C** engage first gear and apply the front brake
☐ **D** glance at the neutral light on your instrument panel

Before starting the engine you should ensure the motorcycle is in neutral. This can be done by, moving the motorcycle to check that the rear wheel turns freely and making sure the neutral warning light is lit when the ignition is turned on.

## 371 Mark *two* answers
**You are approaching this junction. As the motorcyclist you should**

☐ **A** prepare to slow down
☐ **B** sound your horn
☐ **C** keep near the left kerb
☐ **D** speed up to clear the junction
☐ **E** stop, as the car has right of way

Look out for road signs indicating side roads, even if you aren't turning off. A driver who is emerging might not be able to see you due to parked cars or heavy traffic. Always be prepared, and stop if necessary. Remember, no one has priority at unmarked crossroads.

## 372 Mark *one* answer
**What can you do to improve your safety on the road as a motorcyclist?**

☐ **A** Anticipate the actions of others
☐ **B** Stay just above the speed limits
☐ **C** Keep positioned close to the kerbs
☐ **D** Remain well below speed limits

Always ride defensively. This means looking and planning ahead as well as anticipating the actions of other road users.

## 373 Mark *three* answers
**Which THREE of these can cause skidding?**

☐ **A** Braking too gently
☐ **B** Leaning too far over when cornering
☐ **C** Staying upright when cornering
☐ **D** Braking too hard
☐ **E** Changing direction suddenly

In order to keep control of your motorcycle and prevent skidding you must plan well ahead to prevent harsh, late braking. Try to avoid braking while changing direction, as this reduces the tyres' grip on the road. Take the road and weather conditions into consideration and adjust your speed if necessary.

## 374 Mark *two* answers
**It is very cold and the road looks wet. You cannot hear any road noise. You should**

- ☐ **A** continue riding at the same speed
- ☐ **B** ride slower in as high a gear as possible
- ☐ **C** ride in as low a gear as possible
- ☐ **D** keep revving your engine
- ☐ **E** slow down as there may be black ice

Rain freezing on roads is called black ice. It can be hard to see. Indications of black ice are when you can't hear tyre noise and the steering becomes very light. You need to keep your speed down and avoid harsh steering, braking and acceleration. Riding in as high a gear as possible will help to reduce the risk of wheel-spin.

## 375 Mark *one* answer
**When riding a motorcycle you should wear full protective clothing**

- ☐ **A** at all times
- ☐ **B** only on faster, open roads
- ☐ **C** just on long journeys
- ☐ **D** only during bad weather

Protective clothing is designed to protect you from the cold and wet and also gives some protection from injury.

## 376 Mark *two* answers
**You have to make a journey in fog. What are the TWO most important things you should do before you set out?**

- ☐ **A** Fill up with fuel
- ☐ **B** Make sure that you have a warm drink with you
- ☐ **C** Check that your lights are working
- ☐ **D** Check the battery
- ☐ **E** Make sure that your visor is clean

When you're riding a motorcycle, keep your visor as clean as possible to give you a clear view of the road. It's a good idea to carry a clean, damp cloth in a polythene bag for this purpose.

You need to ensure that your lights are clean and can be seen clearly by other road users. This is especially important when visibility is reduced, for example in fog or heavy rain.

## 377 Mark *one* answer
**The best place to park your motorcycle is**

- ☐ **A** on soft tarmac
- ☐ **B** on bumpy ground
- ☐ **C** on grass
- ☐ **D** on firm, level ground

Parking your motorcycle on soft ground might cause the stand to sink and the bike to fall over. The ground should also be level to ensure that the bike is stable. Where off-road parking or motorcycle parking areas are available, use them.

**378** Mark *one* answer
**When riding in windy conditions, you should**

☐ **A** stay close to large vehicles
☐ **B** keep your speed up
☐ **C** keep your speed down
☐ **D** stay close to the gutter

Strong winds can blow motorcycles off course and even across the road. In windy conditions you need to, slow down, avoid riding on exposed roads and watch for gaps in buildings and hedges where you may be affected by a sudden blast of wind.

**379** Mark *one* answer
**In normal riding your position on the road should be**

☐ **A** about a foot from the kerb
☐ **B** about central in your lane
☐ **C** on the right of your lane
☐ **D** near the centre of the road

If you're riding a motorcycle it's very important to ride where other road users can see you. In normal weather you should ride in the centre of your lane. This will help you to avoid uneven road surfaces in the gutter and allow others to overtake on the right if they wish.

**380** Mark *one* answer
**Your motorcycle is parked on a two-way road. You should get on from the**

☐ **A** right and apply the rear brake
☐ **B** left and leave the brakes alone
☐ **C** left and apply the front brake
☐ **D** right and leave the brakes alone

When you get onto a motorcycle you should get on from the left side to avoid putting yourself in danger from passing traffic. Also apply the front brake to prevent the motorcycle rolling either forwards or backwards.

**381** Mark *one* answer
**To gain basic skills in how to ride a motorcycle you should**

☐ **A** practise off-road with an approved training body
☐ **B** ride on the road on the first dry day
☐ **C** practise off-road in a public park or in a quiet cul-de-sac
☐ **D** ride on the road as soon as possible

All new motorcyclists must complete a course of basic training with an approved training body before going on the road. This training is given on a site which has been authorised by the Driving Standards Agency as being suitable for off-road training.

## 382 Mark *one* answer

**You should not ride with your clutch lever pulled in for longer than necessary because it**

☐ **A** increases wear on the gearbox
☐ **B** increases petrol consumption
☐ **C** reduces your control of the motorcycle
☐ **D** reduces the grip of the tyres

Riding with the clutch lever pulled in is known as coasting. It gives you less steering control, reduces traction, and can cause you to pick up speed. When you're travelling downhill your motorcycle will pick up speed quickly. If you are coasting the engine won't be able to assist the braking.

## 383 Mark *one* answer

**You are approaching a road with a surface of loose chippings. What should you do?**

☐ **A** Ride normally
☐ **B** Speed up
☐ **C** Slow down
☐ **D** Stop suddenly

The handling of your motorcycle will be greatly affected by the road surface. Look well ahead and be especially alert if the road looks uneven or has loose chippings. Slow down in good time as braking harshly in these conditions will cause you to skid. Avoid making sudden changes of direction for the same reason.

## 384 Mark *one* answer

**It rains after a long dry, hot spell. This may cause the road surface to**

☐ **A** be unusually slippery
☐ **B** give better grip
☐ **C** become covered in grit
☐ **D** melt and break up

Oil and other substances build up on the road surface during long dry spells and when it rains this surface becomes very slippery.

## 385 Mark *three* answers

**The main causes of a motorcycle skidding are**

☐ **A** heavy and sharp braking
☐ **B** excessive acceleration
☐ **C** leaning too far when cornering
☐ **D** riding in wet weather
☐ **E** riding in the winter

Skids are a lot easier to get into than they are to get out of.

Riding at a speed that suits the conditions, looking ahead for hazards and braking in good time will all help you to avoid skidding or losing control of your vehicle.

**386** Mark *one* answer
**To stop your motorcycle quickly in an emergency you should apply**

☐ **A** the rear brake only
☐ **B** the front brake only
☐ **C** the front brake just before the rear
☐ **D** the rear brake just before the front

You should plan ahead to avoid the need to stop suddenly. But if an emergency should arise you must be able to stop safely. Applying the correct amount of braking effort to each wheel will help you to stop safely and in control.

---

**387** Mark *one* answer
**You leave the choke on for too long. This causes the engine to run too fast. When is this likely to make your motorcycle most difficult to control?**

☐ **A** Accelerating
☐ **B** Going uphill
☐ **C** Slowing down
☐ **D** On motorways

Forgetting to switch the choke off will cause the engine to run too fast. This makes it difficult to control the motorcycle, especially when slowing down, for example when approaching junctions and bends.

**388** Mark *one* answer
**You should NOT look down at the front wheel when riding because it can**

☐ **A** make your steering lighter
☐ **B** improve your balance
☐ **C** use less fuel
☐ **D** upset your balance

When riding look ahead and around you, but don't look down at the front wheel as this can severely upset your balance.

---

**389** Mark *one* answer
**In normal riding conditions you should brake**

☐ **A** by using the rear brake first and then the front
☐ **B** when the motorcycle is being turned or ridden through a bend
☐ **C** by pulling in the clutch before using the front brake
☐ **D** when the motorcycle is upright and moving in a straight line

A motorcycle is most stable when it's upright and moving in a straight line. This is the best time to brake. Normally both brakes should be used, with the front brake being applied just before the rear.

## 390 Mark *three* answers
**Which THREE of the following will affect your stopping distance?**

- ☐ **A** How fast you are going
- ☐ **B** The tyres on your motorcycle
- ☐ **C** The time of day
- ☐ **D** The weather
- ☐ **E** The street lighting

There are several factors that can affect the distance it takes to stop your motorcycle. In wet weather you should double the separation distance from the vehicle in front. Your tyres will have less grip on the road and you therefore need to allow more time to stop. Always ride in accordance with the conditions.

## 391 Mark *one* answer
**You are on a motorway at night. You MUST have your headlights switched on unless**

- ☐ **A** there are vehicles close in front of you
- ☐ **B** you are travelling below 50mph
- ☐ **C** the motorway is lit
- ☐ **D** your motorcycle is broken down on the hard shoulder

Always use your headlights at night on a motorway unless you have stopped on the hard shoulder. If you have to use the hard shoulder, switch off the headlights but leave the parking lights on so that other road users can see your motorcycle.

## 392 Mark *one* answer
**You have to park on the road in fog. You should**

- ☐ **A** leave parking lights on
- ☐ **B** leave no lights on
- ☐ **C** leave dipped headlights on
- ☐ **D** leave main beam headlights on

If you have to park on the road in foggy conditions it's important that your motorcycle can be seen by other road users. Try to find a place to park off the road. If this isn't possible leave your motorcycle facing in the same direction as the traffic. Make sure that your lights are clean and that you leave your parking lights on.

## 393 Mark *one* answer
**You ride over broken glass and get a sudden puncture. What should you do?**

- ☐ **A** Close the throttle and roll to a stop
- ☐ **B** Brake to a stop as quickly as possible
- ☐ **C** Release your grip on the handlebars
- ☐ **D** Steer from side to side to keep your balance

Your motorcycle will be very unstable if a tyre bursts. Try to keep a straight course and stop as gently as possible.

## 394 Mark *one* answer
**You are riding in wet weather.
You see diesel fuel on the road.
What should you do?**

☐ **A** Swerve to avoid the area
☐ **B** Accelerate through quickly
☐ **C** Brake sharply to a stop
☐ **D** Slow down in good time

Spilt diesel will show up in wet weather as a rainbow-coloured pattern on the road. You should try to avoid riding over this area if you can. Slow down in good time but don't swerve suddenly or change direction without taking proper observation.

## 395 Mark *one* answer
**Spilt fuel on the road can be very dangerous for you as a motorcyclist. How can this hazard be seen?**

☐ **A** By a rainbow pattern on the surface
☐ **B** By a series of skid marks
☐ **C** By a pitted road surface
☐ **D** By a highly polished surface

This rainbow-coloured pattern can be seen much more easily on a wet road. You should avoid riding over these areas if possible. If you have to go over them do so with extreme caution.

## 396 Mark *one* answer
**You leave the choke on for too long. This could make the engine run faster than normal. This will make your motorcycle**

☐ **A** handle much better
☐ **B** corner much safer
☐ **C** stop much more quickly
☐ **D** more difficult to control

Leaving the choke on for longer than necessary will usually make the engine run too fast. This can lead to loss of control, which is especially dangerous when approaching junctions and bends in the road and whenever you need to slow down.

## 397 Mark *four* answers
**Which FOUR types of road surface increase the risk of skidding for motorcyclists?**

☐ **A** White lines
☐ **B** Dry tarmac
☐ **C** Tar banding
☐ **D** Yellow grid lines
☐ **E** Loose chippings

When riding it's important to look out for slippery surfaces. These include, potholes, drain covers (especially in the wet), oily and greasy surfaces, road markings, tram tracks, wet mud and leaves. You will then have more time to brake or change course if you need to.

**398** Mark *one* answer
**You are riding on a wet road. When braking you should**

- ☐ **A** apply the rear brake well before the front
- ☐ **B** apply the front brake just before the rear
- ☐ **C** avoid using the front brake at all
- ☐ **D** avoid using the rear brake at all

On wet roads you will need to be especially careful: brake earlier and more smoothly. Always try to brake when the motorcycle is upright. This is particularly important in wet conditions.

**399** Mark *one* answer
**The road is wet. You are passing a line of queuing traffic and riding on the painted road markings. You should take extra care, particularly when**

- ☐ **A** signalling
- ☐ **B** braking
- ☐ **C** carrying a passenger
- ☐ **D** checking your mirrors

Take extra care when braking or cornering on wet roads and try to avoid slippery objects, such as drain covers and painted road markings.

**400** Mark *one* answer
**You are going ahead and will have to cross tram lines. Why should you be especially careful?**

- ☐ **A** Tram lines are always 'live'
- ☐ **B** Trams will be stopping here
- ☐ **C** Pedestrians will be crossing here
- ☐ **D** The steel rails can be slippery

These rails can affect your steering and be a hazard when braking. The smooth surface of the rails makes them slippery and dangerous for motorcyclists, especially when wet. Try to cross them at right angles.

**401** Mark *one* answer
**You have to brake sharply and your motorcycle starts to skid. You should**

- ☐ **A** continue braking and select a low gear
- ☐ **B** apply the brakes harder for better grip
- ☐ **C** select neutral and use the front brake only
- ☐ **D** release the brakes and reapply

If you skid as a result of braking harshly you need to ease off the brakes to stop the skid. Then reapply them progressively to stop.

**402** Mark *one* answer
**You see a rainbow-coloured pattern across the road. What will this warn you of?**

- ☐ **A** A soft uneven road surface
- ☐ **B** A polished road surface
- ☐ **C** Fuel spilt on the road
- ☐ **D** Water on the road

If fuel, especially diesel, is spilt on the road it will make the surface very slippery. In wet weather this can be seen as a rainbow-coloured pattern on the road.

**403** Mark *one* answer

**Traction Control Systems (TCS) are fitted to some motorcycles. What does this help to prevent?**

☐ **A** Wheelspin when accelerating
☐ **B** Skidding when braking too hard
☐ **C** Uneven front tyre wear
☐ **D** Uneven rear tyre wear

Traction Control Systems (TCS) help to prevent the rear wheel from spinning, especially when accelerating on a slippery surface.

**404** Mark *one* answer

**Braking too hard has caused both wheels to skid. What should you do?**

☐ **A** Release both brakes together
☐ **B** Release the front then the rear brake
☐ **C** Release the front brake only
☐ **D** Release the rear brake only

Braking too hard will cause a skid. Release the brakes immediately to allow the wheels to turn, then reapply them as firmly as the road surface and conditions will allow.

**405** Mark *one* answer

**Your motorcycle does NOT have linked brakes. What should you do when braking to a normal stop?**

☐ **A** Only apply the front brake
☐ **B** Rely just on the rear brake
☐ **C** Apply both brakes smoothly
☐ **D** Apply either of the brakes gently

In normal riding you should always use both brakes. Braking when the motorcycle is upright and travelling in a straight line helps you to keep control. If your motorcycle has linked brakes refer to the owners manual.

**406** Mark *one* answer

**You are sitting on a stationary motorcycle and checking your riding position. You should be able to**

☐ **A** just touch the ground with your toes
☐ **B** place both feet on the ground
☐ **C** operate the centre stand
☐ **D** adjust your mirrors by stretching

When sitting astride a stationary motorcycle you should be able to place both feet on the ground to support yourself and your machine.

## 407 Mark *one* answer

**It has rained after a long dry spell. You should be very careful because the road surface will be unusually**

- ☐ **A** rough
- ☐ **B** dry
- ☐ **C** sticky
- ☐ **D** slippery

During a long hot, dry spell the road surface will become coated with rubber and dust. When it rains after this the road surface will be unusually slippery. Take extra care, particularly at junctions, bends and roundabouts, and allow double the usual stopping distance.

## 408 Mark *one* answer

**Riding with the side stand down could cause you to crash. This is most likely to happen when**

- ☐ **A** going uphill
- ☐ **B** accelerating
- ☐ **C** braking
- ☐ **D** cornering

Cornering with the side stand down could lead to a serious crash. Most motorcycles have a device that stops the engine if you try to ride off with the side stand down, but don't rely on this.

## 409 Mark *one* answer

**You are entering a bend. Your side stand is not fully raised. This could**

- ☐ **A** cause you to crash
- ☐ **B** improve your balance
- ☐ **C** alter the motorcycle's centre of gravity
- ☐ **D** make the motorcycle more stable

If the stand isn't fully up it could dig into the road and cause a serious crash. Always check that it is fully raised before moving off. Most side stands have a safety device or cut-out switch, but do NOT rely on this. CHECK FOR YOURSELF!

## 410 Mark *three* answers

**In which THREE of these situations may you overtake another vehicle on the left?**

- ☐ **A** When you are in a one-way street
- ☐ **B** When approaching a motorway slip road where you will be turning off
- ☐ **C** When the vehicle in front is signalling to turn right
- ☐ **D** When a slower vehicle is travelling in the right-hand lane of a dual carriageway
- ☐ **E** In slow-moving traffic queues when traffic in the right-hand lane is moving more slowly

At certain times of the day, traffic might be heavy. If traffic is moving slowly in queues and vehicles in the right-hand lane are moving more slowly, you may overtake on the left. Don't keep changing lanes to try and beat the queue.

## 411 Mark *one* answer
**You are travelling in very heavy rain. Your overall stopping distance is likely to be**

☐ **A** doubled
☐ **B** halved
☐ **C** up to ten times greater
☐ **D** no different

As well as visibility being reduced, the road will be extremely wet. This will reduce the grip the tyres have on the road and increase the distance it takes to stop. Double your separation distance.

## 412 Mark *two* answers
**Which TWO of the following are correct? When overtaking at night you should**

☐ **A** wait until a bend so that you can see the oncoming headlights
☐ **B** sound your horn twice before moving out
☐ **C** be careful because you can see less
☐ **D** beware of bends in the road ahead
☐ **E** put headlights on full beam

Only overtake the vehicle in front if it's really necessary. At night the risks are increased due to the poor visibility. Don't overtake if there's a possibility of
- road junctions
- bends ahead
- the brow of a bridge or hill, except on a dual carriageway
- pedestrian crossings
- double white lines ahead
- vehicles changing direction
- any other potential hazard.

## 413 Mark *one* answer
**When may you wait in a box junction?**

☐ **A** When you are stationary in a queue of traffic
☐ **B** When approaching a pelican crossing
☐ **C** When approaching a zebra crossing
☐ **D** When oncoming traffic prevents you turning right

The purpose of a box junction is to keep the junction clear by preventing vehicles from stopping in the path of crossing traffic.

You must not enter a box junction unless your exit is clear. But, you may enter the box and wait if you want to turn right and are only prevented from doing so by oncoming traffic.

## 414 Mark *one* answer
**Which of these plates normally appear with this road sign?**

☐ **A** Humps for ½ mile
☐ **B** Hump Bridge
☐ **C** Low Bridge
☐ **D** Soft Verge

Road humps are used to slow down the traffic. They are found in places where there are often pedestrians, such as
- in shopping areas
- near schools
- in residential areas.

Watch out for people close to the kerb or crossing the road.

## 415 Mark *one* answer
**Traffic-calming measures are used to**

☐ **A** stop road rage
☐ **B** help overtaking
☐ **C** slow traffic down
☐ **D** help parking

Traffic-calming measures are used to make the roads safer for vulnerable road users, such as cyclists, pedestrians and children. These can be designed as chicanes, road humps or other obstacles that encourage drivers and riders to slow down.

## 416 Mark *one* answer
**You are on a motorway in fog. The left-hand edge of the motorway can be identified by reflective studs. What colour are they?**

☐ **A** Green
☐ **B** Amber
☐ **C** Red
☐ **D** White

Be especially careful if you're on a motorway in fog. Reflective studs are used to help you in poor visibility. Different colours are used so that you'll know which lane you are in. These are
- red on the left-hand side of the road
- white between lanes
- amber on the right-hand edge of the carriageway
- green between the carriageway and slip roads.

## 417 Mark *two* answers
**A rumble device is designed to**

☐ **A** give directions
☐ **B** prevent cattle escaping
☐ **C** alert you to low tyre pressure
☐ **D** alert you to a hazard
☐ **E** encourage you to reduce speed

A rumble device usually consists of raised markings or strips across the road. It gives an audible, visual and tactile warning of a hazard. These strips are found in places where traffic has constantly ignored warning or restriction signs. They are there for a good reason. Slow down and be ready to deal with a hazard.

## 418 Mark *one* answer
**You have to make a journey in foggy conditions. You should**

☐ **A** follow other vehicles' tail lights closely
☐ **B** avoid using dipped headlights
☐ **C** leave plenty of time for your journey
☐ **D** keep two seconds behind other vehicles

If you're planning to make a journey when it's foggy, listen to the weather reports on the radio or television. Don't travel if visibility is very poor or your trip isn't necessary.

If you do travel, leave plenty of time for your journey. If someone is expecting you at the other end, let them know that you'll be taking longer than normal to arrive.

## 419 Mark *one* answer

**You are overtaking a car at night. You must be sure that**

☐ **A** you flash your headlights before overtaking
☐ **B** you select a higher gear
☐ **C** you have switched your lights to full beam before overtaking
☐ **D** you do not dazzle other road users

To prevent your lights from dazzling the driver of the car in front, wait until you've overtaken before switching to full beam.

## 420 Mark *one* answer

**You are on a road which has speed humps. A driver in front is travelling slower than you. You should**

☐ **A** sound your horn
☐ **B** overtake as soon as you can
☐ **C** flash your headlights
☐ **D** slow down and stay behind

Be patient and stay behind the car in front. Normally you should not overtake other vehicles in traffic-calmed areas. If you overtake here your speed may exceed that which is safe along that road, defeating the purpose of the traffic-calming measures.

## 421 Mark *one* answer

**You see these markings on the road. Why are they there?**

☐ **A** To show a safe distance between vehicles
☐ **B** To keep the area clear of traffic
☐ **C** To make you aware of your speed
☐ **D** To warn you to change direction

These lines may be painted on the road on the approach to a roundabout, village or a particular hazard. The lines are raised and painted yellow and their purpose is to make you aware of your speed. Reduce your speed in good time so that you avoid having to brake harshly over the last few metres before reaching the junction.

## 422 Mark *three* answers

**Areas reserved for trams may have**

☐ **A** metal studs around them
☐ **B** white line markings
☐ **C** zigzag markings
☐ **D** a different coloured surface
☐ **E** yellow hatch markings
☐ **F** a different surface texture

Trams can run on roads used by other vehicles and pedestrians. The part of the road used by the trams is known as the reserved area and this should be kept clear. It has a coloured surface and is usually edged with white road markings. It might also have different surface texture.

## 423 Mark *one* answer

**You see a vehicle coming towards you on a single-track road. You should**

- ☐ **A** go back to the main road
- ☐ **B** do an emergency stop
- ☐ **C** stop at a passing place
- ☐ **D** put on your hazard warning lights

You must take extra care when on single track roads. You may not be able to see around bends due to high hedges or fences. Proceed with caution and expect to meet oncoming vehicles around the next bend. If you do, pull into or opposite a passing place.

## 424 Mark *one* answer

**The road is wet. Why might a motorcyclist steer round drain covers on a bend?**

- ☐ **A** To avoid puncturing the tyres on the edge of the drain covers
- ☐ **B** To prevent the motorcycle sliding on the metal drain covers
- ☐ **C** To help judge the bend using the drain covers as marker points
- ☐ **D** To avoid splashing pedestrians on the pavement

Other drivers or riders may have to change course due to the size or characteristics of their vehicle. Understanding this will help you to anticipate their actions. Motorcyclists and cyclists will be checking the road ahead for uneven or slippery surfaces, especially in wet weather. They may need to move across their lane to avoid surface hazards such as potholes and drain covers.

## 425 Mark *one* answer

**After this hazard you should test your brakes. Why is this?**

- ☐ **A** You will be on a slippery road
- ☐ **B** Your brakes will be soaking wet
- ☐ **C** You will be going down a long hill
- ☐ **D** You will have just crossed a long bridge

A ford is a crossing over a stream that's shallow enough to go through. After you've gone through a ford or deep puddle the water will affect your brakes. To dry them out apply a light brake pressure while moving slowly. Don't travel at normal speeds until you are sure your brakes are working properly again.

## 426 Mark *one* answer

**Why should you always reduce your speed when travelling in fog?**

- ☐ **A** The brakes do not work as well
- ☐ **B** You will be dazzled by other headlights
- ☐ **C** The engine will take longer to warm up
- ☐ **D** It is more difficult to see events ahead

You won't be able to see as far ahead in fog as you can on a clear day. You will need to reduce your speed so that, if a hazard looms out of the fog, you have the time and space to take avoiding action.

Travelling in fog is hazardous. If you can, try and delay your journey until it has cleared.

**427** Mark *one* answer

**On a motorway you may ONLY stop on the hard shoulder**

☐ **A** in an emergency
☐ **B** If you feel tired and need to rest
☐ **C** if you go past the exit that you wanted to take
☐ **D** to pick up a hitchhiker

You must not stop on the hard shoulder except in an emergency. Never use it to have a rest or a picnic, pick up hitchhikers, answer a mobile phone, or check a road map. You must not travel back along the hard shoulder if you go past your intended exit.

**428** Mark *one* answer

**You are intending to leave the motorway at the next exit. Before you reach the exit you should normally position your motorcycle**

☐ **A** in the middle lane
☐ **B** in the left-hand lane
☐ **C** on the hard shoulder
☐ **D** in any lane

You'll see the first advance warning sign for a junction one mile from the exit. If you're travelling at 60mph you'll only have about 50 seconds before you reach the countdown markers. Move in to the left-hand lane in good time if you're not there already. Don't cut across traffic at the last moment.

**429** Mark *one* answer

**You are joining a motorway from a slip road. You should**

☐ **A** adjust your speed to the speed of the traffic on the motorway
☐ **B** accelerate as quickly as you can and ride straight out
☐ **C** ride onto the hard shoulder until a gap appears
☐ **D** expect drivers on the motorway to give way to you

Give way to the traffic already on the motorway and join it where there's a suitable gap in the traffic. Don't expect traffic on the motorway to give way to you, but try to avoid stopping at the end of the slip road.

**430** Mark *one* answer

**A motorcycle is not allowed on a motorway if it has an engine size smaller than**

☐ **A** 50cc
☐ **B** 125cc
☐ **C** 150cc
☐ **D** 250cc

Very small motorcycles are not allowed to use motorways due to their restricted speed, as this may cause a hazard to other vehicles.

**431** Mark *one* answer

**To ride on a motorway your motorcycle must be**

☐ **A** 50cc or more   ☐ **B** 100cc or more
☐ **C** 125cc or more   ☐ **D** 250cc or more

Traffic on motorways travels at high speeds. Vehicles need to be capable of keeping up with the flow of traffic. For this reason low-powered vehicles are prohibited.

**432** Mark *one* answer

**On a three-lane motorway why should you normally ride in the left-hand lane?**

☐ **A** The left-hand lane is only for lorries and motorcycles
☐ **B** The left-hand lane should only be used by smaller vehicles
☐ **C** The lanes on the right are for overtaking
☐ **D** Motorcycles are not allowed in the far right-hand lane

Change lanes only if necessary. When you do change lanes make sure you observe, signal and manoeuvre in good time. Always remember your 'lifesaver' check. This is a final, quick rearward glance before you pull out.

**433** Mark *one* answer

**You are riding at 70mph on a three-lane motorway. There is no traffic ahead. Which lane should you use?**

☐ **A** Any lane
☐ **B** Middle lane
☐ **C** Right-hand lane
☐ **D** Left-hand lane

Use the left-hand lane if it's free, regardless of the speed you're travelling.

**434** Mark *one* answer   **NI**

**You are riding on a motorway. Unless signs show otherwise you must NOT exceed**

☐ **A** 50mph
☐ **B** 60mph
☐ **C** 70mph
☐ **D** 80mph

Ride in accordance with the conditions. Bad weather or heavy traffic may mean you have to lower your speed.

**435** Mark *one* answer

**Why is it particularly important to carry out a check of your motorcycle before making a long motorway journey?**

☐ **A** You will have to do more harsh braking on motorways
☐ **B** Motorway service stations do not deal with breakdowns
☐ **C** The road surface will wear down the tyres faster
☐ **D** Continuous high speeds may increase the risk of your motorcycle breaking down

Before starting a motorway journey, make sure your motorcycle can cope with the demands of high-speed riding. Things you need to check include, oil, water and tyres. When you're travelling a long way it's a good idea to plan rest stops in advance.

## 436 Mark *one* answer
**When joining a motorway you must always**

- ☐ **A** use the hard shoulder
- ☐ **B** stop at the end of the acceleration lane
- ☐ **C** come to a stop before joining the motorway
- ☐ **D** give way to traffic already on the motorway

You should give way to traffic already on the motorway. Where possible they may move over to let you in but don't force your way into the traffic stream. The traffic may be travelling at high speed so you should match your speed to fit in.

## 437 Mark *one* answer
**What is the national speed limit for cars and motorcycles in the centre lane of a three-lane motorway?**

- ☐ **A** 40mph
- ☐ **B** 50mph
- ☐ **C** 60mph
- ☐ **D** 70mph

Unless shown otherwise, the speed limit on a motorway applies to all the lanes. Look out for any signs of speed limit changes due to roadworks or traffic flow control.

## 438 Mark *one* answer
**What is the national speed limit on motorways for cars and motorcycles?**

- ☐ **A** 30mph
- ☐ **B** 50mph
- ☐ **C** 60mph
- ☐ **D** 70mph

Travelling at the national speed limit doesn't allow you to hog the right-hand lane. Always use the left-hand lane whenever possible. When leaving a motorway get into the left-hand lane well before your exit. Reduce your speed on the slip road and look out for sharp bends or curves and traffic queuing at roundabouts.

## 439 Mark *one* answer
**The left-hand lane on a three-lane motorway is for use by**

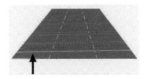

- ☐ **A** any vehicle
- ☐ **B** large vehicles only
- ☐ **C** emergency vehicles only
- ☐ **D** slow vehicles only

On a motorway all traffic should use the left-hand lane unless overtaking. Use the centre or right-hand lanes if you need to overtake. If you're overtaking a number of slower vehicles move back to the left-hand lane when you're safely past. Check your mirrors frequently and don't stay in the middle or right-hand lane if the left-hand lane is free.

**440** Mark *one* answer
**Which of these IS NOT allowed to travel in the right-hand lane of a three-lane motorway?**

☐ **A** A small delivery van
☐ **B** A motorcycle
☐ **C** A vehicle towing a trailer
☐ **D** A motorcycle and side-car

A vehicle with a trailer is restricted to 60mph. For this reason it isn't allowed in the right-hand lane as it might hold up the faster-moving traffic that wishes to overtake in that lane.

**441** Mark *one* answer
**You break down on a motorway. You need to call for help. Why may it be better to use an emergency roadside telephone rather than a mobile phone?**

☐ **A** It connects you to a local garage
☐ **B** Using a mobile phone will distract other drivers
☐ **C** It allows easy location by the emergency services
☐ **D** Mobile phones do not work on motorways

On a motorway it is best to use a roadside emergency telephone so that the emergency services are able to locate you easily. The nearest telephone is shown by an arrow on marker posts at the edge of the hard shoulder. If you use a mobile, they will need to know your exact location. Before you call, find out the number on the nearest marker post. This number will identify your exact location.

**442** Mark *one* answer
**After a breakdown you need to rejoin the main carriageway of a motorway from the hard shoulder. You should**

☐ **A** move out onto the carriageway then build up your speed
☐ **B** move out onto the carriageway using your hazard lights
☐ **C** gain speed on the hard shoulder before moving out onto the carriageway
☐ **D** wait on the hard shoulder until someone flashes their headlights at you

Wait for a safe gap in the traffic before you move out. Indicate your intention and use the hard shoulder to gain speed but don't force your way into the traffic.

**443** Mark *one* answer
**A crawler lane on a motorway is found**

☐ **A** on a steep gradient
☐ **B** before a service area
☐ **C** before a junction
☐ **D** along the hard shoulder

Slow-moving, large vehicles might slow down the progress of other traffic. On a steep gradient this extra lane is provided for these slow-moving vehicles to allow the faster-moving traffic to flow more easily.

## 444 Mark *one* answer
**What do these motorway signs show?**

- ☐ **A** They are countdown markers to a bridge
- ☐ **B** They are distance markers to the next telephone
- ☐ **C** They are countdown markers to the next exit
- ☐ **D** They warn of a police control ahead

The exit from a motorway is indicated by countdown markers. These are positioned 90 metres (100 yards) apart, the first being 270 metres (300 yards) from the start of the slip road. Move into the left-hand lane well before you reach the start of the slip road.

## 445 Mark *one* answer
**On a motorway the amber reflective studs can be found between**

- ☐ **A** the hard shoulder and the carriageway
- ☐ **B** the acceleration lane and the carriageway
- ☐ **C** the central reservation and the carriageway
- ☐ **D** each pair of the lanes

On motorways reflective studs are located into the road to help you in the dark and in conditions of poor visibility. Amber-coloured studs are found on the right-hand edge of the main carriageway, next to the central reservation.

## 446 Mark *one* answer
**What colour are the reflective studs between the lanes on a motorway?**

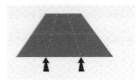

- ☐ **A** Green
- ☐ **B** Amber
- ☐ **C** White
- ☐ **D** Red

White studs are found between the lanes on motorways. The light from your headlights is reflected back and this is especially useful in bad weather, when visibility is restricted.

## 447 Mark *one* answer
**What colour are the reflective studs between a motorway and its slip road?**

- ☐ **A** Amber
- ☐ **B** White
- ☐ **C** Green
- ☐ **D** Red

The studs between the carriageway and the hard shoulder are normally red. These change to green where there is a slip road. They will help you identify slip roads when visibility is poor or when it is dark.

**448** Mark *one* answer
**You have broken down on a motorway. To find the nearest emergency telephone you should always walk**

☐ **A** with the traffic flow
☐ **B** facing oncoming traffic
☐ **C** in the direction shown on the marker posts
☐ **D** in the direction of the nearest exit

Along the hard shoulder there are marker posts at 100-metre intervals. These will direct you to the nearest emergency telephone.

**449** Mark *one* answer
**You are joining a motorway. Why is it important to make full use of the slip road?**

☐ **A** Because there is space available to turn round if you need to
☐ **B** To allow you direct access to the overtaking lanes
☐ **C** To build up a speed similar to traffic on the motorway
☐ **D** Because you can continue on the hard shoulder

Try to join the motorway without affecting the progress of the traffic already travelling on it. Always give way to traffic already on the motorway. At busy times you may have to slow down to merge into slow-moving traffic.

**450** Mark *one* answer
**How should you use the emergency telephone on a motorway?**

☐ **A** Stay close to the carriageway
☐ **B** Face the oncoming traffic
☐ **C** Keep your back to the traffic
☐ **D** Stand on the hard shoulder

Traffic is passing you at speed. If the draught from a large lorry catches you by surprise it could blow you off balance and even onto the carriageway. By facing the oncoming traffic you can see approaching lorries and so be prepared for their draught. You are also in a position to see other hazards approaching.

**451** Mark *one* answer
**You are on a motorway. What colour are the reflective studs on the left of the carriageway?**

☐ **A** Green
☐ **B** Red
☐ **C** White
☐ **D** Amber

Red studs are placed between the edge of the carriageway and the hard shoulder. Where slip roads leave or join the motorway the studs are green.

## 452 Mark *one* answer

**On a three-lane motorway which lane should you normally use?**

☐ **A** Left
☐ **B** Right
☐ **C** Centre
☐ **D** Either the right or centre

On a three-lane motorway you should travel in the left-hand lane unless you're overtaking. This applies regardless of the speed at which you're travelling.

## 453 Mark *one* answer

**When going through a contraflow system on a motorway you should**

☐ **A** ensure that you do not exceed 30mph
☐ **B** keep a good distance from the vehicle ahead
☐ **C** switch lanes to keep the traffic flowing
☐ **D** stay close to the vehicle ahead to reduce queues

There's likely to be a speed restriction in force. Keep to this.
Don't
• switch lanes
• get too close to traffic in front of you.
Be aware there will be no permanent barrier between you and the oncoming traffic.

## 454 Mark *one* answer

**You are on a three-lane motorway. There are red reflective studs on your left and white ones to your right. Where are you?**

☐ **A** In the right-hand lane
☐ **B** In the middle lane
☐ **C** On the hard shoulder
☐ **D** In the left-hand lane

The colours of the reflective studs on the motorway and their locations are
• red – between the hard shoulder and the carriageway
• white – lane markings
• amber – between the edge of the carriageway and the central reservation
• green – along slip road exits and entrances
• bright green/yellow – roadworks and contraflow systems.

## 455 Mark *one* answer

**You are approaching roadworks on a motorway. What should you do?**

☐ **A** Speed up to clear the area quickly
☐ **B** Always use the hard shoulder
☐ **C** Obey all speed limits
☐ **D** Stay very close to the vehicle in front

Collisions can often happen at roadworks. Be aware of the speed limits, slow down in good time and keep your distance from the vehicle in front.

## 456 Mark *four* answers
**Which FOUR of these must NOT use motorways?**

- ☐ **A** Learner car drivers
- ☐ **B** Motorcycles over 50cc
- ☐ **C** Double-deck buses
- ☐ **D** Farm tractors
- ☐ **E** Horse riders
- ☐ **F** Cyclists

In addition, motorways MUST NOT be used by pedestrians, motorcycles under 50cc, certain slow-moving vehicles without permission, and invalid carriages weighing less than 254kg (560lbs).

## 457 Mark *four* answers
**Which FOUR of these must NOT use motorways?**

- ☐ **A** Learner car drivers
- ☐ **B** Motorcycles over 50cc
- ☐ **C** Double-deck buses
- ☐ **D** Farm tractors
- ☐ **E** Learner motorcyclists
- ☐ **F** Cyclists

Learner car drivers and motorcyclists are not allowed on the motorway until they have passed their practical test.

Motorways have rules that you need to know before you venture out for the first time. When you've passed your practical test it's a good idea to have some lessons on motorways. Check with your instructor about this.

## 458 Mark *one* answer
**Immediately after joining a motorway you should normally**

- ☐ **A** try to overtake
- ☐ **B** re-adjust your mirrors
- ☐ **C** position your vehicle in the centre lane
- ☐ **D** keep in the left-hand lane

Stay in the left-hand lane long enough to get used to the higher speeds of motorway traffic.

## 459 Mark *one* answer
**What is the right-hand lane used for on a three-lane motorway?**

- ☐ **A** Emergency vehicles only
- ☐ **B** Overtaking
- ☐ **C** Vehicles towing trailers
- ☐ **D** Coaches only

You should keep to the left and only use the right-hand lane if you're passing slower-moving traffic.

**460** Mark *one* answer

**What should you use the hard shoulder of a motorway for?**

- ☐ **A** Stopping in an emergency
- ☐ **B** Leaving the motorway
- ☐ **C** Stopping when you are tired
- ☐ **D** Joining the motorway

Don't use the hard shoulder for stopping unless it is an emergency. If you want to stop for any other reason go to the next exit or service station.

**461** Mark *one* answer

**You are in the right-hand lane on a motorway. You see these overhead signs. This means**

- ☐ **A** move to the left and reduce your speed to 50mph
- ☐ **B** there are roadworks 50 metres (55 yards) ahead
- ☐ **C** use the hard shoulder until you have passed the hazard
- ☐ **D** leave the motorway at the next exit

You MUST obey this sign. There might not be any visible signs of a problem ahead. However, there might be queuing traffic or another hazard which you cannot yet see.

**462** Mark *one* answer

**You are allowed to stop on a motorway when you**

- ☐ **A** need to walk and get fresh air
- ☐ **B** wish to pick up hitchhikers
- ☐ **C** are told to do so by flashing red lights
- ☐ **D** need to use a mobile telephone

You MUST stop if there are red lights flashing above every lane on the motorway. However, if any of the other lanes do not show flashing red lights or red cross you may move into that lane and continue if it is safe to do so.

**463** Mark *one* answer

**You are travelling along the left-hand lane of a three-lane motorway. Traffic is joining from a slip road. You should**

- ☐ **A** race the other vehicles
- ☐ **B** move to another lane
- ☐ **C** maintain a steady speed
- ☐ **D** switch on your hazard flashers

You should move to another lane if it is safe to do so. This can greatly assist the flow of traffic joining the motorway, especially at peak times.

**464** Mark *one* answer
**A basic rule when on motorways is**

☐ **A** use the lane that has least traffic
☐ **B** keep to the left-hand lane
 unless overtaking
☐ **C** overtake on the side that is clearest
☐ **D** try to keep above 50mph to
 prevent congestion

You should normally travel in the left-hand lane unless you are overtaking a slower-moving vehicle. When you are past that vehicle move back into the left-hand lane as soon as it's safe to do so. Don't cut across in front of the vehicle that you're overtaking.

**465** Mark *one* answer
**On motorways you should never overtake on the left unless**

☐ **A** you can see well ahead that the hard
 shoulder is clear
☐ **B** the traffic in the right-hand lane is
 signalling right
☐ **C** you warn drivers behind by signalling left
☐ **D** there is a queue of slow-moving traffic to
 your right that is moving more slowly than
 you are

Only overtake on the left if traffic is moving slowly in queues and the traffic on your right is moving more slowly than the traffic in your lane.

**466** Mark *one* answer  **NI**
**Motorway emergency telephones are usually linked to the police. In some areas they are now linked to**

☐ **A** the Highways Agency Control Centre
☐ **B** the Driver Vehicle Licensing Agency
☐ **C** the Driving Standards Agency
☐ **D** the local Vehicle Registration Office

In some areas motorway telephones are now linked to a Highways Agency Control Centre, instead of the police. Highways Agency Traffic Officers work in partnership with the police and assist at motorway emergencies and incidents. They are recognised by a high-visibility orange and yellow jacket and high-visibility vehicle with yellow and black chequered markings.

**467** Mark *one* answer
**An Emergency Refuge Area is an area**

☐ **A** on a motorway for use in cases of
 emergency or breakdown
☐ **B** for use if you think you will be involved in
 a road rage incident
☐ **C** on a motorway for a police patrol to park
 and watch traffic
☐ **D** for construction and road workers to store
 emergency equipment

Emergency Refuge Areas may be found at the side of the hard shoulder about 500 metres apart. If you break down you should use them rather than the hard shoulder if you are able. When re-joining the motorway you must remember to take extra care especially when the hard shoulder is being used as a running lane within an Active Traffic Management area. Try to match your speed to that of traffic in the lane you are joining.

## 468 Mark *one* answer
**What is an Emergency Refuge Area on a motorway for?**

- ☐ **A** An area to park in when you want to use a mobile phone
- ☐ **B** To use in cases of emergency or breakdown
- ☐ **C** For an emergency recovery vehicle to park in a contra-flow system
- ☐ **D** To drive in when there is queuing traffic ahead

In cases of breakdown or emergency try to get your vehicle into an Emergency Refuge Area. This is safer than just stopping on the hard shoulder as it gives you greater distance from the main carriageway. If you are able to re-join the motorway you must take extra care, especially when the hard shoulder is being used as a running lane.

---

## 469 Mark *one* answer **NI**
**Highways Agency Traffic Officers**

- ☐ **A** will not be able to assist at a breakdown or emergency
- ☐ **B** are not able to stop and direct anyone on a motorway
- ☐ **C** will tow a broken down vehicle and it's passengers home
- ☐ **D** are able to stop and direct anyone on a motorway

Highways Agency Traffic Officers (HATOs) are able to stop and direct traffic on most motorways and some 'A' class roads. They work in partnership with the police at motorway incidents and provide a highly-trained and visible service. Their role is to help keep traffic moving and make your journey as safe and reliable as possible. They are recognised by an orange and yellow jacket and their vehicle has yellow and black markings.

## 470 Mark *one* answer **NI**
**You are on a motorway. A red cross is displayed above the hard shoulder. What does this mean?**

- ☐ **A** Pull up in this lane to answer your mobile phone
- ☐ **B** Use this lane as a running lane
- ☐ **C** This lane can be used if you need a rest
- ☐ **D** You should not travel in this lane

Active Traffic Management schemes are being introduced on motorways. Within these areas at certain times the hard shoulder will be used as a running lane. A red cross above the hard shoulder shows that this lane should NOT be used, except for emergencies and breakdowns.

**471** Mark *one* answer  NI

**You are on a motorway in an Active Traffic Management (ATM) area. A mandatory speed limit is displayed above the hard shoulder. What does this mean?**

- ☐ **A** You should not travel in this lane
- ☐ **B** The hard shoulder can be used as a running lane
- ☐ **C** You can park on the hard shoulder if you feel tired
- ☐ **D** You can pull up in this lane to answer a mobile phone

A mandatory speed limit sign above the hard shoulder shows that it can be used as a running lane between junctions. You must stay within the speed limit. Look out for vehicles that may have broken down and could be blocking the hard shoulder.

**472** Mark *one* answer  NI

**The aim of an Active Traffic Management scheme on a motorway is to**

- ☐ **A** prevent overtaking
- ☐ **B** reduce rest stops
- ☐ **C** prevent tailgating
- ☐ **D** reduce congestion

Active Traffic Management schemes are intended to reduce congestion and make journey times more reliable. In these areas the hard shoulder may be used as a running lane to ease congestion at peak times or in the event of an incident. It may appear that you could travel faster for a short distance, but keeping traffic flow at a constant speed may improve your journey time.

**473** Mark *one* answer  NI

**You are in an Active Traffic Management area on a motorway. When the Actively Managed mode is operating**

- ☐ **A** speed limits are only advisory
- ☐ **B** the national speed limit will apply
- ☐ **C** the speed limit is always 30mph
- ☐ **D** all speed limit signals are set

When an Active Traffic Management (ATM) scheme is operating on a motorway you MUST follow the mandatory instructions shown on the gantries above each lane. This includes the hard shoulder.

## 474 Mark *one* answer

**You are travelling on a motorway. A red cross is shown above the hard shoulder. What does this mean?**

- ☐ **A** Use this lane as a rest area
- ☐ **B** Use this as a normal running lane
- ☐ **C** Do not use this lane to travel in
- ☐ **D** National speed limit applies in this lane

When a red cross is shown above the hard shoulder it should only be used for breakdowns or emergencies. Within Active Traffic Management (ATM) areas the hard shoulder may sometimes be used as a running lane. Speed limit signs directly above the hard shoulder will show that it's open.

## 475 Mark *one* answer

**Why can it be an advantage for traffic speed to stay constant over a longer distance?**

- ☐ **A** You will do more stop-start driving
- ☐ **B** You will use far more fuel
- ☐ **C** You will be able to use more direct routes
- ☐ **D** Your overall journey time will normally improve

When traffic travels at a constant speed over a longer distance, journey times normally improve. You may feel that you could travel faster for short periods but this won't generally improve your overall journey time. Signs will show the maximum speed at which you should travel.

## 476 Mark *one* answer

**You should not normally travel on the hard shoulder of a motorway. When can you use it?**

- ☐ **A** When taking the next exit
- ☐ **B** When traffic is stopped
- ☐ **C** When signs direct you to
- ☐ **D** When traffic is slow moving

Normally you should only use the hard shoulder for emergencies and breakdowns, and at roadworks when signs direct you to do so. Active Traffic Management (ATM) areas are being introduced to ease traffic congestion. In these areas the hard shoulder may be used as a running lane when speed limit signs are shown directly above.

## 477 Mark *one* answer

**For what reason may you use the right-hand lane of a motorway?**

- ☐ **A** For keeping out of the way of lorries
- ☐ **B** For travelling at more than 70mph
- ☐ **C** For turning right
- ☐ **D** For overtaking other vehicles

The right-hand lane of the motorway is for overtaking.

Sometimes you may be directed into a right-hand lane as a result of roadworks or a traffic incident. This will be indicated by signs or officers directing the traffic.

**478** Mark *one* answer

**On a motorway what is used to reduce traffic bunching?**

☐ **A** Variable speed limits
☐ **B** Contraflow systems
☐ **C** National speed limits
☐ **D** Lane closures

Congestion can be reduced by keeping traffic at a constant speed. At busy times maximum speed limits are displayed on overhead gantries. These can be varied quickly depending on the amount of traffic. By keeping to a constant speed on busy sections of motorway overall journey times are normally improved.

**479** Mark *three* answers

**When should you stop on a motorway?**

☐ **A** If you have to read a map
☐ **B** When you are tired and need a rest
☐ **C** If red lights show above every lane
☐ **D** When told to by the police
☐ **E** If your mobile phone rings
☐ **F** When signalled by a Highways Agency Traffic Officer

There are some occasions when you may have to stop on the carriageway of a motorway. These include when being signalled by the police or a Highways Agency Traffic Officer, when flashing red lights show above every lane and in traffic jams.

**480** Mark *one* answer

**When may you stop on a motorway?**

☐ **A** If you have to read a map
☐ **B** When you are tired and need a rest
☐ **C** If your mobile phone rings
☐ **D** In an emergency or breakdown

You should not normally stop on a motorway but there may be occasions when you need to do so. If you are unfortunate enough to break down make every effort to pull up on the hard shoulder.

**481** Mark *one* answer    NI

**You are travelling on a motorway. Unless signs show a lower speed limit you must NOT exceed**

☐ **A** 50mph
☐ **B** 60mph
☐ **C** 70mph
☐ **D** 80mph

The national speed limit for a car or motorcycle on the motorway is 70mph. Lower speed limits may be in force, for example at roadworks, so look out for the signs. Variable speed limits operate in some areas to control very busy stretches of motorway. The speed limit may change depending on the volume of traffic.

## 482 Mark *one* answer

**Motorway emergency telephones are usually linked to the police. In some areas they are now linked to**

☐ **A** the local ambulance service
☐ **B** an Highways Agency control centre
☐ **C** the local fire brigade
☐ **D** a breakdown service control centre

The controller will ask you
- the make and colour of your vehicle
- whether you are a member of an emergency breakdown service
- the number shown on the emergency telephone casing
- whether you are travelling alone.

## 483 Mark *one* answer

**You are on a motorway. There are red flashing lights above every lane. You must**

☐ **A** pull onto the hard shoulder
☐ **B** slow down and watch for further signals
☐ **C** leave at the next exit
☐ **D** stop and wait

Red flashing lights above every lane mean you must not go on any further. You'll also see a red cross illuminated. Stop and wait. Don't
- change lanes
- continue
- pull onto the hard shoulder (unless in an emergency).

## 484 Mark *one* answer

**You are on a three-lane motorway. A red cross is shown above the hard shoulder and mandatory speed limits above all other lanes. This means**

☐ **A** the hard shoulder can be used as a rest area if you feel tired
☐ **B** the hard shoulder is for emergency or breakdown use only
☐ **C** the hard shoulder can be used as a normal running lane
☐ **D** the hard shoulder has a speed limit of 50mph

A red cross above the hard shoulder shows it is closed as a running lane and should only be used for emergencies or breakdowns. At busy times within an Active Traffic Management (ATM) area the hard shoulder may be used as a running lane. This will be shown by a mandatory speed limit on the gantry above.

## 485 Mark *one* answer  **NI**

**You are on a three-lane motorway and see this sign. It means you can use**

- ☐ **A** any lane except the hard shoulder
- ☐ **B** the hard shoulder only
- ☐ **C** the three right hand lanes only
- ☐ **D** all the lanes including the hard shoulder

Mandatory speed limit signs above all lanes including the hard shoulder, show that you are in an Active Traffic Management (ATM) area. In this case you can use the hard shoulder as a running lane. You must stay within the speed limit shown. Look out for any vehicles that may have broken down and be blocking the hard shoulder.

## 486 Mark *one* answer

**You are travelling on a motorway. You decide you need a rest. You should**

- ☐ **A** stop on the hard shoulder
- ☐ **B** pull in at the nearest service area
- ☐ **C** pull up on a slip road
- ☐ **D** park on the central reservation

If you feel tired stop at the nearest service area. If it's too far away leave the motorway at the next exit and find a safe place to stop. You must not stop on the carriageway or hard shoulder of a motorway except in an emergency, in a traffic queue, when signalled to do so by a police or enforcement officer, or by traffic signals. Plan your journey so that you have regular rest stops.

## 487 Mark *one* answer

**You are on a motorway. You become tired and decide you need to rest. What should you do?**

- ☐ **A** Stop on the hard shoulder
- ☐ **B** Pull up on a slip road
- ☐ **C** Park on the central reservation
- ☐ **D** Leave at the next exit

Ideally you should plan your journey so that you have regular rest stops. If you do become tired leave at the next exit, or pull in at a service area if this is sooner.

**488** Mark *one* answer

**You are riding slowly in a town centre. Before turning left you should glance over your left shoulder to**

- ☐ **A** check for cyclists
- ☐ **B** help keep your balance
- ☐ **C** look for traffic signs
- ☐ **D** check for potholes

When riding slowly you must remember cyclists. They can travel quickly and fit through surprisingly narrow spaces. Before you turn left in slow-moving traffic it's important to check that a cyclist isn't trying to overtake on your left.

**489** Mark *two* answers

**As a motorcycle rider which TWO lanes must you NOT use?**

- ☐ **A** Crawler lane
- ☐ **B** Overtaking lane
- ☐ **C** Acceleration lane
- ☐ **D** Cycle lane
- ☐ **E** Tram lane

In some towns motorcycles are permitted to use bus lanes. Check the signs carefully.

**490** Mark *one* answer

**What does this sign mean?**

- ☐ **A** No parking for solo motorcycles
- ☐ **B** Parking for solo motorcycles
- ☐ **C** Passing place for motorcycles
- ☐ **D** Police motorcycles only

In some towns and cities there are special areas reserved for parking motorcycles. Look out for these signs.

**491** Mark *one* answer

**You are riding on a busy dual carriageway. When changing lanes you should**

- ☐ **A** rely totally on mirrors
- ☐ **B** always increase your speed
- ☐ **C** signal so others will give way
- ☐ **D** use mirrors and shoulder checks

Before changing direction, as well as using your mirrors, you need to take a quick sideways glance to check for vehicles in any of your blind spots. These are areas behind and to the side of you which are not covered by the mirrors.

**492** Mark *one* answer

**You are looking for somewhere to park your motorcycle. The area is full EXCEPT for spaces marked 'disabled use'. You can**

☐ **A** use these spaces when elsewhere is full
☐ **B** park if you stay with your motorcycle
☐ **C** use these spaces, disabled or not
☐ **D** not park there unless permitted

Don't be selfish. These spaces are intended for people with limited mobility. Find somewhere else to park, even if it means that you have to walk further.

**493** Mark *one* answer

**You are on a road with passing places. It is only wide enough for one vehicle. There is a car coming towards you. What should you do?**

☐ **A** Pull into a passing place on your right
☐ **B** Force the other driver to reverse
☐ **C** Turn round and ride back to the main road
☐ **D** Pull into a passing place on your left

If you meet another vehicle in a narrow road and the passing place is on your left, pull into it. If the passing place is on the right, wait opposite it.

**494** Mark *one* answer

**You are both turning right at this crossroads. It is safer to keep the car to your right so you can**

☐ **A** see approaching traffic
☐ **B** keep close to the kerb
☐ **C** keep clear of following traffic
☐ **D** make oncoming vehicles stop

When turning right at this crossroads you should keep the oncoming car on your right. This will give you a clear view of the road ahead and any oncoming traffic.

**495** Mark *three* answers

**When filtering through slow-moving or stationary traffic you should**

☐ **A** watch for hidden vehicles emerging from side roads
☐ **B** continually use your horn as a warning
☐ **C** look for vehicles changing course suddenly
☐ **D** always ride with your hazard lights on
☐ **E** stand up on the footrests for a good view ahead
☐ **F** look for pedestrians walking between vehicles

Other road users may not expect or look for motorcycles filtering through slow-moving or stationary traffic. Your view will be reduced by the vehicles around you. Watch out for, pedestrians walking between the vehicles, vehicles suddenly changing direction and vehicles pulling out of side roads.

## 496 Mark *one* answer

**You are riding towards roadworks. The temporary traffic lights are at red. The road ahead is clear. What should you do?**

- ☐ **A** Ride on with extreme caution
- ☐ **B** Ride on at normal speed
- ☐ **C** Carry on if approaching cars have stopped
- ☐ **D** Wait for the green light

You must obey all traffic signs and signals. Just because the lights are temporary it does not mean that you can disregard them.

## 497 Mark *one* answer

**You intend to go abroad and will be riding on the right-hand side of the road. What should you fit to your motorcycle?**

- ☐ **A** Twin headlights
- ☐ **B** Headlight deflectors
- ☐ **C** Tinted yellow brake lights
- ☐ **D** Tinted red indicator lenses

When abroad and riding on the right, deflectors are usually required to prevent your headlight dazzling approaching drivers.

## 498 Mark *one* answer

**You want to tow a trailer with your motorcycle. Your engine must be more than**

- ☐ **A** 50cc
- ☐ **B** 125cc
- ☐ **C** 525cc
- ☐ **D** 1000cc

You must remember that towing a trailer requires special care. You must obey the restrictions which apply to all vehicles towing trailers. Do not forget it is there, especially when negotiating bends and junctions.

## 499 Mark *one* answer

**What is the national speed limit on a single carriageway?**

- ☐ **A** 40mph
- ☐ **B** 50mph
- ☐ **C** 60mph
- ☐ **D** 70mph

You don't have to ride at the speed limit. Use your own judgement and ride at a speed that suits the prevailing road, weather and traffic conditions.

## 500 Mark *three* answers

**On which THREE occasions MUST you stop your motorcycle?**

- ☐ **A** When involved in a collision
- ☐ **B** At a red traffic light
- ☐ **C** When signalled to do so by a police officer
- ☐ **D** At a junction with double broken white lines
- ☐ **E** At a clear pelican crossing when the amber light is flashing

Don't stop or hold up traffic unnecessarily. However there are occasions when you MUST stop by law. These include, when signalled to do so by a police officer, at a red traffic light and if you have a collision. There are many other instances where you may have to stop.

## 501 Mark *one* answer
**What is the meaning of this sign?**

- ☐ **A** Local speed limit applies
- ☐ **B** No waiting on the carriageway
- ☐ **C** National speed limit applies
- ☐ **D** No entry to vehicular traffic

This sign doesn't tell you the speed limit in figures. You should know the speed limit for the type of road that you're on. Study your copy of The Highway Code.

## 502 Mark *one* answer
**What is the national speed limit for cars and motorcycles on a dual carriageway?**

- ☐ **A** 30mph
- ☐ **B** 50mph
- ☐ **C** 60mph
- ☐ **D** 70mph

Ensure that you know the speed limit for the road that you're on. The speed limit on a dual carriageway or motorway is 70mph for cars and motorcycles, unless there are signs to indicate otherwise. The speed limits for different types of vehicles are listed in The Highway Code.

## 503 Mark *one* answer
**There are no speed limit signs on the road. How is a 30mph limit indicated?**

- ☐ **A** By hazard warning lines
- ☐ **B** By street lighting
- ☐ **C** By pedestrian islands
- ☐ **D** By double or single yellow lines

There is usually a 30mph speed limit where there are street lights unless there are signs showing another limit.

## 504 Mark *one* answer
**Where you see street lights but no speed limit signs the limit is usually**

- ☐ **A** 30mph
- ☐ **B** 40mph
- ☐ **C** 50mph
- ☐ **D** 60mph

The presence of street lights generally shows that there is a 30mph speed limit, unless signs tell you otherwise.

## 505 Mark *one* answer
**What does this sign mean?**

- ☐ **A** Minimum speed 30mph
- ☐ **B** End of maximum speed
- ☐ **C** End of minimum speed
- ☐ **D** Maximum speed 30mph

A red slash through this sign indicates that the restriction has ended. In this case the restriction was a minimum speed limit of 30mph.

## 506 Mark *one* answer

**There is a tractor ahead of you. You wish to overtake but you are NOT sure if it is safe to do so. You should**

- ☐ **A** follow another overtaking vehicle through
- ☐ **B** sound your horn to the slow vehicle to pull over
- ☐ **C** speed through but flash your lights to oncoming traffic
- ☐ **D** not overtake if you are in doubt

Never overtake if you're not sure whether it's safe. Can you see far enough down the road to ensure that you can complete the manoeuvre safely? If the answer is no, DON'T GO.

## 507 Mark *three* answers

**Which three of the following are most likely to take an unusual course at roundabouts?**

- ☐ **A** Horse riders
- ☐ **B** Milk floats
- ☐ **C** Delivery vans
- ☐ **D** Long vehicles
- ☐ **E** Estate cars
- ☐ **F** Cyclists

Long vehicles might have to take a slightly different position when approaching the roundabout or going around it. This is to stop the rear of the vehicle cutting in and mounting the kerb.

Horse riders and cyclists might stay in the left-hand lane although they are turning right. Be aware of this and allow them room.

## 508 Mark *one* answer

**On a clearway you must not stop**

- ☐ **A** at any time
- ☐ **B** when it is busy
- ☐ **C** in the rush hour
- ☐ **D** during daylight hours

Clearways are in place so that traffic can flow without the obstruction of parked vehicles. Just one parked vehicle will cause an obstruction for all other traffic. You MUST NOT stop where a clearway is in force, not even to pick up or set down passengers.

## 509 Mark *one* answer

**What is the meaning of this sign?**

- ☐ **A** No entry
- ☐ **B** Waiting restrictions
- ☐ **C** National speed limit
- ☐ **D** School crossing patrol

This sign indicates that there are waiting restrictions. It is normally accompanied by details of when restrictions are in force.

Details of most signs which are in common use are shown in The Highway Code and a more comprehensive selection is available in Know Your Traffic Signs.

# 510 Mark *one* answer
**You can park on the right-hand side of a road at night**

- ☐ **A** in a one-way street
- ☐ **B** with your sidelights on
- ☐ **C** more than 10 metres (32 feet) from a junction
- ☐ **D** under a lamp-post

Red rear reflectors show up when headlights shine on them. These are useful when you are parked at night but will only reflect if you park in the same direction as the traffic flow. Normally you should park on the left, but if you're in a one-way street you may also park on the right-hand side.

---

# 511 Mark *one* answer
**On a three-lane dual carriageway the right-hand lane can be used for**

- ☐ **A** overtaking only, never turning right
- ☐ **B** overtaking or turning right
- ☐ **C** fast-moving traffic only
- ☐ **D** turning right only, never overtaking

You should normally use the left-hand lane on any dual carriageway unless you are overtaking or turning right.

When overtaking on a dual carriageway, look for vehicles ahead that are turning right. They're likely to be slowing or stopped. You need to see them in good time so that you can take appropriate action.

# 512 Mark *one* answer
**You are approaching a busy junction. There are several lanes with road markings. At the last moment you realise that you are in the wrong lane. You should**

- ☐ **A** continue in that lane
- ☐ **B** force your way across
- ☐ **C** stop until the area has cleared
- ☐ **D** use clear arm signals to cut across

There are times where road markings can be obscured by queuing traffic, or you might be unsure which lane you need to be in.

If you realise that you're in the wrong lane, don't cut across lanes or bully other drivers to let you in. Follow the lane you're in and find somewhere safe to turn around if you need to.

---

# 513 Mark *one* answer
**Where may you overtake on a one-way street?**

- ☐ **A** Only on the left-hand side
- ☐ **B** Overtaking is not allowed
- ☐ **C** Only on the right-hand side
- ☐ **D** Either on the right or the left

You can overtake other traffic on either side when travelling in a one-way street. Make full use of your mirrors and ensure that it's clear all around before you attempt to overtake. Look for signs and road markings and use the most suitable lane for your destination.

## 514 Mark *one* answer
**When going straight ahead at a roundabout you should**

☐ **A** indicate left before leaving the roundabout
☐ **B** not indicate at any time
☐ **C** indicate right when approaching the roundabout
☐ **D** indicate left when approaching the roundabout

When you want to go straight on at a roundabout, don't signal as you approach it, but indicate left just after you pass the exit before the one you wish to take.

## 515 Mark *one* answer
**Which vehicle might have to use a different course to normal at roundabouts?**

☐ **A** Sports car
☐ **B** Van
☐ **C** Estate car
☐ **D** Long vehicle

A long vehicle may have to straddle lanes either on or approaching a roundabout so that the rear wheels don't cut in over the kerb.

If you're following a long vehicle, stay well back and give it plenty of room.

## 516 Mark *one* answer
**You may only enter a box junction when**

☐ **A** there are less than two vehicles in front of you
☐ **B** the traffic lights show green
☐ **C** your exit road is clear
☐ **D** you need to turn left

Yellow box junctions are marked on the road to prevent the road becoming blocked. Don't enter one unless your exit road is clear. You may only wait in the yellow box if your exit road is clear but oncoming traffic is preventing you from completing the turn.

## 517 Mark *one* answer
**You may wait in a yellow box junction when**

☐ **A** oncoming traffic is preventing you from turning right
☐ **B** you are in a queue of traffic turning left
☐ **C** you are in a queue of traffic to go ahead
☐ **D** you are on a roundabout

The purpose of this road marking is to keep the junction clear of queuing traffic. You may only wait in the marked area when you're turning right and your exit lane is clear but you can't complete the turn because of oncoming traffic.

**518** Mark *three* answers
**You MUST stop when signalled to do so by which THREE of these?**

- ☐ **A** A police officer
- ☐ **B** A pedestrian
- ☐ **C** A school crossing patrol
- ☐ **D** A bus driver
- ☐ **E** A red traffic light

Looking well ahead and 'reading' the road will help you to anticipate hazards. This will enable you to stop safely at traffic lights or if ordered to do so by an authorised person.

**519** Mark *one* answer
**Someone is waiting to cross at a zebra crossing. They are standing on the pavement. You should normally**

- ☐ **A** go on quickly before they step onto the crossing
- ☐ **B** stop before you reach the zigzag lines and let them cross
- ☐ **C** stop, let them cross, wait patiently
- ☐ **D** ignore them as they are still on the pavement

By standing on the pavement, the pedestrian is showing an intention to cross. If you are looking well down the road you will give yourself enough time to slow down and stop safely. Don't forget to check your mirrors before slowing down.

**520** Mark *one* answer
**At toucan crossings, apart from pedestrians you should be aware of**

- ☐ **A** emergency vehicles emerging
- ☐ **B** buses pulling out
- ☐ **C** trams crossing in front
- ☐ **D** cyclists riding across

The use of cycles is being encouraged and more toucan crossings are being installed. These crossings enable pedestrians and cyclists to cross the path of other traffic. Watch out as cyclists will approach the crossing faster than pedestrians.

**521** Mark *two* answers
**Who can use a toucan crossing?**

- ☐ **A** Trains
- ☐ **B** Cyclists
- ☐ **C** Buses
- ☐ **D** Pedestrians
- ☐ **E** Trams

Toucan crossings are similar to pelican crossings but there is no flashing amber phase. Cyclists share the crossing with pedestrians and are allowed to cycle across when the green cycle symbol is shown.

## 522 Mark *one* answer
**At a pelican crossing, what does a flashing amber light mean?**

□ **A** You must not move off until the lights stop flashing

□ **B** You must give way to pedestrians still on the crossing

□ **C** You can move off, even if pedestrians are still on the crossing

□ **D** You must stop because the lights are about to change to red

If there is no-one on the crossing when the amber light is flashing, you may proceed over the crossing. You don't need to wait for the green light to show.

## 523 Mark *one* answer
**You are waiting at a pelican crossing. The red light changes to flashing amber. This means you must**

□ **A** wait for pedestrians on the crossing to clear

□ **B** move off immediately without any hesitation

□ **C** wait for the green light before moving off

□ **D** get ready and go when the continuous amber light shows

This light allows time for the pedestrians already on the crossing to get to the other side in their own time, without being rushed. Don't rev your engine or start to move off while they are still crossing.

## 524 Mark *one* answer
**When can you park on the left opposite these road markings?**

□ **A** If the line nearest to you is broken

□ **B** When there are no yellow lines

□ **C** To pick up or set down passengers

□ **D** During daylight hours only

You MUST NOT park or stop on a road marked with double white lines (even where one of the lines is broken) except to pick up or set down passengers.

## 525 Mark *one* answer
**You are intending to turn right at a crossroads. An oncoming driver is also turning right. It will normally be safer to**

□ **A** keep the other vehicle to your RIGHT and turn behind it (offside to offside)

□ **B** keep the other vehicle to your LEFT and turn in front of it (nearside to nearside)

□ **C** carry on and turn at the next junction instead

□ **D** hold back and wait for the other driver to turn first

At some junctions the layout may make it difficult to turn offside to offside. If this is the case, be prepared to pass nearside to nearside, but take extra care as your view ahead will be obscured by the vehicle turning in front of you.

## 526 Mark *one* answer

**You are on a road that has no traffic signs. There are street lights. What is the speed limit?**

☐ **A** 20mph
☐ **B** 30mph
☐ **C** 40mph
☐ **D** 60mph

If you aren't sure of the speed limit a good indication is the presence of street lights. If there is street lighting the speed limit will be 30mph unless otherwise indicated.

## 527 Mark *three* answers

**You are going along a street with parked vehicles on the left-hand side. For which THREE reasons should you keep your speed down?**

☐ **A** So that oncoming traffic can see you more clearly
☐ **B** You may set off car alarms
☐ **C** Vehicles may be pulling out
☐ **D** Drivers' doors may open
☐ **E** Children may run out from between the vehicles

Travel slowly and carefully where there are parked vehicles in a built-up area.
Beware of
 • vehicles pulling out, especially bicycles and other motorcycles
 • pedestrians, especially children, who may run out from between cars
 • drivers opening their doors.

## 528 Mark *one* answer

**You meet an obstruction on your side of the road. You should**

☐ **A** carry on, you have priority
☐ **B** give way to oncoming traffic
☐ **C** wave oncoming vehicles through
☐ **D** accelerate to get past first

Take care if you have to pass a parked vehicle on your side of the road. Give way to oncoming traffic if there isn't enough room for you both to continue safely.

## 529 Mark two answers

**You are on a two-lane dual carriageway. For which TWO of the following would you use the right-hand lane?**

☐ **A** Turning right
☐ **B** Normal progress
☐ **C** Staying at the minimum allowed speed
☐ **D** Constant high speed
☐ **E** Overtaking slower traffic
☐ **F** Mending punctures

Normally you should travel in the left-hand lane and only use the right-hand lane for overtaking or turning right. Move back into the left lane as soon as it's safe but don't cut in across the path of the vehicle you've just passed.

**530** Mark *one* answer
**Who has priority at an unmarked crossroads?**

☐ **A** The larger vehicle
☐ **B** No one has priority
☐ **C** The faster vehicle
☐ **D** The smaller vehicle

Practise good observation in all directions before you emerge or make a turn. Proceed only when you're sure it's safe to do so.

**531** Mark *one* answer    NI
**What is the nearest you may park to a junction?**

☐ **A** 10 metres (32 feet)
☐ **B** 12 metres (39 feet)
☐ **C** 15 metres (49 feet)
☐ **D** 20 metres (66 feet)

Don't park within 10 metres (32 feet) of a junction (unless in an authorised parking place). This is to allow drivers emerging from, or turning into, the junction a clear view of the road they are joining. It also allows them to see hazards such as pedestrians or cyclists at the junction.

**532** Mark *three* answers    NI
**In which THREE places must you NOT park?**

☐ **A** Near the brow of a hill
☐ **B** At or near a bus stop
☐ **C** Where there is no pavement
☐ **D** Within 10 metres (32 feet) of a junction
☐ **E** On a 40mph road

Other traffic will have to pull out to pass you. They may have to use the other side of the road, and if you park near the brow of a hill, they may not be able to see oncoming traffic. It's important not to park at or near a bus stop as this could inconvenience passengers, and may put them at risk as they get on or off the bus. Parking near a junction could restrict the view for emerging vehicles.

**533** Mark *one* answer
**You are waiting at a level crossing. A train has passed but the lights keep flashing. You must**

☐ **A** carry on waiting
☐ **B** phone the signal operator
☐ **C** edge over the stop line and look for trains
☐ **D** park and investigate

If the lights at a level crossing continue to flash after a train has passed, you should still wait as there might be another train coming. Time seems to pass slowly when you're held up in a queue. Be patient and wait until the lights stop flashing.

## 534 Mark *one* answer
**At a crossroads there are no signs or road markings. Two vehicles approach. Which has priority?**

- ☐ **A** Neither of the vehicles
- ☐ **B** The vehicle travelling the fastest
- ☐ **C** Oncoming vehicles turning right
- ☐ **D** Vehicles approaching from the right

At a crossroads where there are no 'give way' signs or road markings be very careful. No vehicle has priority, even if the sizes of the roads are different.

## 535 Mark *one* answer
**What does this sign tell you?**

- ☐ **A** That it is a no-through road
- ☐ **B** End of traffic-calming zone
- ☐ **C** Free parking zone ends
- ☐ **D** No waiting zone ends

The blue and red circular sign on its own means that waiting restrictions are in force. This sign shows that you are leaving the controlled zone and waiting restrictions no longer apply.

## 536 Mark *one* answer
**You are entering an area of roadworks. There is a temporary speed limit displayed. You should**

- ☐ **A** not exceed the speed limit
- ☐ **B** obey the limit only during rush hour
- ☐ **C** ignore the displayed limit
- ☐ **D** obey the limit except at night

Where there are extra hazards such as roadworks, it's often necessary to slow traffic down by imposing a temporary speed limit. These speed limits aren't advisory, they must be obeyed.

## 537 Mark *two* answers
**In which TWO places should you NOT park?**

- ☐ **A** Near a school entrance
- ☐ **B** Near a police station
- ☐ **C** In a side road
- ☐ **D** At a bus stop
- ☐ **E** In a one-way street

It may be tempting to park where you shouldn't while you run a quick errand. Careless parking is a selfish act and could endanger other road users.

**538** Mark *one* answer
**You are travelling on a well-lit road at night in a built-up area. By using dipped headlights you will be able to**

☐ **A** see further along the road
☐ **B** go at a much faster speed
☐ **C** switch to main beam quickly
☐ **D** be easily seen by others

You may be difficult to see when you're travelling at night, even on a well lit road. If you use dipped headlights rather than sidelights other road users will see you more easily.

**539** Mark *one* answer
**The dual carriageway you are turning right onto has a very narrow central reservation. What should you do?**

☐ **A** Proceed to the central reservation and wait
☐ **B** Wait until the road is clear in both directions
☐ **C** Stop in the first lane so that other vehicles give way
☐ **D** Emerge slightly to show your intentions

When the central reservation is narrow you should treat a dual carriageway as one road. Wait until the road is clear in both directions before emerging to turn right. If you try to treat it as two separate roads and wait in the middle, you are likely to cause an obstruction and possibly a collision.

**540** Mark *one* answer
**What is the national speed limit on a single carriageway road for cars and motorcycles?**

☐ **A** 30mph
☐ **B** 50mph
☐ **C** 60mph
☐ **D** 70mph

Exceeding the speed limit is dangerous and can result in you receiving penalty points on your licence. It isn't worth it. You should know the speed limit for the road that you're on by observing the road signs. Different speed limits apply if you are towing a trailer.

**541** Mark *one* answer
**You park at night on a road with a 40mph speed limit. You should park**

☐ **A** facing the traffic
☐ **B** with parking lights on
☐ **C** with dipped headlights on
☐ **D** near a street light

You MUST use parking lights when parking at night on a road or lay-by with a speed limit greater than 30mph. You MUST also park in the direction of the traffic flow and not close to a junction.

**542** Mark *one* answer

**You will see these red and white markers when approaching**

- ☐ **A** the end of a motorway
- ☐ **B** a concealed level crossing
- ☐ **C** a concealed speed limit sign
- ☐ **D** the end of a dual carriageway

If there is a bend just before the level crossing you may not be able to see the level crossing barriers or waiting traffic. These signs give you an early warning that you may find these hazards just around the bend.

---

**543** Mark *one* answer    **NI**

**You are travelling on a motorway. You MUST stop when signalled to do so by which of these?**

- ☐ **A** Flashing amber lights above your lane
- ☐ **B** A Highways Agency Traffic Officer
- ☐ **C** Pedestrians on the hard shoulder
- ☐ **D** A driver who has broken down

You will find Highways Agency Traffic Officers on many of Britain's motorways. They work in partnership with the police, helping to keep traffic moving and to make your journey as safe as possible. It is an offence not to comply with the directions given by a Traffic Officer.

**544** Mark *one* answer

**At a busy unmarked crossroads, which of the following has priority?**

- ☐ **A** Vehicles going straight ahead
- ☐ **B** Vehicles turning right
- ☐ **C** None of the vehicles
- ☐ **D** The vehicles that arrived first

If there are no road signs or markings do not assume that you have priority. Remember that other drivers may assume they have the right to go. No type of vehicle has priority but it's courteous to give way to large vehicles. Also look out in particular for cyclists and motorcyclists.

---

**545** Mark *one* answer

**You are going straight ahead at a roundabout. How should you signal?**

- ☐ **A** Signal right on the approach and then left to leave the roundabout
- ☐ **B** Signal left after you leave the roundabout and enter the new road
- ☐ **C** Signal right on the approach to the roundabout and keep the signal on
- ☐ **D** Signal left just after you pass the exit before the one you will take

To go straight ahead at a roundabout you should normally approach in the left-hand lane. You will not normally need to signal, but look out for the road markings. At some roundabouts the left lane on approach is marked as 'left turn only', so make sure you use the correct lane to go ahead. Signal before you leave as other road users need to know your intentions.

## 546 Mark *one* answer

**How should you give an arm signal to turn left?**

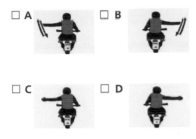

☐ A

☐ B

☐ C

☐ D

Arm signals can be effective during daylight, especially when you're wearing bright clothing. Practise giving arm signals when you're learning. You need to be able to keep full control of your motorcycle with one hand off the handlebars.

## 547 Mark *one* answer

**You are giving an arm signal ready to turn left. Why should you NOT continue with the arm signal while you turn?**

☐ **A** Because you might hit a pedestrian on the corner

☐ **B** Because you will have less steering control

☐ **C** Because you will need to keep the clutch applied

☐ **D** Because other motorists will think that you are stopping on the corner

Consider giving an arm signal if it will help other road users. Situations where you might do this include, approaching a pedestrian crossing, in bright sunshine when your indicators may be difficult to see, when your indicators may be obscured in a traffic queue and where your indicators could cause confusion, such as when pulling up close to a side road. Don't maintain an arm signal when turning. Maintain full control by keeping both hands on the handlebars when you turn.

**548** Mark *one* answer

**This sign is of particular importance to motorcyclists. It means**

- ☐ **A** side winds
- ☐ **B** airport
- ☐ **C** slippery road
- ☐ **D** service area

Strong crosswinds can suddenly blow you off course. Keep your speed down when it's very windy, especially on exposed roads.

**549** Mark *one* answer

**Which one of these signs are you allowed to ride past on a solo motorcycle?**

Most regulatory signs are circular, a red circle tells you what you must NOT do.

**550** Mark *one* answer

**Which of these signals should you give when slowing or stopping your motorcycle?**

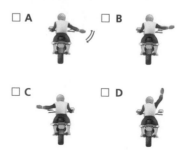

Arm signals can be given to reinforce your flashing indicators, especially if the indicator signal could cause confusion, for example if you intend to pull up close to a side road.

**551** Mark *one* answer

**When drivers flash their headlights at you it means**

- ☐ **A** that there is a radar speed trap ahead
- ☐ **B** that they are giving way to you
- ☐ **C** that they are warning you of their presence
- ☐ **D** that there is something wrong with your motorcycle

A driver flashing their headlights has the same meaning as sounding the horn, it's a warning of their presence.

## 552 Mark *one* answer

**Why should you make sure that you cancel your indicators after turning?**

☐ **A** To avoid flattening the battery
☐ **B** To avoid misleading other road users
☐ **C** To avoid dazzling other road users
☐ **D** To avoid damage to the indicator relay

Always check that you have cancelled your indicators after turning. Failing to cancel your indicators could lead to a serious or even fatal collision. Other road users may pull out in front of you if they think you are going to turn off before you reach them.

## 553 Mark *one* answer

**Your indicators are difficult to see due to bright sunshine. When using them you should**

☐ **A** also give an arm signal
☐ **B** sound your horn
☐ **C** flash your headlight
☐ **D** keep both hands on the handlebars

Arm signals should be used to confirm your intentions when you aren't sure that your indicators can be seen by other road users. Use the signals shown in The Highway Code and return your hand to the handlebars before you turn.

## 554 Mark *one* answer

**You are riding on a motorway. There is a slow-moving vehicle ahead. On the back you see this sign. What should you do?**

☐ **A** Pass on the right
☐ **B** Pass on the left
☐ **C** Leave at the next exit
☐ **D** Drive no further

If this vehicle is in your lane you will have to move to the left. Use your mirrors and signal if necessary. When it's safe move into the lane on your left. You should always look well ahead so that you can spot such hazards early, giving yourself time to react safely.

## 555 Mark *one* answer

**You MUST obey signs giving orders. These signs are mostly in**

☐ **A** green rectangles
☐ **B** red triangles
☐ **C** blue rectangles
☐ **D** red circles

There are three basic types of traffic sign, those that warn, inform or give orders. Generally, triangular signs warn, rectangular ones give information or directions, and circular signs usually give orders. An exception is the eight-sided 'STOP' sign.

## 556 Mark *one* answer
**Traffic signs giving orders are generally which shape?**

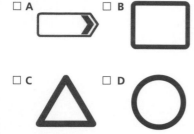

☐ A  ☐ B  ☐ C  ☐ D

Road signs in the shape of a circle give orders. Those with a red circle are mostly prohibitive. The 'STOP' sign is octagonal to give it greater prominence. Signs giving orders MUST always be obeyed.

## 557 Mark *one* answer
**Which type of sign tells you NOT to do something?**

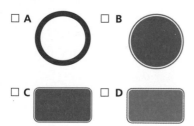

☐ A  ☐ B  ☐ C  ☐ D

Signs in the shape of a circle give orders. A sign with a red circle means that you aren't allowed to do something. Study Know Your Traffic Signs to ensure that you understand what the different traffic signs mean.

## 558 Mark *one* answer
**What does this sign mean?**

☐ **A** Maximum speed limit with traffic calming
☐ **B** Minimum speed limit with traffic calming
☐ **C** '20 cars only' parking zone
☐ **D** Only 20 cars allowed at any one time

If you're in places where there are likely to be pedestrians such as outside schools, near parks, residential areas and shopping areas, you should be extra-cautious and keep your speed down.

Many local authorities have taken measures to slow traffic down by creating traffic-calming measures such as speed humps. They are there for a reason; slow down.

## 559 Mark *one* answer
**Which sign means no motor vehicles are allowed?**

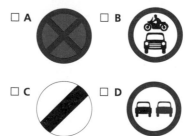

☐ A  ☐ B  ☐ C  ☐ D

You would generally see this sign at the approach to a pedestrian-only zone.

## 560 Mark *one* answer
**Which of these signs means no motor vehicles?**

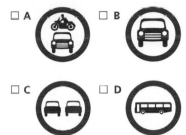

☐ A ☐ B
☐ C ☐ D

If you are driving a motor vehicle or riding a motorcycle you MUST NOT travel past this sign. This area has been designated for use by pedestrians.

## 561 Mark *one* answer
**What does this sign mean?**

☐ **A** New speed limit 20mph
☐ **B** No vehicles over 30 tonnes
☐ **C** Minimum speed limit 30mph
☐ **D** End of 20mph zone

Where you see this sign the 20mph restriction ends. Check all around for possible hazards and only increase your speed if it's safe to do so.

## 562 Mark *one* answer
**What does this sign mean?**

☐ **A** No overtaking
☐ **B** No motor vehicles
☐ **C** Clearway (no stopping)
☐ **D** Cars and motorcycles only

A sign will indicate which types of vehicles are prohibited from certain roads. Make sure that you know which signs apply to the vehicle you're using.

## 563 Mark *one* answer
**What does this sign mean?**

☐ **A** No parking
☐ **B** No road markings
☐ **C** No through road
☐ **D** No entry

'No entry' signs are used in places such as one-way streets to prevent vehicles driving against the traffic. To ignore one would be dangerous, both for yourself and other road users, as well as being against the law.

## 564 Mark *one* answer
**What does this sign mean?**

- ☐ **A** Bend to the right
- ☐ **B** Road on the right closed
- ☐ **C** No traffic from the right
- ☐ **D** No right turn

The 'no right turn' sign may be used to warn road users that there is a 'no entry' prohibition on a road to the right ahead.

## 565 Mark *one* answer
**Which sign means 'no entry'?**

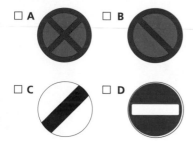

☐ A

☐ B

☐ C

☐ D

Look out for traffic signs. Disobeying or not seeing a sign could be dangerous. It may also be an offence for which you could be prosecuted.

## 566 Mark *one* answer
**What does this sign mean?**

- ☐ **A** Route for trams only
- ☐ **B** Route for buses only
- ☐ **C** Parking for buses only
- ☐ **D** Parking for trams only

Avoid blocking tram routes. Trams are fixed on their route and can't manoeuvre around other vehicles and pedestrians. Modern trams travel quickly and are quiet so you might not hear them approaching.

## 567 Mark *one* answer
**Which type of vehicle does this sign apply to?**

- ☐ **A** Wide vehicles
- ☐ **B** Long vehicles
- ☐ **C** High vehicles
- ☐ **D** Heavy vehicles

The triangular shapes above and below the dimensions indicate a height restriction that applies to the road ahead.

## 568 Mark *one* answer
**Which sign means NO motor vehicles allowed?**

□ A    □ B

□ C    □ D

This sign is used to enable pedestrians to walk free from traffic. It's often found in shopping areas.

## 569 Mark *one* answer
**What does this sign mean?**

□ **A** You have priority
□ **B** No motor vehicles
□ **C** Two-way traffic
□ **D** No overtaking

Road signs that prohibit overtaking are placed in locations where passing the vehicle in front is dangerous. If you see this sign don't attempt to overtake. The sign is there for a reason and you must obey it.

## 570 Mark *one* answer
**What does this sign mean?**

□ **A** Keep in one lane
□ **B** Give way to oncoming traffic
□ **C** Do not overtake
□ **D** Form two lanes

If you're behind a slow-moving vehicle be patient. Wait until the restriction no longer applies and you can overtake safely.

## 571 Mark *one* answer
**Which sign means no overtaking?**

□ A    □ B

□ C    □ D

This sign indicates that overtaking here is not allowed and you could face prosecution if you ignore this prohibition.

## 572 Mark *one* answer
**What does this sign mean?**

☐ **A** Waiting restrictions apply
☐ **B** Waiting permitted
☐ **C** National speed limit applies
☐ **D** Clearway (no stopping)

There will be a plate or additional sign to tell you when the restrictions apply.

## 573 Mark *one* answer
**What does this sign mean?**

☐ **A** End of restricted speed area
☐ **B** End of restricted parking area
☐ **C** End of clearway
☐ **D** End of cycle route

Even though you have left the restricted area, make sure that you park where you won't endanger other road users or cause an obstruction.

## 574 Mark *one* answer
**Which sign means 'no stopping'?**

☐ **A**    ☐ **B**

☐ **C**    ☐ **D**

Stopping where this clearway restriction applies is likely to cause congestion. Allow the traffic to flow by obeying the signs.

## 575 Mark *one* answer
**What does this sign mean?**

☐ **A** Roundabout
☐ **B** Crossroads
☐ **C** No stopping
☐ **D** No entry

This sign is in place to ensure a clear route for traffic. Don't stop except in an emergency.

**576** Mark *one* answer
**You see this sign ahead. It means**

□ **A** national speed limit applies
□ **B** waiting restrictions apply
□ **C** no stopping
□ **D** no entry

Clearways are stretches of road where you aren't allowed to stop unless in an emergency. You'll see this sign. Stopping where these restrictions apply may be dangerous and likely to cause an obstruction. Restrictions might apply for several miles and this may be indicated on the sign.

**577** Mark *one* answer
**What does this sign mean?**

□ **A** Distance to parking place ahead
□ **B** Distance to public telephone ahead
□ **C** Distance to public house ahead
□ **D** Distance to passing place ahead

If you intend to stop and rest, this sign allows you time to reduce speed and pull over safely.

**578** Mark *one* answer
**What does this sign mean?**

□ **A** Vehicles may not park on the verge or footway
□ **B** Vehicles may park on the left-hand side of the road only
□ **C** Vehicles may park fully on the verge or footway
□ **D** Vehicles may park on the right-hand side of the road only

In order to keep roads free from parked cars, there are some areas where you're allowed to park on the verge. Only do this where you see the sign. Parking on verges or footways anywhere else could lead to a fine.

## 579 Mark *one* answer
**What does this traffic sign mean?**

- ☐ **A** No overtaking allowed
- ☐ **B** Give priority to oncoming traffic
- ☐ **C** Two-way traffic
- ☐ **D** One-way traffic only

Priority signs are normally shown where the road is narrow and there isn't enough room for two vehicles to pass. These can be at narrow bridges, road works and where there's a width restriction.

Make sure that you know who has priority, don't force your way through. Show courtesy and consideration to other road users.

## 580 Mark *one* answer
**What is the meaning of this traffic sign?**

- ☐ **A** End of two-way road
- ☐ **B** Give priority to vehicles coming towards you
- ☐ **C** You have priority over vehicles coming towards you
- ☐ **D** Bus lane ahead

Don't force your way through. Show courtesy and consideration to other road users. Although you have priority, make sure oncoming traffic is going to give way before you continue.

## 581 Mark *one* answer
**What does this sign mean?**

- ☐ **A** No overtaking
- ☐ **B** You are entering a one-way street
- ☐ **C** Two-way traffic ahead
- ☐ **D** You have priority over vehicles from the opposite direction

Don't force your way through if oncoming vehicles fail to give way. If necessary, slow down and give way to avoid confrontation or a collision.

## 582 Mark *one* answer
**What shape is a 'STOP' sign at a junction?**

To make it easy to recognise, the 'STOP' sign is the only sign of this shape. You must stop and take effective observation before proceeding.

## 583 Mark *one* answer

**At a junction you see this sign partly covered by snow. What does it mean?**

- ☐ **A** Cross roads
- ☐ **B** Give way
- ☐ **C** Stop
- ☐ **D** Turn right

The 'STOP' sign is the only road sign that is octagonal. This is so that it can be recognised and obeyed even if it is obscured, for example by snow.

## 584 Mark *one* answer

**What does this sign mean?**

- ☐ **A** Service area 30 miles ahead
- ☐ **B** Maximum speed 30mph
- ☐ **C** Minimum speed 30mph
- ☐ **D** Lay-by 30 miles ahead

This sign is shown where slow-moving vehicles would impede the flow of traffic, for example in tunnels. However, if you need to slow down or even stop to avoid an incident or potential collision, you should do so.

## 585 Mark *one* answer

**What does this sign mean?**

- ☐ **A** Give way to oncoming vehicles
- ☐ **B** Approaching traffic passes you on both sides
- ☐ **C** Turn off at the next available junction
- ☐ **D** Pass either side to get to the same destination

These signs are often seen in one-way streets that have more than one lane. When you see this sign, use the route that's the most convenient and doesn't require a late change of direction.

## 586 Mark *one* answer

**What does this sign mean?**

- ☐ **A** Route for trams
- ☐ **B** Give way to trams
- ☐ **C** Route for buses
- ☐ **D** Give way to buses

Take extra care when you encounter trams. Look out for road markings and signs that alert you to them. Modern trams are very quiet and you may not hear them approaching.

## 587 Mark *one* answer
**What does a circular traffic sign with a blue background do?**

- ☐ **A** Give warning of a motorway ahead
- ☐ **B** Give directions to a car park
- ☐ **C** Give motorway information
- ☐ **D** Give an instruction

Signs with blue circles give a positive instruction. These are often found in urban areas and include signs for mini-roundabouts and directional arrows.

## 588 Mark *one* answer
**Where would you see a contraflow bus and cycle lane?**

- ☐ **A** On a dual carriageway
- ☐ **B** On a roundabout
- ☐ **C** On an urban motorway
- ☐ **D** On a one-way street

In a contraflow lane the traffic permitted to use it travels in the opposite direction to traffic in the other lanes on the road.

## 589 Mark *one* answer
**What does this sign mean?**

- ☐ **A** Bus station on the right
- ☐ **B** Contraflow bus lane
- ☐ **C** With-flow bus lane
- ☐ **D** Give way to buses

There will also be markings on the road surface to indicate the bus lane. You must not use this lane for parking or overtaking.

## 590 Mark *one* answer
**What does a sign with a brown background show?**

- ☐ **A** Tourist directions
- ☐ **B** Primary roads
- ☐ **C** Motorway routes
- ☐ **D** Minor routes

Signs with a brown background give directions to places of interest. They will often be seen on a motorway directing you along the easiest route to the attraction.

## 591 Mark *one* answer
**This sign means**

- ☐ **A** tourist attraction
- ☐ **B** beware of trains
- ☐ **C** level crossing
- ☐ **D** beware of trams

These signs indicate places of interest and are designed to guide you by the easiest route. They are particularly useful if you are unfamiliar with the area.

---

## 592 Mark *one* answer
**What are triangular signs for?**

- ☐ **A** To give warnings
- ☐ **B** To give information
- ☐ **C** To give orders
- ☐ **D** To give directions

This type of sign will warn you of hazards ahead.
Make sure you look at each sign that you pass on the road, so that you do not miss any vital instructions or information.

## 593 Mark *one* answer
**What does this sign mean?**

- ☐ **A** Turn left ahead
- ☐ **B** T-junction
- ☐ **C** No through road
- ☐ **D** Give way

This type of sign will warn you of hazards ahead. Make sure you look at each sign and road markings that you pass, so that you do not miss any vital instructions or information. This particular sign shows there is a T-junction with priority over vehicles from the right.

---

## 594 Mark *one* answer
**What does this sign mean?**

- ☐ **A** Multi-exit roundabout
- ☐ **B** Risk of ice
- ☐ **C** Six roads converge
- ☐ **D** Place of historical interest

It will take up to ten times longer to stop when it's icy. Where there is a risk of icy conditions you need to be aware of this and take extra care. If you think the road may be icy, don't brake or steer harshly as your tyres could lose their grip on the road.

**595** Mark *one* answer

**What does this sign mean?**

- ☐ **A** Crossroads
- ☐ **B** Level crossing with gate
- ☐ **C** Level crossing without gate
- ☐ **D** Ahead only

The priority through the junction is shown by the broader line. You need to be aware of the hazard posed by traffic crossing or pulling out onto a major road.

**596** Mark *one* answer

**What does this sign mean?**

- ☐ **A** Ring road
- ☐ **B** Mini-roundabout
- ☐ **C** No vehicles
- ☐ **D** Roundabout

As you approach a roundabout look well ahead and check all signs. Decide which exit you wish to take and move into the correct position as you approach the roundabout, signalling as required.

**597** Mark *four* answers

**Which FOUR of these would be indicated by a triangular road sign?**

- ☐ **A** Road narrows
- ☐ **B** Ahead only
- ☐ **C** Low bridge
- ☐ **D** Minimum speed
- ☐ **E** Children crossing
- ☐ **F** T-junction

Warning signs are there to make you aware of potential hazards on the road ahead. Act on the signs so you are prepared and can take whatever action is necessary.

**598** Mark *one* answer

**What does this sign mean?**

- ☐ **A** Cyclists must dismount
- ☐ **B** Cycles are not allowed
- ☐ **C** Cycle route ahead
- ☐ **D** Cycle in single file

Where there's a cycle route ahead, a sign will show a bicycle in a red warning triangle. Watch out for children on bicycles and cyclists rejoining the main road.

## 599 Mark *one* answer

**Which sign means that pedestrians may be walking along the road?**

☐ **A**
☐ **B**

☐ **C**
☐ **D**

When you pass pedestrians in the road, leave plenty of room. You might have to use the right-hand side of the road, so look well ahead, as well as in your mirrors, before pulling out. Take great care if there is a bend in the road obscuring your view ahead.

## 600 Mark *one* answer

**Which of these signs means there is a double bend ahead?**

☐ **A**
☐ **B**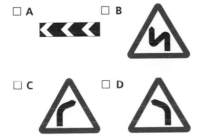

☐ **C**
☐ **D**

Triangular signs give you a warning of hazards ahead. They are there to give you time to prepare for the hazard, for example by adjusting your speed.

## 601 Mark *one* answer

**What does this sign mean?**

☐ **A** Wait at the barriers
☐ **B** Wait at the crossroads
☐ **C** Give way to trams
☐ **D** Give way to farm vehicles

Obey the 'give way' signs. Trams are unable to steer around you if you misjudge when it is safe to enter the junction.

## 602 Mark *one* answer

**What does this sign mean?**

☐ **A** Humpback bridge
☐ **B** Humps in the road
☐ **C** Entrance to tunnel
☐ **D** Soft verges

These have been put in place to slow the traffic down. They're usually found in residential areas. Slow down to an appropriate speed.

## 603 Mark *one* answer

**Which of these signs means the end of a dual carriageway?**

☐ A 　　☐ B

☐ C 　　☐ D

If you're overtaking make sure you move back safely into the left-hand lane before you reach the end of the dual carriageway.

## 604 Mark *one* answer

**What does this sign mean?**

☐ **A** End of dual carriageway
☐ **B** Tall bridge
☐ **C** Road narrows
☐ **D** End of narrow bridge

Don't leave moving into the left-hand lane until the last moment. Plan ahead and don't rely on other traffic letting you in.

## 605 Mark *one* answer

**What does this sign mean?**

☐ **A** Crosswinds
☐ **B** Road noise
☐ **C** Airport
☐ **D** Adverse camber

A warning sign with a picture of a windsock will indicate there may be strong crosswinds. This sign is often found on exposed roads.

## 606 Mark *one* answer

**What does this traffic sign mean?**

☐ **A** Slippery road ahead
☐ **B** Tyres liable to punctures ahead
☐ **C** Danger ahead
☐ **D** Service area ahead

This sign is there to alert you to the likelihood of danger ahead. It may be accompanied by a plate indicating the type of hazard. Be ready to reduce your speed and take avoiding action.

## 607 Mark *one* answer

**You are about to overtake when you see this sign. You should**

Hidden dip

- ☐ **A** overtake the other driver as quickly as possible
- ☐ **B** move to the right to get a better view
- ☐ **C** switch your headlights on before overtaking
- ☐ **D** hold back until you can see clearly ahead

You won't be able to see any hazards that might be hidden in the dip. As well as oncoming traffic the dip may conceal
- cyclists
- horse riders
- parked vehicles
- pedestrians
in the road.

## 608 Mark *one* answer

**What does this sign mean?**

- ☐ **A** Level crossing with gate or barrier
- ☐ **B** Gated road ahead
- ☐ **C** Level crossing without gate or barrier
- ☐ **D** Cattle grid ahead

Some crossings have gates but no attendant or signals. You should stop, look both ways, listen and make sure that there is no train approaching. If there is a telephone, contact the signal operator to make sure that it's safe to cross.

## 609 Mark *one* answer

**What does this sign mean?**

- ☐ **A** No trams ahead
- ☐ **B** Oncoming trams
- ☐ **C** Trams crossing ahead
- ☐ **D** Trams only

This sign warns you to beware of trams. If you don't usually drive in a town where there are trams, remember to look out for them at junctions and look for tram rails, signs and signals.

## 610 Mark *one* answer

**What does this sign mean?**

- ☐ **A** Adverse camber
- ☐ **B** Steep hill downwards
- ☐ **C** Uneven road
- ☐ **D** Steep hill upwards

This sign will give you an early warning that the road ahead will slope downhill. Prepare to alter your speed and gear. Looking at the sign from left to right will show you whether the road slopes uphill or downhill.

## 611 Mark *one* answer
**What does this sign mean?**

- ☐ **A** Uneven road surface
- ☐ **B** Bridge over the road
- ☐ **C** Road ahead ends
- ☐ **D** Water across the road

This sign is found where a shallow stream crosses the road. Heavy rainfall could increase the flow of water. If the water looks too deep or the stream has spread over a large distance, stop and find another route.

## 612 Mark *one* answer
**What does this sign mean?**

- ☐ **A** Turn left for parking area
- ☐ **B** No through road on the left
- ☐ **C** No entry for traffic turning left
- ☐ **D** Turn left for ferry terminal

If you intend to take a left turn, this sign shows you that you can't get through to another route using the left-turn junction ahead.

## 613 Mark *one* answer
**What does this sign mean?**

- ☐ **A** T-junction
- ☐ **B** No through road
- ☐ **C** Telephone box ahead
- ☐ **D** Toilet ahead

You will not be able to find a through route to another road. Use this road only for access.

## 614 Mark *one* answer
**Which sign means 'no through road'?**

☐ A   ☐ B

☐ C   ☐ D

This sign is found at the entrance to a road that can only be used for access.

## 615 Mark *one* answer
**Which is the sign for a ring road?**

☐ A  ☐ B

☐ C ☐ D

Ring roads are designed to relieve congestion in towns and city centres.

---

## 616 Mark *one* answer
**What does this sign mean?**

☐ **A** The right-hand lane ahead is narrow
☐ **B** Right-hand lane for buses only
☐ **C** Right-hand lane for turning right
☐ **D** The right-hand lane is closed

Yellow and black temporary signs may be used to inform you of roadworks or lane restrictions. Look well ahead. If you have to change lanes, do so in good time.

## 617 Mark *one* answer
**What does this sign mean?**

☐ **A** Change to the left lane
☐ **B** Leave at the next exit
☐ **C** Contraflow system
☐ **D** One-way street

If you use the right-hand lane in a contraflow system, you'll be travelling with no permanent barrier between you and the oncoming traffic. Observe speed limits and keep a good distance from the vehicle ahead.

---

## 618 Mark *one* answer
**What does this sign mean?**

☐ **A** Leave motorway at next exit
☐ **B** Lane for heavy and slow vehicles
☐ **C** All lorries use the hard shoulder
☐ **D** Rest area for lorries

Where there's a long, steep, uphill gradient on a motorway, a crawler lane may be provided. This helps the traffic to flow by diverting the slower heavy vehicles into a dedicated lane on the left.

## 619 Mark *one* answer
**A red traffic light means**

- ☐ **A** you should stop unless turning left
- ☐ **B** stop, if you are able to brake safely
- ☐ **C** you must stop and wait behind the stop line
- ☐ **D** proceed with caution

Make sure you learn and understand the sequence of traffic lights. Whatever light appears you will then know what light is going to appear next and be able to take the appropriate action. For example if amber is showing on its own you'll know that red will appear next, giving you ample time to slow and stop safely.

## 620 Mark *one* answer
**At traffic lights, amber on its own means**

- ☐ **A** prepare to go
- ☐ **B** go if the way is clear
- ☐ **C** go if no pedestrians are crossing
- ☐ **D** stop at the stop line

When amber is showing on its own red will appear next. The amber light means STOP, unless you have already crossed the stop line or you are so close to it that pulling up might cause a collision.

## 621 Mark *one* answer
**You are at a junction controlled by traffic lights. When should you NOT proceed at green?**

- ☐ **A** When pedestrians are waiting to cross
- ☐ **B** When your exit from the junction is blocked
- ☐ **C** When you think the lights may be about to change
- ☐ **D** When you intend to turn right

As you approach the lights look into the road you wish to take. Only proceed if your exit road is clear. If the road is blocked hold back, even if you have to wait for the next green signal.

## 622 Mark *one* answer
**You are in the left-hand lane at traffic lights. You are waiting to turn left. At which of these traffic lights must you NOT move on?**

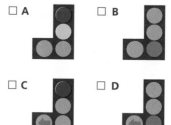

At some junctions there may be a separate signal for different lanes. These are called 'filter' lights. They're designed to help traffic flow at major junctions. Make sure that you're in the correct lane and proceed if the way is clear and the green light shows for your lane.

## 623 Mark *one* answer

**What does this sign mean?**

- ☐ **A** Traffic lights out of order
- ☐ **B** Amber signal out of order
- ☐ **C** Temporary traffic lights ahead
- ☐ **D** New traffic lights ahead

Where traffic lights are out of order you might see this sign. Proceed with caution as nobody has priority at the junction.

## 624 Mark *one* answer

**When traffic lights are out of order, who has priority?**

- ☐ **A** Traffic going straight on
- ☐ **B** Traffic turning right
- ☐ **C** Nobody
- ☐ **D** Traffic turning left

When traffic lights are out of order you should treat the junction as an unmarked crossroads. Be cautious as you may need to give way or stop. Keep a look out for traffic attempting to cross the junction at speed.

## 625 Mark *three* answers

**These flashing red lights mean STOP. In which THREE of the following places could you find them?**

- ☐ **A** Pelican crossings
- ☐ **B** Lifting bridges
- ☐ **C** Zebra crossings
- ☐ **D** Level crossings
- ☐ **E** Motorway exits
- ☐ **F** Fire stations

You must always stop when the red lights are flashing, whether or not the way seems to be clear.

## 626 Mark *one* answer

**What do these zigzag lines at pedestrian crossings mean?**

- ☐ **A** No parking at any time
- ☐ **B** Parking allowed only for a short time
- ☐ **C** Slow down to 20mph
- ☐ **D** Sounding horns is not allowed

The approach to, and exit from, a pedestrian crossing is marked with zigzag lines. You must not park on them or overtake the leading vehicle when approaching the crossing. Parking here would block the view for pedestrians and the approaching traffic.

## 627 Mark *one* answer
**When may you cross a double solid white line in the middle of the road?**

- ☐ **A** To pass traffic that is queuing back at a junction
- ☐ **B** To pass a car signalling to turn left ahead
- ☐ **C** To pass a road maintenance vehicle travelling at 10mph or less
- ☐ **D** To pass a vehicle that is towing a trailer

You may cross the solid white line to pass a stationary vehicle, pedal cycle, horse or road maintenance vehicle if they are travelling at 10mph or less. You may also cross the solid line to enter into a side road or access a property.

## 628 Mark *one* answer
**What does this road marking mean?**

- ☐ **A** Do not cross the line
- ☐ **B** No stopping allowed
- ☐ **C** You are approaching a hazard
- ☐ **D** No overtaking allowed

Road markings will warn you of a hazard ahead. A single, broken line along the centre of the road, with long markings and short gaps, is a hazard warning line. Don't cross it unless you can see that the road is clear well ahead.

## 629 Mark *one* answer
**Where would you see this road marking?**

- ☐ **A** At traffic lights
- ☐ **B** On road humps
- ☐ **C** Near a level crossing
- ☐ **D** At a box junction

Due to the dark colour of the road, changes in level aren't easily seen. White triangles painted on the road surface give you an indication of where there are road humps.

## 630 Mark *one* answer
**Which is a hazard warning line?**

☐ A 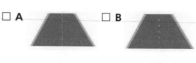 ☐ B

☐ C  ☐ D

You need to know the difference between the normal centre line and a hazard warning line. If there is a hazard ahead, the markings are longer and the gaps shorter. This gives you advanced warning of an unspecified hazard ahead.

## 631 Mark *one* answer

**At this junction there is a stop sign with a solid white line on the road surface. Why is there a stop sign here?**

- ☐ **A** Speed on the major road is de-restricted
- ☐ **B** It is a busy junction
- ☐ **C** Visibility along the major road is restricted
- ☐ **D** There are hazard warning lines in the centre of the road

If your view is restricted at a road junction you must stop. There may also be a 'stop' sign. Don't emerge until you're sure there's no traffic approaching.
IF YOU DON'T KNOW, DON'T GO.

## 632 Mark *one* answer

**You see this line across the road at the entrance to a roundabout. What does it mean?**

- ☐ **A** Give way to traffic from the right
- ☐ **B** Traffic from the left has right of way
- ☐ **C** You have right of way
- ☐ **D** Stop at the line

Slow down as you approach the roundabout and check for traffic from the right. If you need to stop and give way, stay behind the broken line until it is safe to emerge onto the roundabout.

## 633 Mark *one* answer

**How will a police officer in a patrol vehicle normally get you to stop?**

- ☐ **A** Flash the headlights, indicate left and point to the left
- ☐ **B** Wait until you stop, then approach you
- ☐ **C** Use the siren, overtake, cut in front and stop
- ☐ **D** Pull alongside you, use the siren and wave you to stop

You must obey signals given by the police. If a police officer in a patrol vehicle wants you to pull over they will indicate this without causing danger to you or other traffic.

## 634 Mark *one* answer

**You approach a junction. The traffic lights are not working. A police officer gives this signal. You should**

- ☐ **A** turn left only
- ☐ **B** turn right only
- ☐ **C** stop level with the officer's arm
- ☐ **D** stop at the stop line

If a police officer or traffic warden is directing traffic you must obey them. They will use the arm signals shown in The Highway Code. Learn what these mean and act accordingly.

## 635 Mark *one* answer

**The driver of the car in front is giving this arm signal. What does it mean?**

- ☐ **A** The driver is slowing down
- ☐ **B** The driver intends to turn right
- ☐ **C** The driver wishes to overtake
- ☐ **D** The driver intends to turn left

There might be an occasion where another driver uses an arm signal. This may be because the vehicle's indicators are obscured by other traffic. In order for such signals to be effective all drivers should know the meaning of them. Be aware that the 'left turn' signal might look similar to the 'slowing down' signal.

## 636 Mark *one* answer

**Where would you see these road markings?**

- ☐ **A** At a level crossing
- ☐ **B** On a motorway slip road
- ☐ **C** At a pedestrian crossing
- ☐ **D** On a single-track road

When driving on a motorway or slip road, you must not enter into an area marked with chevrons and bordered by a solid white line for any reason, except in an emergency.

## 637 Mark *one* answer

**What does this motorway sign mean?**

- ☐ **A** Change to the lane on your left
- ☐ **B** Leave the motorway at the next exit
- ☐ **C** Change to the opposite carriageway
- ☐ **D** Pull up on the hard shoulder

On the motorway, signs sometimes show temporary warnings due to traffic or weather conditions. They may be used to indicate
- lane closures
- temporary speed limits
- weather warnings.

## 638 Mark *one* answer

**What does this motorway sign mean?**

- ☐ **A** Temporary minimum speed 50mph
- ☐ **B** No services for 50 miles
- ☐ **C** Obstruction 50 metres (164 feet) ahead
- ☐ **D** Temporary maximum speed 50mph

Look out for signs above your lane or on the central reservation. These will give you important information or warnings about the road ahead. Due to the high speed of motorway traffic these signs may light up some distance from any hazard. Don't ignore the signs just because the road looks clear to you.

## 639 Mark *one* answer
**What does this sign mean?**

- ☐ **A** Through traffic to use left lane
- ☐ **B** Right-hand lane T-junction only
- ☐ **C** Right-hand lane closed ahead
- ☐ **D** 11 tonne weight limit

You should move into the lanes as directed by the sign. Here the right-hand lane is closed and the left-hand and centre lanes are available. Merging in turn is recommended when it's safe and traffic is going slowly, for example at road works or a road traffic incident. When vehicles are travelling at speed this is not advisable and you should move into the appropriate lane in good time.

## 640 Mark *one* answer
**On a motorway this sign means**

- ☐ **A** move over onto the hard shoulder
- ☐ **B** overtaking on the left only
- ☐ **C** leave the motorway at the next exit
- ☐ **D** move to the lane on your left

It is important to know and obey temporary signs on the motorway: they are there for a reason. You may not be able to see the hazard straight away, as the signs give warnings well in advance, due to the speed of traffic on the motorway.

## 641 Mark *one* answer
**What does '25' mean on this motorway sign?**

- ☐ **A** The distance to the nearest town
- ☐ **B** The route number of the road
- ☐ **C** The number of the next junction
- ☐ **D** The speed limit on the slip road

Before you set out on your journey use a road map to plan your route. When you see advance warning of your junction, make sure you get into the correct lane in plenty of time. Last-minute harsh braking and cutting across lanes at speed is extremely hazardous.

## 642 Mark *one* answer
**The right-hand lane of a three-lane motorway is**

- ☐ **A** for lorries only
- ☐ **B** an overtaking lane
- ☐ **C** the right-turn lane
- ☐ **D** an acceleration lane

You should stay in the left-hand lane of a motorway unless overtaking. The right-hand lane of a motorway is an overtaking lane and not a 'fast lane'.

After overtaking, move back to the left when it is safe to do so.

## 643 Mark *one* answer
**Where can you find reflective amber studs on a motorway?**

- ☐ **A** Separating the slip road from the motorway
- ☐ **B** On the left-hand edge of the road
- ☐ **C** On the right-hand edge of the road
- ☐ **D** Separating the lanes

At night or in poor visibility reflective studs on the road help you to judge your position on the carriageway.

## 644 Mark *one* answer
**Where on a motorway would you find green reflective studs?**

- ☐ **A** Separating driving lanes
- ☐ **B** Between the hard shoulder and the carriageway
- ☐ **C** At slip road entrances and exits
- ☐ **D** Between the carriageway and the central reservation

Knowing the colours of the reflective studs on the road will help you judge your position, especially at night, in foggy conditions or when visibility is poor.

## 645 Mark *one* answer
**You are travelling along a motorway. You see this sign. You should**

- ☐ **A** leave the motorway at the next exit
- ☐ **B** turn left immediately
- ☐ **C** change lane
- ☐ **D** move onto the hard shoulder

You'll see this sign if the motorway is closed ahead. Pull into the nearside lane as soon as it is safe to do so. Don't leave it to the last moment.

## 646 Mark *one* answer
**What does this sign mean?**

- ☐ **A** No motor vehicles
- ☐ **B** End of motorway
- ☐ **C** No through road
- ☐ **D** End of bus lane

When you leave the motorway make sure that you check your speedometer. You may be going faster than you realise. Slow down and look out for speed limit signs.

## 647 Mark *one* answer

**Which of these signs means that the national speed limit applies?**

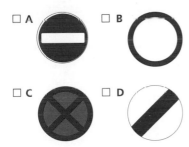

☐ A

☐ B

☐ C

☐ D

You should know the speed limit for the road on which you are travelling, and the vehicle that you are driving. The different speed limits are shown in The Highway Code.

## 648 Mark *one* answer

**What is the maximum speed on a single carriageway road?**

☐ **A** 50mph
☐ **B** 60mph
☐ **C** 40mph
☐ **D** 70mph

If you're travelling on a dual carriageway that becomes a single carriageway road, reduce your speed gradually so that you aren't exceeding the limit as you enter. There might not be a sign to remind you of the limit, so make sure you know what the speed limits are for different types of roads and vehicles.

## 649 Mark *one* answer

**What does this sign mean?**

☐ **A** End of motorway
☐ **B** End of restriction
☐ **C** Lane ends ahead
☐ **D** Free recovery ends

Temporary restrictions on motorways are shown on signs which have flashing amber lights. At the end of the restriction you will see this sign without any flashing lights.

## 650 Mark *one* answer

**This sign is advising you to**

☐ **A** follow the route diversion
☐ **B** follow the signs to the picnic area
☐ **C** give way to pedestrians
☐ **D** give way to cyclists

When a diversion route has been put in place, drivers are advised to follow a symbol which may be a triangle, square, circle or diamond shape on a yellow background.

## 651 Mark *one* answer

**Why would this temporary speed limit sign be shown?**

- ☐ **A** To warn of the end of the motorway
- ☐ **B** To warn you of a low bridge
- ☐ **C** To warn you of a junction ahead
- ☐ **D** To warn of road works ahead

In the interests of road safety, temporary speed limits are imposed at all major road works. Signs like this, giving advanced warning of the speed limit, are normally placed about three quarters of a mile ahead of where the speed limit comes into force.

## 652 Mark *one* answer

**This traffic sign means there is**

- ☐ **A** a compulsory maximum speed limit
- ☐ **B** an advisory maximum speed limit
- ☐ **C** a compulsory minimum speed limit
- ☐ **D** an advised separation distance

The sign gives you an early warning of a speed restriction. If you are travelling at a higher speed, slow down in good time. You could come across queuing traffic due to roadworks or a temporary obstruction.

## 653 Mark *one* answer

**You see this sign at a crossroads. You should**

- ☐ **A** maintain the same speed
- ☐ **B** carry on with great care
- ☐ **C** find another route
- ☐ **D** telephone the police

When traffic lights are out of order treat the junction as an unmarked crossroad. Be very careful as no one has priority and be prepared to stop.

## 654 Mark *one* answer

**You are signalling to turn right in busy traffic. How would you confirm your intention safely?**

- ☐ **A** Sound the horn
- ☐ **B** Give an arm signal
- ☐ **C** Flash your headlights
- ☐ **D** Position over the centre line

In some situations you may feel your indicators cannot be seen by other road users. If you think you need to make your intention more clearly seen, give the arm signal shown in The Highway Code.

## 655 Mark *one* answer
**What does this sign mean?**

- ☐ **A** Motorcycles only
- ☐ **B** No cars
- ☐ **C** Cars only
- ☐ **D** No motorcycles

You must comply with all traffic signs and be especially aware of those signs which apply specifically to the type of vehicle you are using.

## 656 Mark *one* answer
**You are on a motorway. You see this sign on a lorry that has stopped in the right-hand lane. You should**

- ☐ **A** move into the right-hand lane
- ☐ **B** stop behind the flashing lights
- ☐ **C** pass the lorry on the left
- ☐ **D** leave the motorway at the next exit

Sometimes work is carried out on the motorway without closing the lanes. When this happens, signs are mounted on the back of lorries to warn other road users of roadworks ahead.

## 657 Mark *one* answer
**You are on a motorway. Red flashing lights appear above your lane only. What should you do?**

- ☐ **A** Continue in that lane and look for further information
- ☐ **B** Move into another lane in good time
- ☐ **C** Pull onto the hard shoulder
- ☐ **D** Stop and wait for an instruction to proceed

Flashing red lights above your lane show that your lane is closed. You should move into another lane as soon as you can do so safely.

## 658 Mark *one* answer
**A red traffic light means**

- ☐ **A** you must stop behind the white stop line
- ☐ **B** you may go straight on if there is no other traffic
- ☐ **C** you may turn left if it is safe to do so
- ☐ **D** you must slow down and prepare to stop if traffic has started to cross

The white line is generally positioned so that pedestrians have room to cross in front of waiting traffic. Don't move off while pedestrians are crossing, even if the lights change to green.

**659** Mark *one* answer
**The driver of this car is giving an arm signal. What are they about to do?**

- ☐ **A** Turn to the right
- ☐ **B** Turn to the left
- ☐ **C** Go straight ahead
- ☐ **D** Let pedestrians cross

In some situations drivers may need to give arm signals, in addition to indicators, to make their intentions clear. For arm signals to be effective, all road users should know their meaning.

**660** Mark *one* answer
**When may you sound the horn?**

- ☐ **A** To give you right of way
- ☐ **B** To attract a friend's attention
- ☐ **C** To warn others of your presence
- ☐ **D** To make slower drivers move over

Never sound the horn aggressively. You MUST NOT sound it when driving in a built-up area between 11.30pm and 7am or when you are stationary, an exception to this is when another road user poses a danger. Do not scare animals by sounding your horn.

**661** Mark *one* answer
**You must not use your horn when you are stationary**

- ☐ **A** unless a moving vehicle may cause you danger
- ☐ **B** at any time whatsoever
- ☐ **C** unless it is used only briefly
- ☐ **D** except for signalling that you have just arrived

When stationary only sound your horn if you think there is a risk of danger from another road user. Don't use it just to attract someone's attention. This causes unnecessary noise and could be misleading.

**662** Mark *one* answer
**What does this sign mean?**

- ☐ **A** You can park on the days and times shown
- ☐ **B** No parking on the days and times shown
- ☐ **C** No parking at all from Monday to Friday
- ☐ **D** End of the urban clearway restrictions

Urban clearways are provided to keep traffic flowing at busy times. You may stop only briefly to set down or pick up passengers. Times of operation will vary from place to place so always check the signs.

## 663 Mark *one* answer
**What does this sign mean?**

- ☐ **A** Quayside or river bank
- ☐ **B** Steep hill downwards
- ☐ **C** Uneven road surface
- ☐ **D** Road liable to flooding

You should be careful in these locations as the road surface is likely to be wet and slippery. There may be a steep drop to the water, and there may not be a barrier along the edge of the road.

## 664 Mark *one* answer
**Which sign means you have priority over oncoming vehicles?**

☐ A  ☐ B

☐ C ☐ D

Even though you have priority, be prepared to give way if other drivers don't. This will help to avoid congestion, confrontation or even a collision.

## 665 Mark *one* answer
**A white line like this along the centre of the road is a**

- ☐ **A** bus lane marking
- ☐ **B** hazard warning
- ☐ **C** give way marking
- ☐ **D** lane marking

The centre of the road is usually marked by a broken white line, with lines that are shorter than the gaps. When the lines become longer than the gaps this is a hazard warning line. Look well ahead for these, especially when you are planning to overtake or turn off.

## 666 Mark *one* answer

**What is the reason for the yellow criss-cross lines painted on the road here?**

- ☐ **A** To mark out an area for trams only
- ☐ **B** To prevent queuing traffic from blocking the junction on the left
- ☐ **C** To mark the entrance lane to a car park
- ☐ **D** To warn you of the tram lines crossing the road

Yellow 'box junctions' like this are often used where it's busy. Their purpose is to keep the junction clear for crossing traffic. Don't enter the painted area unless your exit is clear. The exception to this is when you are turning right and are only prevented from doing so by oncoming traffic or by other vehicles waiting to turn right.

## 667 Mark *one* answer

**What is the reason for the area marked in red and white along the centre of this road?**

- ☐ **A** It is to separate traffic flowing in opposite directions
- ☐ **B** It marks an area to be used by overtaking motorcyclists
- ☐ **C** It is a temporary marking to warn of the roadworks
- ☐ **D** It is separating the two sides of the dual carriageway

Areas of 'hatched markings' such as these are to separate traffic streams which could be a danger to each other. They are often seen on bends or where the road becomes narrow. If the area is bordered by a solid white line, you must not enter it except in an emergency.

## 668 Mark *one* answer

**Other drivers may sometimes flash their headlights at you. In which situation are they allowed to do this?**

- ☐ **A** To warn of a radar speed trap ahead
- ☐ **B** To show that they are giving way to you
- ☐ **C** To warn you of their presence
- ☐ **D** To let you know there is a fault with your vehicle

If other drivers flash their headlights this isn't a signal to show priority. The flashing of headlights has the same meaning as sounding the horn, it's a warning of their presence.

## 669 Mark *one* answer
**In some narrow residential streets you may find a speed limit of**

- ☐ **A** 20mph
- ☐ **B** 25mph
- ☐ **C** 35mph
- ☐ **D** 40mph

In some built-up areas, you may find the speed limit reduced to 20mph. Driving at a slower speed will help give you the time and space to see and deal safely with hazards such as pedestrians and parked cars.

## 670 Mark *one* answer
**At a junction you see this signal. It means**

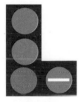

- ☐ **A** cars must stop
- ☐ **B** trams must stop
- ☐ **C** both trams and cars must stop
- ☐ **D** both trams and cars can continue

The white light shows that trams must stop, but the green light shows that other vehicles may go if the way is clear. You may not live in an area where there are trams but you should still learn the signs. You never know when you may go to a town with trams.

## 671 Mark *one* answer
**Where would you find these road markings?**

- ☐ **A** At a railway crossing
- ☐ **B** At a junction
- ☐ **C** On a motorway
- ☐ **D** On a pedestrian crossing

These markings show the direction in which the traffic should go at a mini-roundabout.

## 672 Mark *one* answer
**There is a police car following you. The police officer flashes the headlights and points to the left. What should you do?**

- ☐ **A** Turn left at the next junction
- ☐ **B** Pull up on the left
- ☐ **C** Stop immediately
- ☐ **D** Move over to the left

You must pull up on the left as soon as it's safe to do so and switch off your engine.

## 673 Mark *one* answer

**You see this amber traffic light ahead. Which light or lights, will come on next?**

☐ **A** Red alone
☐ **B** Red and amber together
☐ **C** Green and amber together
☐ **D** Green alone

At junctions controlled by traffic lights you must stop behind the white line until the lights change to green. Red and amber lights showing together also mean stop.

You may proceed when the light is green unless your exit road is blocked or pedestrians are crossing in front of you.

If you're approaching traffic lights that are visible from a distance and the light has been green for some time they are likely to change. Be ready to slow down and stop.

## 674 Mark *one* answer

**This broken white line painted in the centre of the road means**

☐ **A** oncoming vehicles have priority over you
☐ **B** you should give priority to oncoming vehicles
☐ **C** there is a hazard ahead of you
☐ **D** the area is a national speed limit zone

A long white line with short gaps means that you are approaching a hazard. If you do need to cross it, make sure that the road is clear well ahead.

## 675 Mark *one* answer

**You see this signal overhead on the motorway. What does it mean?**

☐ **A** Leave the motorway at the next exit
☐ **B** All vehicles use the hard shoulder
☐ **C** Sharp bend to the left ahead
☐ **D** Stop, all lanes ahead closed

You will see this sign if there has been an incident ahead and the motorway is closed. You MUST obey the sign. Make sure that you prepare to leave as soon as you see the warning sign.

Don't pull over at the last moment or cut across other traffic.

**676** Mark *one* answer

**What is the purpose of these yellow criss-cross lines on the road?**

- ☐ **A** To make you more aware of the traffic lights
- ☐ **B** To guide you into position as you turn
- ☐ **C** To prevent the junction becoming blocked
- ☐ **D** To show you where to stop when the lights change

You MUST NOT enter a box junction until your exit road or lane is clear. The exception to this is if you want to turn right and are only prevented from doing so by oncoming traffic or by other vehicles waiting to turn right.

**677** Mark *one* answer

**What MUST you do when you see this sign?**

- ☐ **A** Stop, only if traffic is approaching
- ☐ **B** Stop, even if the road is clear
- ☐ **C** Stop, only if children are waiting to cross
- ☐ **D** Stop, only if a red light is showing

STOP signs are situated at junctions where visibility is restricted or there is heavy traffic. They MUST be obeyed. You MUST stop.

Take good all-round observation before moving off.

**678** Mark *one* answer

**Which shape is used for a 'give way' sign?**

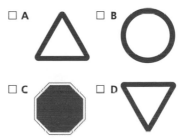

☐ A ☐ B
☐ C ☐ D

Other warning signs are the same shape and colour, but the 'give way' sign triangle points downwards. When you see this sign you MUST give way to traffic on the road which you are about to enter.

**679** Mark *one* answer
**What does this sign mean?**

☐ **A** Buses turning
☐ **B** Ring road
☐ **C** Mini-roundabout
☐ **D** Keep right

When you see this sign, look out for any direction signs and judge whether you need to signal your intentions. Do this in good time so that other road users approaching the roundabout know what you're planning to do.

**680** Mark *one* answer
**What does this sign mean?**

☐ **A** Two-way traffic straight ahead
☐ **B** Two-way traffic crosses a one-way road
☐ **C** Two-way traffic over a bridge
☐ **D** Two-way traffic crosses a two-way road

Be prepared for traffic approaching from junctions on either side of you. Try to avoid unnecessary changing of lanes just before the junction.

**681** Mark *one* answer
**What does this sign mean?**

☐ **A** Two-way traffic ahead across a one-way road
☐ **B** Traffic approaching you has priority
☐ **C** Two-way traffic straight ahead
☐ **D** Motorway contraflow system ahead

This sign may be at the end of a dual carriageway or a one-way street. It is there to warn you of oncoming traffic.

**682** Mark *one* answer
**What does this sign mean?**

☐ **A** Humpback bridge
☐ **B** Traffic-calming hump
☐ **C** Low bridge
☐ **D** Uneven road

You will need to slow down. At humpback bridges your view ahead will be restricted and the road will often be narrow on the bridge. If the bridge is very steep or your view is restricted sound your horn to warn others of your approach. Going too fast over the bridge is highly dangerous to other road users and could even cause your wheels to leave the road, with a resulting loss of control.

**683** Mark *one* answer

**Which of the following signs informs you that you are coming to a 'no through road'?**

☐ **A**
☐ **B**

☐ **C**
☐ **D**

This sign is found at the entrance to a road that can only be used for access.

---

**684** Mark *one* answer

**What does this sign mean?**

☐ **A** Direction to park-and-ride car park
☐ **B** No parking for buses or coaches
☐ **C** Directions to bus and coach park
☐ **D** Parking area for cars and coaches

To ease the congestion in town centres, some cities and towns provide park-and-ride schemes. These allow you to park in a designated area and ride by bus into the centre.

Park-and-ride schemes are usually cheaper and easier than car parking in the town centre.

**685** Mark *one* answer

**You are approaching traffic lights. Red and amber are showing. This means**

☐ **A** pass the lights if the road is clear
☐ **B** there is a fault with the lights – take care
☐ **C** wait for the green light before you cross the stop line
☐ **D** the lights are about to change to red

Be aware that other traffic might still be clearing the junction. Make sure the way is clear before continuing.

---

**686** Mark *one* answer

**This marking appears on the road just before a**

☐ **A** 'no entry' sign
☐ **B** 'give way' sign
☐ **C** 'stop' sign
☐ **D** 'no through road' sign

Where you see this road marking you should give way to traffic on the main road. It might not be used at junctions where there is relatively little traffic. However, if there is a double broken line across the junction the 'give way' rules still apply.

## 687 Mark *one* answer

**At a railway level crossing the red light signal continues to flash after a train has gone by. What should you do?**

☐ **A** Phone the signal operator
☐ **B** Alert drivers behind you
☐ **C** Wait
☐ **D** Proceed with caution

You MUST always obey red flashing stop lights. If a train passes but the lights continue to flash, another train will be passing soon. Cross only when the lights go off and the barriers open.

## 688 Mark *one* answer

**You are in a tunnel and you see this sign. What does it mean?**

☐ **A** Direction to emergency pedestrian exit
☐ **B** Beware of pedestrians, no footpath ahead
☐ **C** No access for pedestrians
☐ **D** Beware of pedestrians crossing ahead

If you have to leave your vehicle in a tunnel and leave by an emergency exit, do so as quickly as you can. Follow the signs directing you to the nearest exit point. If there are several people using the exit, don't panic but try to leave in a calm and orderly manner.

## 689 Mark *one* answer

**Which of these signs shows that you are entering a one-way system?**

☐ **A**    ☐ **B**

☐ **C**    ☐ **D**

If the road has two lanes you can use either lane and overtake on either side. Use the lane that's more convenient for your destination unless signs or road markings indicate otherwise.

## 690 Mark *one* answer

**What does this sign mean?**

☐ **A** With-flow bus and cycle lane
☐ **B** Contraflow bus and cycle lane
☐ **C** No buses and cycles allowed
☐ **D** No waiting for buses and cycles

Buses and cycles can travel in this lane. In this case they will flow in the same direction as other traffic. If it's busy they may be passing you on the left, so watch out for them. Times on the sign will show its hours of operation. No times shown, or no sign at all, means it's 24 hours. In some areas other vehicles, such as taxis and motorcycles, are allowed to use bus lanes. The sign will show these.

## 691 Mark *one* answer
**Which of these signs warns you of a zebra crossing?**

☐ **A**   ☐ **B**

☐ **C**   ☐ **D**

Look well ahead and check the pavements and surrounding areas for pedestrians. Look for anyone walking towards the crossing. Check your mirrors for traffic behind, in case you have to slow down or stop.

## 692 Mark *one* answer
**What does this sign mean?**

☐ **A** No footpath
☐ **B** No pedestrians
☐ **C** Zebra crossing
☐ **D** School crossing

You need to be aware of the various signs that relate to pedestrians. Some of the signs look similar but have very different meanings. Make sure you know what they all mean and be ready for any potential hazard.

## 693 Mark *one* answer
**What does this sign mean?**

☐ **A** School crossing patrol
☐ **B** No pedestrians allowed
☐ **C** Pedestrian zone – no vehicles
☐ **D** Zebra crossing ahead

Look well ahead and be ready to stop for any pedestrians crossing, or about to cross, the road. Also check the pavements for anyone who looks like they might step or run into the road.

## 694 Mark *one* answer
**Which sign means there will be two-way traffic crossing your route ahead?**

☐ **A**   ☐ **B**

☐ **C**   ☐ **D**

This sign is found in or at the end of a one-way system. It warns you that traffic will be crossing your path from both directions.

## 695 Mark *one* answer

**Which arm signal tells you that the car you are following is going to pull up?**

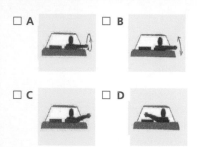

☐ A  ☐ B  ☐ C  ☐ D

There may be occasions when drivers need to give an arm signal to confirm an indicator. This could include in bright sunshine, at a complex road layout, when stopping at a pedestrian crossing or when turning right just after passing a parked vehicle. You should understand what each arm signal means. If you give arm signals, make them clear, correct and decisive.

## 696 Mark *one* answer

**Which of these signs means turn left ahead?**

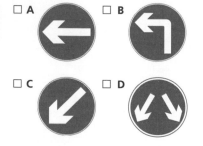

☐ A  ☐ B  ☐ C  ☐ D

Blue circles tell you what you must do and this sign gives a clear instruction to turn left ahead. You should be looking out for signs at all times and know what they mean.

## 697 Mark *one* answer

**Which sign shows that traffic can only travel in one direction on the road you're on?**

☐ A  ☐ B  ☐ C  ☐ D

This sign means that traffic can only travel in one direction. The others show different priorities on a two-way road.

## 698 Mark *one* answer

**You have just driven past this sign. You should be aware that**

☐ **A** it is a single track road
☐ **B** you cannot stop on this road
☐ **C** there is only one lane in use
☐ **D** all traffic is going one way

In a one-way system traffic may be passing you on either side. Always be aware of all traffic signs and understand their meaning. Look well ahead and react to them in good time.

**699** Mark **one** answer

**You are approaching a red traffic light. What will the signal show next?**

☐ **A** Red and amber
☐ **B** Green alone
☐ **C** Amber alone
☐ **D** Green and amber

If you know which light is going to show next you can plan your approach accordingly. This can help prevent excessive braking or hesitation at the junction.

---

**700** Mark **one** answer

**What does this sign mean?**

☐ **A** Low bridge ahead
☐ **B** Tunnel ahead
☐ **C** Ancient monument ahead
☐ **D** Traffic danger spot ahead

When approaching a tunnel switch on your dipped headlights. Be aware that your eyes might need to adjust to the sudden darkness. You may need to reduce your speed.

## 701 Mark *three* answers
**Which of the following information is found on your motorcycle registration document?**

☐ **A** Make and model
☐ **B** Service history record
☐ **C** Ignition key security number
☐ **D** Engine size and number
☐ **E** Purchase price
☐ **F** Year of first registration

Each motorcycle has a registration document which describes the vehicle's make, model and other details; it also gives details of the registered keeper. If you buy a new motorcycle the dealer will register your motorcycle with the licensing authority, who will send the registration document to you.

## 702 Mark *one* answer **NI**
**Compulsory Basic Training (CBT) can only be carried out by**

☐ **A** any ADI (Approved Driving Instructor)
☐ **B** any road safety officer
☐ **C** any DSA (Driving Standards Agency) approved training body
☐ **D** any motorcycle main dealer

CBT courses can only be given by training bodies that are approved by DSA. The standard of training is monitored by DSA examiners. The course is designed to give you basic skills before going on the road.

## 703 Mark *one* answer
**Before riding anyone else's motorcycle you should make sure that**

☐ **A** the owner has third party insurance cover
☐ **B** your own motorcycle has insurance cover
☐ **C** the motorcycle is insured for your use
☐ **D** the owner has the insurance documents with them

If you borrow a motorcycle you must make sure that you are insured. Find out yourself. Don't take anyone else's word for it.

## 704 Mark *one* answer
**Vehicle excise duty is often called 'Road Tax' or 'The Tax Disc'. You must**

☐ **A** keep it with your registration document
☐ **B** display it clearly on your motorcycle
☐ **C** keep it concealed safely in your motorcycle
☐ **D** carry it on you at all times

You must display a current, valid tax disc on your vehicle. It can't be transferred from one vehicle to another. A vehicle that is exempt from duty must display a valid nil licence instead.

## 705 Mark *one* answer **NI**
**Motorcycles must FIRST have an MOT test certificate when they are**

☐ **A** one year old
☐ **B** three years old
☐ **C** five years old
☐ **D** seven years old

Any motorcycle you ride must be in good condition and roadworthy. If it's over three years old it must have a valid MOT test certificate.

**706** Mark *three* answers
**Which THREE pieces of information are found on a registration document?**

- ☐ **A** Registered keeper
- ☐ **B** Make of the motorcycle
- ☐ **C** Service history details
- ☐ **D** Date of the MOT
- ☐ **E** Type of insurance cover
- ☐ **F** Engine size

Every motorcycle used on the road has a registration document issued by the Driver and Vehicle Licensing Agency (DVLA) or Driver and Vehicle Agency (DVA) in Northern Ireland. It is used to record any change of ownership and gives, date of first registration, registration number, previous keeper, registered keeper, make of motorcycle, engine size and frame number, year of manufacture and colour.

**707** Mark *three* answers
**You have a duty to contact the licensing authority when**

- ☐ **A** you go abroad on holiday
- ☐ **B** you change your motorcycle
- ☐ **C** you change your name
- ☐ **D** your job status is changed
- ☐ **E** your permanent address changes
- ☐ **F** your job involves travelling abroad

The licensing authority will need to keep their records up to date. They send out a reminder when your road tax is due and need your current address for this purpose. Every motorcycle in the country is registered, so it is possible to trace its history.

**708** Mark *two* answers
**Your motorcycle is insured third party only. This covers**

- ☐ **A** damage to your motorcycle
- ☐ **B** damage to other vehicles
- ☐ **C** injury to yourself
- ☐ **D** injury to others
- ☐ **E** all damage and injury

Third party insurance cover is usually cheaper than fully comprehensive. However, it does not cover any damage to your own motorcycle or property and it does not provide cover if your motorcycle is stolen.

**709** Mark *one* answer
**What is the legal minimum insurance cover you must have to ride on public roads?**

- ☐ **A** Third party, fire and theft
- ☐ **B** Fully comprehensive
- ☐ **C** Third party only
- ☐ **D** Personal injury cover

The minimum insurance cover required by law is third party only. This covers other people and vehicles involved in a collision, but not you or your vehicle. Also basic third party insurance won't cover you for theft or fire damage. Make sure you carefully read and understand your policy.

**710** Mark *one* answer

**A Vehicle Registration Document will show**

- ☐ **A** the service history
- ☐ **B** the year of first registration
- ☐ **C** the purchase price
- ☐ **D** the tyre sizes

A Vehicle Registration Document contains a number of details that are unique to a particular vehicle. You must notify DVLA (or DVA in Northern Ireland) of any changes to, for example, the registered keeper, registration number or any modifications to the vehicle.

**711** Mark *one* answer

**What is the purpose of having a vehicle test certificate (MOT)?**

- ☐ **A** To make sure your motorcycle is roadworthy
- ☐ **B** To certify how many miles per gallon it does
- ☐ **C** To prove you own the motorcycle
- ☐ **D** To allow you to park in restricted areas

It is your responsibility to make sure that any motorcycle you ride is in a roadworthy condition. Any faults that develop should be promptly corrected. If your motorcycle fails an MOT test, it should not be used on the road unless you're taking it to have the faults repaired or for a previously arranged retest.

**712** Mark *one* answer  **NI**

**Before taking a practical motorcycle test you need**

- ☐ **A** a full moped licence
- ☐ **B** a full car licence
- ☐ **C** a CBT (Compulsory Basic Training) certificate
- ☐ **D** 12 months riding experience

The purpose of a CBT (Compulsory Basic Training) course is to teach you basic theory and practical skills before riding on the road, on your own, for the first time. They can only be given by Approved Training Bodies (ATBs).

**713** Mark *three* answers

**You must notify the licensing authority when**

- ☐ **A** your health affects your riding
- ☐ **B** your eyesight does not meet a set standard
- ☐ **C** you intend lending your motorcycle
- ☐ **D** your motorcycle requires an MOT certificate
- ☐ **E** you change your motorcycle

The Driver and Vehicle Licensing Agency (DVLA) hold the records of all vehicles, drivers and riders in Great Britain (DVA in Northern Ireland). They need to know of any change in circumstances so they can keep their records up to date. Your health might affect your ability to ride safely. Don't put yourself or other road users at risk.

**714** Mark *two* answers
**You have just passed your practical motorcycle test. This is your first full licence. Within two years you get six penalty points. You will have to**

- ☐ **A** retake only your theory test
- ☐ **B** retake your theory and practical tests
- ☐ **C** retake only your practical test
- ☐ **D** reapply for your full licence immediately
- ☐ **E** reapply for your provisional licence

If, during your first two years of holding a full licence, the number of points on your licence reaches six or more, your licence will be revoked. This includes offences you committed before you passed your test. You may ride only as a learner until you pass both the theory and practical tests again.

**715** Mark *three* answers
**You hold a provisional motorcycle licence. This means you must NOT**

- ☐ **A** exceed 30mph
- ☐ **B** ride on a motorway
- ☐ **C** ride after dark
- ☐ **D** carry a pillion passenger
- ☐ **E** ride without 'L' plates displayed

Provisional entitlement means that restrictions apply to your use of motorcycles. The requirements are there to protect you and other road users. Make sure you are aware of all the restrictions that apply before you ride your motorcycle on the road.

**716** Mark *one* answer
**A full category A1 licence will allow you to ride a motorcycle up to**

- ☐ **A** 125cc
- ☐ **B** 250cc
- ☐ **C** 350cc
- ☐ **D** 425cc

When you pass your test on a motorcycle between 75cc and 125cc you will be issued with a full light motorcycle licence of category A1. You will then be allowed to ride any motorcycle up to 125cc and with a power output of 11Kw (14.6bhp).

**717** Mark *one* answer    NI
**You want a licence to ride a large motorcycle via Direct Access. You will**

- ☐ **A** not require L-plates if you have passed a car test
- ☐ **B** require L-plates only when learning on your own machine
- ☐ **C** require L-plates while learning with a qualified instructor
- ☐ **D** not require L-plates if you have passed a moped test

While training through the Direct Access scheme you must be accompanied by an instructor on another motorcycle and be in radio contact. You must display L-plates on your motorcycle and follow all normal learner restrictions.

**718** Mark *three* answers   `NI`
**A motorcyclist may only carry a pillion passenger when**

- ☐ **A** the rider has successfully completed CBT (Compulsory Basic Training)
- ☐ **B** the rider holds a full licence for the category of motorcycle
- ☐ **C** the motorcycle is fitted with rear footrests
- ☐ **D** the rider has a full car licence and is over 21
- ☐ **E** there is a proper passenger seat fitted
- ☐ **F** there is no sidecar fitted to the machine

Before carrying a passenger on a motorcycle the rider must hold a full licence for the category being ridden. They must also ensure that a proper passenger seat and footrests are fitted.

---

**719** Mark *one* answer   `NI`
**You have a CBT (Compulsory Basic Training) certificate. How long is it valid?**

- ☐ **A** one year
- ☐ **B** two years
- ☐ **C** three years
- ☐ **D** four years

All new learner motorcycle and moped riders must complete a Compulsory Basic Training (CBT) course before riding on the road. This can only be given by an Approved Training Body (ATB). If you don't pass your practical test within two years you will need to retake and pass CBT to continue riding.

**720** Mark *one* answer
**Your road tax disc is due to expire. To renew it you may need a renewal form, the fee, and valid MOT (if required). What else will you need?**

- ☐ **A** Proof of purchase receipt
- ☐ **B** Compulsory Basic Training certificate
- ☐ **C** A valid certificate of insurance
- ☐ **D** A complete service record

You will normally be sent a reminder automatically by the DVLA (DVA in Northern Ireland) close to the time of renewal. Make sure that all your documentation is correct, up to date and valid. You can renew, by post, in person, by phone or online.

---

**721** Mark *one* answer
**You want to carry a pillion passenger on your motorcycle. To do this**

- ☐ **A** your motorcycle must be larger than 125cc
- ☐ **B** they must be a full motorcycle licence-holder
- ☐ **C** you must have passed your test for a full motorcycle licence
- ☐ **D** you must have three years motorcycle riding experience

As a learner motorcyclist you are not allowed to carry a pillion passenger, even if they hold a full motorcycle licence. You MUST NOT carry a pillion, or tow a trailer, until you have passed your test.

**722** Mark *one* answer

**A friend asks you to give them a lift on your motorcycle. What conditions apply?**

- ☐ **A** Your motorcycle must be larger than 125cc
- ☐ **B** You must have three years motorcycle riding experience
- ☐ **C** The pillion must be a full motorcycle licence-holder
- ☐ **D** You must have passed your test for a full motorcycle licence

By law, you can only carry a pillion passenger after you have gained a full motorcycle licence. Even if they hold a full licence it makes no difference. As a learner you are also restricted from towing a trailer.

**723** Mark *one* answer

**Your motorcycle insurance policy has an excess of £100. What does this mean?**

- ☐ **A** The insurance company will pay the first £100 of any claim
- ☐ **B** You will be paid £100 if you do not have a crash
- ☐ **C** Your motorcycle is insured for a value of £100 if it is stolen
- ☐ **D** You will have to pay the first £100 of any claim

This is a method used by insurance companies to keep annual premiums down. Generally, the higher the excess you choose to pay, the lower the annual premium you will be charged.

**724** Mark *one* answer

**An MOT certificate is normally valid for**

- ☐ **A** three years after the date it was issued
- ☐ **B** 10,000 miles
- ☐ **C** one year after the date it was issued
- ☐ **D** 30,000 miles

Make a note of the date that your MOT certificate expires. Some garages remind you that your vehicle is due an MOT but not all do. You may take your vehicle for MOT up to one month in advance and have the certificate post dated.

**725** Mark *one* answer

**A cover note is a document issued before you receive your**

- ☐ **A** driving licence
- ☐ **B** insurance certificate
- ☐ **C** registration document
- ☐ **D** MOT certificate

Sometimes an insurance company will issue a temporary insurance certificate called a cover note. It gives you the same insurance cover as your certificate, but lasts for a limited period, usually one month.

## 726 Mark *two* answers

**You have just passed your practical test. You do not hold a full licence in another category. Within two years you get six penalty points on your licence. What will you have to do?**

☐ **A** Retake only your theory test
☐ **B** Retake your theory and practical tests
☐ **C** Retake only your practical test
☐ **D** Reapply for your full licence immediately
☐ **E** Reapply for your provisional licence

If you accumulate six or more penalty points within two years of gaining your first full licence it will be revoked. The six or more points include any gained due to offences you committed before passing your test. If this happens you may only drive as a learner until you pass both the theory and practical tests again.

## 727 Mark *one* answer

**How long will a Statutory Off Road Notification (SORN) last for?**

☐ **A** 12 months
☐ **B** 24 months
☐ **C** 3 years
☐ **D** 10 years

A SORN declaration allows you to keep a vehicle off road and untaxed for 12 months. If you want to keep your vehicle off road beyond that you must send a further SORN form to DVLA, or DVA in Northern Ireland. If the vehicle is sold SORN will end and the new owner becomes responsible immediately.

## 728 Mark *one* answer　NI

**What is a Statutory Off Road Notification (SORN) declaration?**

☐ **A** A notification to tell VOSA that a vehicle does not have a current MOT
☐ **B** Information kept by the police about the owner of the vehicle
☐ **C** A notification to tell DVLA that a vehicle is not being used on the road
☐ **D** Information held by insurance companies to check the vehicle is insured

If you want to keep a vehicle off the public road you must declare SORN. It is an offence not to do so. You then won't have to pay road tax. If you don't renew the SORN declaration or re-license the vehicle, you will incur a penalty.

## 729 Mark *one* answer　NI

**A Statutory Off Road Notification (SORN) declaration is**

☐ **A** to tell DVLA that your vehicle is being used on the road but the MOT has expired
☐ **B** to tell DVLA that you no longer own the vehicle
☐ **C** to tell DVLA that your vehicle is not being used on the road
☐ **D** to tell DVLA that you are buying a personal number plate

This will enable you to keep a vehicle off the public road for 12 months without having to pay road tax. You must send a further SORN declaration after 12 months.

**730** Mark **one** answer
**A Statutory Off Road Notification (SORN) is valid**

☐ **A** for as long as the vehicle has an MOT
☐ **B** for 12 months only
☐ **C** only if the vehicle is more than 3 years old
☐ **D** provided the vehicle is insured

If you want to keep a vehicle off the public road you must declare SORN. It is an offence not to do so. You then won't have to pay road tax for that vehicle. You will incur a penalty after 12 months if you don't renew the SORN declaration, or re-license the vehicle. If you sell the vehicle the SORN declaration ends and the new owner should declare SORN or re-license the vehicle.

**731** Mark **one** answer
**A Statutory Off Road Notification (SORN) will last**

☐ **A** for the life of the vehicle
☐ **B** for as long as you own the vehicle
☐ **C** for 12 months only
☐ **D** until the vehicle warranty expires

If you are keeping a vehicle, or vehicles, off road and don't want to pay road tax you must declare SORN. You must still do this even if the vehicle is incapable of being used, for example it may be under restoration or being stored. After 12 months you must send another SORN declaration or re-license your vehicle. You will be fined if you don't do this. The SORN will end if you sell the vehicle and the new owner will be responsible immediately.

**732** Mark **one** answer
**What is the maximum specified fine for driving without insurance?**

☐ **A** £50
☐ **B** £500
☐ **C** £1,000
☐ **D** £5,000

It is a serious offence to drive without insurance. As well as a heavy fine you may be disqualified or incur penalty points.

**733** Mark **one** answer
**Who is legally responsible for ensuring that a Vehicle Registration Certificate (V5C) is updated?**

☐ **A** The registered vehicle keeper
☐ **B** The vehicle manufacturer
☐ **C** Your insurance company
☐ **D** The licensing authority

It is your legal responsibility to keep the details of your Vehicle Registration Certificate (V5C) up to date. You should tell the licensing authority of any changes. These include your name, address, or vehicle details. If you don't do this you may have problems when you sell your vehicle.

**734** Mark *one* answer

**For which of these MUST you show your insurance certificate?**

☐ **A** When making a SORN declaration
☐ **B** When buying or selling a vehicle
☐ **C** When a police officer asks you for it
☐ **D** When having an MOT inspection

You MUST be able to produce your valid insurance certificate when requested by a police officer. If you can't do this immediately you may be asked to take it to a police station. Other documents you may be asked to produce are your driving licence and MOT certificate.

**735** Mark *one* answer

**You must have valid insurance before you can**

☐ **A** make a SORN declaration
☐ **B** buy or sell a vehicle
☐ **C** apply for a driving licence
☐ **D** obtain a tax disc

You MUST have valid insurance before you can apply for a tax disc. Your vehicle will also need to have a valid MOT certificate, if applicable. You can apply on-line, at certain post offices or by post. It is illegal and can be dangerous to drive without valid insurance or an MOT.

**736** Mark *one* answer

**Your vehicle needs a current MOT certificate. Until you have one you will NOT be able to**

☐ **A** renew your driving licence
☐ **B** change your insurance company
☐ **C** renew your road tax disc
☐ **D** notify a change of address

If your vehicle is required to have an MOT certificate you will need to make sure this is current before you are able to renew your tax disc (also known as vehicle excise duty). You can renew online, by phone or by post.

**737** Mark *three* answers

**Which THREE of these do you need before you can use a vehicle on the road legally?**

☐ **A** A valid driving licence
☐ **B** A valid tax disc clearly displayed
☐ **C** Proof of your identity
☐ **D** Proper insurance cover
☐ **E** Breakdown cover
☐ **F** A vehicle handbook

Using a vehicle on the road illegally carries a heavy fine and can lead to penalty points on your licence. Things you MUST have include a valid driving licence, a current valid tax disc, and proper insurance cover.

**738** Mark *one* answer

**When you apply to renew your Vehicle Excise Duty (tax disc) you must have**

- ☐ **A** valid insurance
- ☐ **B** the old tax disc
- ☐ **C** the handbook
- ☐ **D** a valid driving licence

Tax discs can be renewed at post offices, vehicle registration offices, online, or by post. When applying make sure you have all the relevant valid documents, including MOT where applicable.

---

**739** Mark *one* answer

**A police officer asks to see your documents. You do not have them with you. You may be asked to take them to a police station within**

- ☐ **A** 5 days
- ☐ **B** 7 days
- ☐ **C** 14 days
- ☐ **D** 21 days

You don't have to carry the documents for your vehicle around with you. If a police officer asks to see them and you don't have them with you, you may be asked to produce them at a police station within seven days.

**740** Mark *one* answer

**When you apply to renew your vehicle excise licence (tax disc) what must you have?**

- ☐ **A** Valid insurance
- ☐ **B** The old tax disc
- ☐ **C** The vehicle handbook
- ☐ **D** A valid driving licence

Tax discs can be renewed online, at most post offices, your nearest vehicle registration office or by post to the licensing authority. Make sure you have or take all the relevant documents with your application.

---

**741** Mark *one* answer

**When should you update your Vehicle Registration Certificate?**

- ☐ **A** When you pass your driving test
- ☐ **B** When you move house
- ☐ **C** When your vehicle needs an MOT
- ☐ **D** When you have a collision

As the registered keeper of a vehicle it is up to you to inform DVLA (DVA in Northern Ireland) of any changes in your vehicle or personal details, for example, change of name or address. You do this by completing the relevant section of the Registration Certificate and sending it to them.

**742** Mark *one* answer

**Your motorcycle has broken down on a motorway. How will you know the direction of the nearest emergency telephone?**

- [ ] **A** By walking with the flow of traffic
- [ ] **B** By following an arrow on a marker post
- [ ] **C** By walking against the flow of traffic
- [ ] **D** By remembering where the last phone was

If you break down on a motorway pull onto the hard shoulder and stop as far over to the left as you can. Switch on hazard lights (if fitted) and go to the nearest emergency telephone. Marker posts spaced every 100 metres will show you where the nearest telephone is.

**743** Mark *one* answer

**You should use the engine cut-out switch to**

- [ ] **A** stop the engine in an emergency
- [ ] **B** stop the engine on short journeys
- [ ] **C** save wear on the ignition switch
- [ ] **D** start the engine if you lose the key

Most motorcycles are fitted with an engine cut-out switch. This is designed to stop the engine in an emergency and so reduce the risk of fire.

**744** Mark *one* answer

**You are riding on a motorway. The car in front switches on its hazard warning lights whilst moving. This means**

- [ ] **A** they are going to take the next exit
- [ ] **B** there is a danger ahead
- [ ] **C** there is a police car in the left lane
- [ ] **D** they are trying to change lanes

When riding on a motorway, or a dual carriageway subject to a national speed limit, vehicles may switch on their hazard warning lights to warn following traffic of an obstruction ahead.

**745** Mark *three* answers

**You have broken down on a motorway. When you use the emergency telephone you will be asked**

- [ ] **A** for the number on the telephone that you are using
- [ ] **B** for your driving licence details
- [ ] **C** for the name of your vehicle insurance company
- [ ] **D** for details of yourself and your motorcycle
- [ ] **E** whether you belong to a motoring organisation

Have these details ready before you phone and be sure to give the correct information. For your own safety face the traffic when you speak on the telephone.

**746** Mark *one* answer

**You are on a motorway. When can you use hazard warning lights?**

☐ **A** When a vehicle is following too closely
☐ **B** When you slow down quickly because of danger ahead
☐ **C** When you are being towed by another vehicle
☐ **D** When riding on the hard shoulder

Hazard lights will warn the traffic behind you that there is a potential hazard ahead. Don't forget to turn them off again when your signal has been seen.

**747** Mark *one* answer

**Your motorcycle breaks down in a tunnel. What should you do?**

☐ **A** Stay with your motorcycle and wait for the police
☐ **B** Stand in the lane behind your motorcycle to warn others
☐ **C** Stand in front of your motorcycle to warn oncoming drivers
☐ **D** Switch on hazard lights then go and call for help immediately

Any broken down vehicle in a tunnel can cause serious congestion and danger to other traffic and drivers. If you break down you should get help without delay. Switch on your hazard warning lights and then go to an emergency telephone point to call for help.

**748** Mark *one* answer

**You are riding through a tunnel. Your motorcycle breaks down. What should you do?**

☐ **A** Switch on hazard warning lights
☐ **B** Remain on your motorcycle
☐ **C** Wait for the police to find you
☐ **D** Rely on CCTV cameras seeing you

If your motorcycle breaks down in a tunnel it could present a danger to other traffic. First switch on your hazard warning lights and then call for help from an emergency telephone point. Don't rely on being found by the police or being seen by a CCTV camera.

**749** Mark *one* answer

**You are travelling on a motorway. A bag falls from your motorcycle. There are valuables in the bag. What should you do?**

☐ **A** Go back carefully and collect the bag as quickly as possible
☐ **B** Stop wherever you are and pick up the bag, but only when there is a safe gap
☐ **C** Stop on the hard shoulder and use the emergency telephone to inform the authorities
☐ **D** Stop on the hard shoulder and then retrieve the bag yourself

You must never walk on a motorway, however important you think retrieving your property may be. Your bag might be creating a hazard but not as great a hazard as you would be.

**750** Mark *one* answer

**You are on a motorway. Luggage falls from your motorcycle. What should you do?**

- ☐ **A** Stop at the next emergency telephone and report the hazard
- ☐ **B** Stop on the motorway and put on hazard lights while you pick it up
- ☐ **C** Walk back up the motorway to pick it up
- ☐ **D** Pull up on the hard shoulder and wave traffic down

If any of your luggage falls onto the road, pull onto the hard shoulder near an emergency telephone and phone for assistance. Don't stop on the carriageway or attempt to retrieve anything.

---

**751** Mark *four* answers

**You are in collision with another vehicle. Someone is injured. Your motorcycle is damaged. Which FOUR of the following should you find out?**

- ☐ **A** Whether the driver owns the other vehicle involved
- ☐ **B** The other driver's name, address and telephone number
- ☐ **C** The make and registration number of the other vehicle
- ☐ **D** The occupation of the other driver
- ☐ **E** The details of the other driver's vehicle insurance
- ☐ **F** Whether the other driver is licensed to drive

If you are involved in a collision where someone is injured, your first priority is to warn other traffic and call the emergency services.

When exchanging details, make sure you have all the information you need before you leave the scene. Don't ride your motorcycle if it is unroadworthy.

**752** Mark *one* answer

**You see a car on the hard shoulder of a motorway with a HELP pennant displayed. This means the driver is most likely to be**

- ☐ **A** a disabled person
- ☐ **B** first aid trained
- ☐ **C** a foreign visitor
- ☐ **D** a rescue patrol person

If a disabled driver's vehicle breaks down and they are unable to walk to an emergency phone, they are advised to stay in their car and switch on the hazard warning lights. They may also display a 'Help' pennant in their vehicle.

---

**753** Mark *two* answers

**For which TWO should you use hazard warning lights?**

- ☐ **A** When you slow down quickly on a motorway because of a hazard ahead
- ☐ **B** When you have broken down
- ☐ **C** When you wish to stop on double yellow lines
- ☐ **D** When you need to park on the pavement

Hazard warning lights are fitted to all modern cars and some motorcycles. They should only be used to warn other road users of a hazard ahead.

**754** Mark *one* answer
**When are you allowed to use hazard warning lights?**

☐ **A** When stopped and temporarily obstructing traffic
☐ **B** When travelling during darkness without headlights
☐ **C** When parked for shopping on double yellow lines
☐ **D** When travelling slowly because you are lost

You must not use hazard warning lights when moving, except when slowing suddenly on a motorway or unrestricted dual carriageway to warn the traffic behind. Never use hazard warning lights to excuse dangerous or illegal parking.

**755** Mark *one* answer
**You are going through a congested tunnel and have to stop. What should you do?**

☐ **A** Pull up very close to the vehicle in front to save space
☐ **B** Ignore any message signs as they are never up to date
☐ **C** Keep a safe distance from the vehicle in front
☐ **D** Make a U-turn and find another route

It's important to keep a safe distance from the vehicle in front at all times. This still applies in congested tunnels even If you are moving very slowly or have stopped. If the vehicle in front breaks down you may need room to manoeuvre past it.

**756** Mark *one* answer
**On the motorway, the hard shoulder should be used**

☐ **A** to answer a mobile phone
☐ **B** when an emergency arises
☐ **C** for a short rest when tired
☐ **D** to check a road atlas

Pull onto the hard shoulder and use the emergency telephone to report your problem. This lets the emergency services know your exact location so they can send help. Never cross the carriageway to use the telephone on the other side.

**757** Mark *one* answer
**You arrive at the scene of a crash. Someone is bleeding badly from an arm wound. There is nothing embedded in it. What should you do?**

☐ **A** Apply pressure over the wound and keep the arm down
☐ **B** Dab the wound
☐ **C** Get them a drink
☐ **D** Apply pressure over the wound and raise the arm

If possible, lay the casualty down. Check for anything that may be in the wound. Apply firm pressure to the wound using clean material, without pressing on anything which might be in it. Raising the arm above the level of the heart will also help to stem the flow of blood.

**758** Mark *one* answer

**You are at an incident where a casualty is unconscious. Their breathing should be checked. This should be done for at least**

☐ **A** 2 seconds
☐ **B** 10 seconds
☐ **C** 1 minute
☐ **D** 2 minutes

Once the airway is open, check breathing. Listen and feel for breath. Do this by placing your cheek over their mouth and nose, and look to see if the chest rises. This should be done for up to 10 seconds.

**759** Mark *one* answer

**Following a collision someone has suffered a burn. The burn needs to be cooled. What is the shortest time it should be cooled for?**

☐ **A** 5 minutes
☐ **B** 10 minutes
☐ **C** 15 minutes
☐ **D** 20 minutes

Check the casualty for shock and if possible try to cool the burn for at least ten minutes. Use a clean, cold non-toxic liquid preferably water.

**760** Mark *one* answer

**After a collision someone has suffered a burn. The burn needs to be cooled. What is the shortest time it should be cooled for?**

☐ **A** 30 seconds
☐ **B** 60 seconds
☐ **C** 5 minutes
☐ **D** 10 minutes

It's important to cool a burn for at least ten minutes. Use a clean, cold non-toxic liquid preferably water. Bear in mind the person may also be in shock.

**761** Mark *one* answer

**A casualty is not breathing normally. Chest compressions should be given. At what rate?**

☐ **A** 50 per minute
☐ **B** 100 per minute
☐ **C** 200 per minute
☐ **D** 250 per minute

If a casualty is not breathing normally chest compressions may be needed to maintain circulation. Place two hands on the centre of the chest and press down about 4–5 centimetres, at the rate of 100 per minute.

**762** Mark *one* answer

**A person has been injured. They may be suffering from shock. What are the warning signs to look for?**

☐ **A** Flushed complexion
☐ **B** Warm dry skin
☐ **C** Slow pulse
☐ **D** Pale grey skin

The effects of shock may not be immediately obvious. Warning signs are rapid pulse, sweating, pale grey skin and rapid shallow breathing.

---

**763** Mark *one* answer

**You suspect that an injured person may be suffering from shock. What are the warning signs to look for?**

☐ **A** Warm dry skin
☐ **B** Sweating
☐ **C** Slow pulse
☐ **D** Skin rash

Sometimes you may not realise that someone is in shock. The signs to look for are rapid pulse, sweating, pale grey skin and rapid shallow breathing.

**764** Mark *one* answer

**An injured person has been placed in the recovery position. They are unconscious but breathing normally. What else should be done?**

☐ **A** Press firmly between the shoulders
☐ **B** Place their arms by their side
☐ **C** Give them a hot sweet drink
☐ **D** Check the airway is clear

After a casualty has been placed in the recovery position, their airway should be checked to make sure it's clear. Don't leave them alone until medical help arrives. Where possible do NOT move a casualty unless there's further danger.

---

**765** Mark *one* answer

**An injured motorcyclist is lying unconscious in the road. You should always**

☐ **A** remove the safety helmet
☐ **B** seek medical assistance
☐ **C** move the person off the road
☐ **D** remove the leather jacket

If someone has been injured, the sooner proper medical attention is given the better. Send someone to phone for help or go yourself. An injured person should only be moved if they're in further danger. An injured motorcyclist's helmet should NOT be removed unless it is essential.

**766** Mark *one* answer

**You are on a motorway. A large box falls onto the road from a lorry. The lorry does not stop. You should**

- ☐ **A** go to the next emergency telephone and report the hazard
- ☐ **B** catch up with the lorry and try to get the driver's attention
- ☐ **C** stop close to the box until the police arrive
- ☐ **D** pull over to the hard shoulder, then remove the box

Lorry drivers can be unaware of objects falling from their vehicles. If you see something fall onto a motorway look to see if the driver pulls over. If they don't stop, do not attempt to retrieve it yourself. Pull on to the hard shoulder near an emergency telephone and report the hazard. You will be connected to the police or a Highways Agency control centre.

**767** Mark *one* answer

**You are going through a long tunnel. What will warn you of congestion or an incident ahead?**

- ☐ **A** Hazard warning lines
- ☐ **B** Other drivers flashing their lights
- ☐ **C** Variable message signs
- ☐ **D** Areas marked with hatch markings

Follow the instructions given by the signs or by tunnel officials.

In congested tunnels a minor incident can soon turn into a major one with serious or even fatal results.

**768** Mark *one* answer

**An adult casualty is not breathing. To maintain circulation, compressions should be given. What is the correct depth to press?**

- ☐ **A** 1 to 2 centimetres
- ☐ **B** 4 to 5 centimetres
- ☐ **C** 10 to 15 centimetres
- ☐ **D** 15 to 20 centimetres

An adult casualty is not breathing normally. To maintain circulation place two hands on the centre of the chest. Then press down 4 to 5 centimetres at a rate of 100 times per minute.

**769** Mark *two* answers

**You are the first to arrive at the scene of a crash. Which TWO of these should you do?**

- ☐ **A** Leave as soon as another motorist arrives
- ☐ **B** Make sure engines are switched off
- ☐ **C** Drag all casualties away from the vehicles
- ☐ **D** Call the emergency services promptly

At a crash scene you can help in practical ways, even if you aren't trained in first aid. Make sure you do not put yourself or anyone else in danger. The safest way to warn other traffic is by switching on your hazard warning lights.

**770** Mark **one** answer
**At the scene of a traffic incident
you should**

☐ **A** not put yourself at risk
☐ **B** go to those casualties who are screaming
☐ **C** pull everybody out of their vehicles
☐ **D** leave vehicle engines switched on

It's important that people at the scene of a collision do not create further risk to themselves or others. If the incident is on a motorway or major road, traffic will be approaching at speed. Do not put yourself at risk when trying to help casualties or warning other road users.

**771** Mark **three** answers
**You are the first person to arrive at an incident where people are badly injured. Which THREE should you do?**

☐ **A** Switch on your own hazard warning lights
☐ **B** Make sure that someone telephones for an ambulance
☐ **C** Try and get people who are injured to drink something
☐ **D** Move the people who are injured clear of their vehicles
☐ **E** Get people who are not injured clear of the scene

If you're the first to arrive at a crash scene the first concerns are the risk of further collision and fire. Ensuring that vehicle engines are switched off will reduce the risk of fire. Use hazard warning lights so that other traffic knows there's a need for caution. Make sure the emergency services are contacted, don't assume this has already been done.

**772** Mark **one** answer
**You arrive at the scene of a motorcycle crash. The rider is injured. When should the helmet be removed?**

☐ **A** Only when it is essential
☐ **B** Always straight away
☐ **C** Only when the motorcyclist asks
☐ **D** Always, unless they are in shock

DO NOT remove a motorcyclist's helmet unless it is essential. Remember they may be suffering from shock. Don't give them anything to eat or drink but do reassure them confidently.

**773** Mark **three** answers
**You arrive at a serious motorcycle crash. The motorcyclist is unconscious and bleeding. Your THREE main priorities should be to**

☐ **A** try to stop the bleeding
☐ **B** make a list of witnesses
☐ **C** check their breathing
☐ **D** take the numbers of other vehicles
☐ **E** sweep up any loose debris
☐ **F** check their airways

Further collisions and fire are the main dangers immediately after a crash. If possible get others to assist you and make the area safe. Help those involved and remember DR ABC, Danger, Response, Airway, Breathing, Compressions. This will help when dealing with any injuries.

**774** Mark *one* answer

**You arrive at an incident. A motorcyclist is unconscious. Your FIRST priority is the casualty's**

☐ **A** breathing
☐ **B** bleeding
☐ **C** broken bones
☐ **D** bruising

At the scene of an incident always be aware of danger from further collisions or fire. The first priority when dealing with an unconscious person is to ensure they can breathe. This may involve clearing their airway if you can see an obstruction, or if they're having difficulty breathing.

**775** Mark *three* answers

**At an incident a casualty is unconscious. Which THREE of these should you check urgently?**

☐ **A** Circulation
☐ **B** Airway
☐ **C** Shock
☐ **D** Breathing
☐ **E** Broken bones

Remember DR ABC. An unconscious casualty may have difficulty breathing. Check that their airway is clear by tilting the head back gently and unblock it if necessary. Then make sure they are breathing. If there is bleeding, stem the flow by placing clean material over any wounds but without pressing on any objects in the wound. Compressions may need to be given to maintain circulation.

**776** Mark *three* answers

**You arrive at the scene of an incident. It has just happened and someone is unconscious. Which THREE of these should be given urgent priority to help them?**

☐ **A** Clear the airway and keep it open
☐ **B** Try to get them to drink water
☐ **C** Check that they are breathing
☐ **D** Look for any witnesses
☐ **E** Stop any heavy bleeding
☐ **F** Take the numbers of vehicles involved

Make sure that the emergency services are called immediately. Once first aid has been given, stay with the casualty.

**777** Mark *three* answers

**At an incident someone is unconscious. Your THREE main priorities should be to**

☐ **A** sweep up the broken glass
☐ **B** take the names of witnesses
☐ **C** count the number of vehicles involved
☐ **D** check the airway is clear
☐ **E** make sure they are breathing
☐ **F** stop any heavy bleeding

Remember this procedure by saying DR ABC. This stands for Danger, Response, Airway, Breathing, Compressions.

# 778 Mark *three* answers
**You have stopped at an incident to give help. Which THREE things should you do?**

- ☐ **A** Keep injured people warm and comfortable
- ☐ **B** Keep injured people calm by talking to them reassuringly
- ☐ **C** Keep injured people on the move by walking them around
- ☐ **D** Give injured people a warm drink
- ☐ **E** Make sure that injured people are not left alone

There are a number of things you can do to help, even without expert training. Be aware of further danger and fire, make sure the area is safe. People may be in shock. Don't give them anything to eat or drink. Keep them warm and comfortable and reassure them. Don't move injured people unless there is a risk of further danger.

# 779 Mark *three* answers
**You arrive at an incident. It has just happened and someone is injured. Which THREE should be given urgent priority?**

- ☐ **A** Stop any severe bleeding
- ☐ **B** Give them a warm drink
- ☐ **C** Check they are breathing
- ☐ **D** Take numbers of vehicles involved
- ☐ **E** Look for witnesses
- ☐ **F** Clear their airway and keep it open

The first priority with a casualty is to make sure their airway is clear and they are breathing. Any wounds should be checked for objects and then bleeding stemmed using clean material. Ensure the emergency services are called, they are the experts. If you're not first aid trained consider getting training. It might save a life.

# 780 Mark *one* answer
**Which of the following should you NOT do at the scene of a collision?**

- ☐ **A** Warn other traffic by switching on your hazard warning lights
- ☐ **B** Call the emergency services immediately
- ☐ **C** Offer someone a cigarette to calm them down
- ☐ **D** Ask drivers to switch off their engines

Keeping casualties or witnesses calm is important, but never offer a cigarette because of the risk of fire. Bear in mind they may be in shock. Don't offer an injured person anything to eat or drink. They may have internal injuries or need surgery.

# 781 Mark *two* answers
**There has been a collision. A driver is suffering from shock. What TWO of these should you do?**

- ☐ **A** Give them a drink
- ☐ **B** Reassure them
- ☐ **C** Not leave them alone
- ☐ **D** Offer them a cigarette
- ☐ **E** Ask who caused the incident

Be aware they could have an injury that is not immediately obvious. Ensure the emergency services are called. Reassure and stay with them until the experts arrive.

# 782 Mark *one* answer
**You have to treat someone for shock at the scene of an incident. You should**

- ☐ **A** reassure them constantly
- ☐ **B** walk them around to calm them down
- ☐ **C** give them something cold to drink
- ☐ **D** cool them down as soon as possible

Stay with the casualty and talk to them quietly and firmly to calm and reassure them. Avoid moving them unnecessarily in case they are injured. Keep them warm, but don't give them anything to eat or drink.

# 783 Mark *one* answer
**You arrive at the scene of a motorcycle crash. No other vehicle is involved. The rider is unconscious and lying in the middle of the road. The FIRST thing you should do is**

- ☐ **A** move the rider out of the road
- ☐ **B** warn other traffic
- ☐ **C** clear the road of debris
- ☐ **D** give the rider reassurance

The motorcyclist is in an extremely vulnerable position, exposed to further danger from traffic. Approaching vehicles need advance warning in order to slow down and safely take avoiding action or stop. Don't put yourself or anyone else at risk. Use the hazard warning lights on your vehicle to alert other road users to the danger.

# 784 Mark *one* answer
**At an incident a small child is not breathing. To restore normal breathing you should breathe into their mouth**

- ☐ **A** sharply
- ☐ **B** gently
- ☐ **C** heavily
- ☐ **D** rapidly

If a young child has stopped breathing, first check that the airway is clear. Then give compressions to the chest using one hand (two fingers for an infant) and begin mouth to mouth resuscitation. Breathe very gently and continue the procedure until they can breathe without help.

# 785 Mark *three* answers
**At an incident a casualty is not breathing. To start the process to restore normal breathing you should**

- ☐ **A** tilt their head forward
- ☐ **B** clear the airway
- ☐ **C** turn them on their side
- ☐ **D** tilt their head back gently
- ☐ **E** pinch the nostrils together
- ☐ **F** put their arms across their chest

It's important to ensure that the airways are clear before you start mouth to mouth resuscitation. Gently tilt their head back and use your finger to check for and remove any obvious obstruction in the mouth.

**786** Mark *one* answer

**You arrive at an incident. There has been an engine fire and someone's hands and arms have been burnt. You should NOT**

☐ **A** douse the burn thoroughly with clean cool non-toxic liquid
☐ **B** lay the casualty down on the ground
☐ **C** remove anything sticking to the burn
☐ **D** reassure them confidently and repeatedly

This could cause further damage and infection to the wound. Your first priority is to cool the burn with a clean, cool, non-toxic liquid, preferably water. Don't forget the casualty may be in shock.

**787** Mark *one* answer

**You arrive at an incident where someone is suffering from severe burns. You should**

☐ **A** apply lotions to the injury
☐ **B** burst any blisters
☐ **C** remove anything stuck to the burns
☐ **D** douse the burns with clean cool non-toxic liquid

Use a liquid that is clean, cold and non-toxic, preferably water. Its coolness will help take the heat out of the burn and relieve the pain. Keep the wound doused for at least ten minutes. If blisters appear don't attempt to burst them as this could lead to infection.

**788** Mark *two* answers

**You arrive at an incident. A pedestrian has a severe bleeding leg wound. It is not broken and there is nothing in the wound. What TWO of these should you do?**

☐ **A** Dab the wound to stop bleeding
☐ **B** Keep both legs flat on the ground
☐ **C** Apply firm pressure to the wound
☐ **D** Raise the leg to lessen bleeding
☐ **E** Fetch them a warm drink

First check for anything that may be in the wound such as glass. If there's nothing in it apply a pad of clean cloth or bandage. Raising the leg will lessen the flow of blood. Don't tie anything tightly round the leg. This will restrict circulation and can result in long-term injury.

**789** Mark *one* answer

**At an incident a casualty is unconscious but still breathing. You should only move them if**

☐ **A** an ambulance is on its way
☐ **B** bystanders advise you to
☐ **C** there is further danger
☐ **D** bystanders will help you to

Do not move a casualty unless there is further danger, for example, from other traffic or fire. They may have unseen or internal injuries. Moving them unnecessarily could cause further injury. Do NOT remove a motorcyclist's helmet unless it's essential.

# 790 Mark *one* answer

**At a collision you suspect a casualty has back injuries. The area is safe. You should**

- ☐ **A** offer them a drink
- ☐ **B** not move them
- ☐ **C** raise their legs
- ☐ **D** not call an ambulance

Talk to the casualty and keep them calm. Do not attempt to move them as this could cause further injury. Call an ambulance at the first opportunity.

# 791 Mark *one* answer

**At an incident it is important to look after any casualties. When the area is safe, you should**

- ☐ **A** get them out of the vehicle
- ☐ **B** give them a drink
- ☐ **C** give them something to eat
- ☐ **D** keep them in the vehicle

When the area is safe and there's no danger from other traffic or fire it's better not to move casualties. Moving them may cause further injury.

# 792 Mark *one* answer

**A tanker is involved in a collision. Which sign shows that it is carrying dangerous goods?**

☐ **A**   ☐ **B**

☐ **C**  ☐ **D**

There will be an orange label on the side and rear of the tanker. Look at this carefully and report what it says when you phone the emergency services. Details of hazard warning plates are given in The Highway Code.

# 793 Mark *three* answers

**You are involved in a collision. Because of this which THREE of these documents may the police ask you to produce?**

- ☐ **A** Vehicle registration document
- ☐ **B** Driving licence
- ☐ **C** Theory test certificate
- ☐ **D** Insurance certificate
- ☐ **E** MOT test certificate
- ☐ **F** Vehicle service record

You MUST stop if you have been involved in a collision which results in injury or damage. The police may ask to see your documents at the time or later at a police station.

## 794 Mark *one* answer

**After a collision someone is unconscious in their vehicle. When should you call the emergency services?**

- ☐ **A** Only as a last resort
- ☐ **B** As soon as possible
- ☐ **C** After you have woken them up
- ☐ **D** After checking for broken bones

It is important to make sure that emergency services arrive on the scene as soon as possible. When a person is unconscious, they could have serious injuries that are not immediately obvious.

## 795 Mark *one* answer

**A casualty has an injured arm. They can move it freely but it is bleeding. Why should you get them to keep it in a raised position?**

- ☐ **A** Because it will ease the pain
- ☐ **B** It will help them to be seen more easily
- ☐ **C** To stop them touching other people
- ☐ **D** It will help to reduce the blood flow

If a casualty is bleeding heavily, raise the limb to a higher position. This will help to reduce the blood flow. Before raising the limb you should make sure that it is not broken.

## 796 Mark *one* answer

**You are going through a tunnel. What systems are provided to warn of any incidents, collisions or congestion?**

- ☐ **A** Double white centre lines
- ☐ **B** Variable message signs
- ☐ **C** Chevron 'distance markers'
- ☐ **D** Rumble strips

Take notice of any instructions given on variable message signs or by tunnel officials. They will warn you of any incidents or congestion ahead and advise you what to do.

## 797 Mark *one* answer

**A collision has just happened. An injured person is lying in a busy road. What is the FIRST thing you should do to help?**

- ☐ **A** Treat the person for shock
- ☐ **B** Warn other traffic
- ☐ **C** Place them in the recovery position
- ☐ **D** Make sure the injured person is kept warm

The most immediate danger is further collisions and fire. You could warn other traffic by displaying an advance warning triangle or sign (but not on a motorway), switching on hazard warning lights or by any other means that does not put you or others at risk.

# 798 Mark *two* answers
**At an incident a casualty has stopped breathing. You should**

□ **A** remove anything that is blocking the mouth
□ **B** keep the head tilted forwards as far as possible
□ **C** raise the legs to help with circulation
□ **D** try to give the casualty something to drink
□ **E** tilt the head back gently to clear the airway

Unblocking the airway and gently tilting the head back will help the casualty to breathe. They will then be in the correct position if mouth-to-mouth resuscitation is required. Don't move a casualty unless there's further danger.

# 799 Mark *four* answers
**You are at the scene of an incident. Someone is suffering from shock. You should**

□ **A** reassure them constantly
□ **B** offer them a cigarette
□ **C** keep them warm
□ **D** avoid moving them if possible
□ **E** avoid leaving them alone
□ **F** give them a warm drink

The signs of shock may not be immediately obvious. Prompt treatment can help to minimise the effects. Lay the casualty down, loosen tight clothing, call an ambulance and check their breathing and pulse.

# 800 Mark *one* answer
**There has been a collision. A motorcyclist is lying injured and unconscious. Unless it's essential, why should you usually NOT attempt to remove their helmet?**

□ **A** Because they may not want you to
□ **B** This could result in more serious injury
□ **C** They will get too cold if you do this
□ **D** Because you could scratch the helmet

When someone is injured, any movement which is not absolutely necessary should be avoided since it could make injuries worse. Unless it is essential, it's generally safer to leave a motorcyclist's helmet in place.

## 801 Mark *one* answer

**If a trailer swerves or snakes when you are towing it you should**

☐ **A** ease off the throttle and reduce your speed
☐ **B** let go of the handlebars and let it correct itself
☐ **C** brake hard and hold the brake on
☐ **D** increase your speed as quickly as possible

Don't be tempted to use harsh braking to stop swerving or snaking as this won't help the situation. You should reduce your speed by easing off the throttle.

## 802 Mark *two* answers

**When riding with a sidecar attached for the first time you should**

☐ **A** keep your speed down
☐ **B** be able to stop more quickly
☐ **C** accelerate quickly round bends
☐ **D** approach corners more carefully

A motorcycle with a sidecar will feel very different to ride than a solo motorcycle. Keep your speed down until you get used to the outfit, especially when negotiating bends and junctions.

## 803 Mark *three* answers

**When carrying extra weight on a motorcycle, you may need to make adjustments to the**

☐ **A** headlight
☐ **B** gears
☐ **C** suspension
☐ **D** tyres
☐ **E** footrests

Carrying extra weight such as luggage or a pillion passenger, will probably affect the aim of the headlight. Adjust this so that it does not dazzle other road users. The feel and balance will also be affected so you may need to adjust the suspension and tyre pressures to help overcome this.

## 804 Mark *one* answer   NI

**To obtain the full category 'A' licence through the accelerated or direct access scheme, your motorcycle must be**

☐ **A** solo with maximum power 25kw (33bhp)
☐ **B** solo with maximum power of 11kw (14.6bhp)
☐ **C** fitted with a sidecar and have minimum power of 35kw (46.6bhp)
☐ **D** solo with minimum power of 35kw (46.6bhp)

From the age of 21 you may take a category A test via the Direct or Accelerated Access schemes. The motorcycle you use for your practical test under the Direct or Accelerated Access scheme is one that has an engine with a minimum power output of 35kw (46.6bhp).

## 805 Mark *one* answer
**Any load that is carried on a luggage rack MUST be**

- [ ] **A** securely fastened when riding
- [ ] **B** carried only when strictly necessary
- [ ] **C** visible when you are riding
- [ ] **D** covered with plastic sheeting

Don't risk losing any luggage while riding: it could fall into the path of following vehicles and cause danger. It is an offence to travel with an insecure load.

## 806 Mark *one* answer
**Pillion passengers should**

- [ ] **A** have a provisional motorcycle licence
- [ ] **B** be lighter than the rider
- [ ] **C** always wear a helmet
- [ ] **D** signal for the rider

Pillion passengers must sit astride the machine on a proper passenger seat and rear footrests should be fitted. They must wear a safety helmet which is correctly fastened.

## 807 Mark *one* answer
**Pillion passengers should**

- [ ] **A** give the rider directions
- [ ] **B** lean with the rider when going round bends
- [ ] **C** check the road behind for the rider
- [ ] **D** give arm signals for the rider

When riding with a pillion passenger, your motorcycle may feel unbalanced and the acceleration and braking distance may also be affected. Make sure your passenger knows they must lean with you while cornering. If they don't, they could cause the motorcycle to become unstable and difficult to control.

## 808 Mark *one* answer
**When you are going around a corner your pillion passenger should**

- [ ] **A** give arm signals for you
- [ ] **B** check behind for other vehicles
- [ ] **C** lean with you on bends
- [ ] **D** lean to one side to see ahead

A pillion passenger should not give signals or look round for you.

If your passenger has never been on a motorcycle before, make sure they know that they need to lean with you while going around bends.

## 809 Mark *one* answer
**Which of these may need to be adjusted when carrying a pillion passenger?**

☐ **A** Indicators
☐ **B** Exhaust
☐ **C** Fairing
☐ **D** Headlight

Your headlight must be properly adjusted to avoid dazzling other road users. You will probably need to do this when carrying a heavy load or the extra weight of a pillion passenger. You may also need to adjust suspension and tyre pressures.

## 810 Mark *one* answer
**You are towing a trailer with your motorcycle. You should remember that your**

☐ **A** stopping distance may increase
☐ **B** fuel consumption will improve
☐ **C** tyre grip will increase
☐ **D** stability will improve

When you tow a trailer remember that you must obey the relevant speed limits. Ensure that the trailer is hitched correctly and that any load in the trailer is secure. You should also bear in mind that your stopping distance may increase.

## 811 Mark *one* answer
**Heavy loads in a motorcycle top box may**

☐ **A** improve stability
☐ **B** cause low-speed wobble
☐ **C** cause a puncture
☐ **D** improve braking

Carrying heavy loads in your top box could make your motorcycle unstable because the weight is high up and at the very back of the machine. Take extra care.

## 812 Mark *one* answer
**Who is responsible for making sure that a motorcycle is not overloaded?**

☐ **A** The rider of the motorcycle
☐ **B** The owner of the items being carried
☐ **C** The licensing authority
☐ **D** The owner of the motorcycle

Correct loading is the responsibility of the rider. Overloading a motorcycle can seriously affect the control and handling. It could result in a crash with serious or even fatal consequences.

## 813 Mark *one* answer

**Before fitting a sidecar to a motorcycle you should**

- ☐ **A** have the wheels balanced
- ☐ **B** have the engine tuned
- ☐ **C** pass the extended bike test
- ☐ **D** check that the motorcycle is suitable

Make sure that the sidecar is fixed securely and properly aligned. If your motorcycle is registered on or after 1 August 1981 the sidecar must be fitted on the left-hand side of the motorcycle.

## 814 Mark *one* answer

**You are using throwover saddlebags. Why is it important to make sure they are evenly loaded?**

- ☐ **A** They will be uncomfortable for you to sit on
- ☐ **B** They will slow your motorcycle down
- ☐ **C** They could make your motorcycle unstable
- ☐ **D** They will be uncomfortable for a pillion passenger to sit on

Panniers or saddlebags should be loaded so that you carry about the same weight in each bag. Uneven loading could affect your balance, especially when cornering.

## 815 Mark *one* answer

**You are carrying a bulky tank bag. What could this affect?**

- ☐ **A** Your ability to steer
- ☐ **B** Your ability to accelerate
- ☐ **C** Your view ahead
- ☐ **D** Your insurance premium

If your tank bag is too bulky it could get in the way of your arms or restrict the movement of the handlebars.

## 816 Mark *one* answer          NI

**To carry a pillion passenger you must**

- ☐ **A** hold a full car licence
- ☐ **B** hold a full motorcycle licence
- ☐ **C** be over the age of 21
- ☐ **D** be over the age of 25

The law requires you to have a full licence for the category of motorcycle you are riding before you can carry a pillion passenger.

## 817 Mark *one* answer

**When carrying a heavy load on your luggage rack, you may need to adjust your**

- ☐ **A** carburettor
- ☐ **B** fuel tap
- ☐ **C** seating position
- ☐ **D** tyre pressures

The load will increase the overall weight that your motorcycle is carrying. You may need to adjust your tyre pressures according to the manufacturer's instructions to allow for this. You may also need to adjust your headlight beam alignment.

## 818 Mark *one* answer
**You are carrying a pillion passenger. When following other traffic, which of the following should you do?**

☐ **A** Keep to your normal following distance
☐ **B** Get your passenger to keep checking behind
☐ **C** Keep further back than you normally would
☐ **D** Get your passenger to signal for you

The extra weight of a passenger may increase your stopping distance. Allow for this when following another vehicle by increasing the separation distance.

## 819 Mark *one* answer
**You should only carry a child as a pillion passenger when**

☐ **A** they are over 14 years old
☐ **B** they are over 16 years old
☐ **C** they can reach the floor from the seat
☐ **D** they can reach the handholds and footrests

Any passenger you carry must be able to reach footrests and handholds properly to remain safe on your machine. Ensure they are wearing protective weatherproof kit and a properly fitting helmet.

## 820 Mark *one* answer
**You have fitted a sidecar to your motorcycle. You should make sure that the sidecar**

☐ **A** has a registration plate
☐ **B** is correctly aligned
☐ **C** has a waterproof cover
☐ **D** has a solid cover

If the sidecar is not correctly aligned to the mounting points it will result in the outfit being difficult to control and even dangerous.
   Riding with a sidecar attached requires a different technique to riding a solo motorcycle and you should keep your speed down while learning this skill.

## 821 Mark *one* answer
**You are riding a motorcycle and sidecar. The extra weight**

☐ **A** will allow you to corner more quickly
☐ **B** will allow you to brake later for hazards
☐ **C** may increase your stopping distance
☐ **D** will improve your fuel consumption

You will need to adapt your riding technique when riding a motorcycle fitted with a sidecar. The extra weight will affect the handling and may increase your overall stopping distance.

# 822 Mark *one* answer

**You are carrying a pillion passenger. To allow for the extra weight which of the following is most likely to need adjustment?**

- ☐ **A** Preload on the front forks
- ☐ **B** Preload on the rear shock absorber(s)
- ☐ **C** The balance of the rear wheel
- ☐ **D** The front and rear wheel alignment

When carrying a passenger or other extra weight, you may need to make adjustments, particularly to the rear shock absorber(s), tyre pressures and headlight alignment. Check your owner's handbook for details.

# 823 Mark *one* answer

**A trailer on a motorcycle must be no wider than**

- ☐ **A** 0.5 metres (1 foot 8 inches)
- ☐ **B** 1 metre (3 feet 3 inches)
- ☐ **C** 1.5 metres (4 feet 11 inches)
- ☐ **D** 2 metres (6 feet 6 inches)

When you're towing a trailer you must remember that you may not be able to filter through traffic. Don't forget that the trailer is there, especially when riding round bends and negotiating junctions.

# 824 Mark *one* answer

**You want to tow a trailer with your motorcycle. Which one applies?**

- ☐ **A** The motorcycle should be attached to a sidecar
- ☐ **B** The trailer should weigh more than the motorcycle
- ☐ **C** The trailer should be fitted with brakes
- ☐ **D** The trailer should NOT be more than 1 metre (3 feet 3 inches) wide

To tow a trailer behind a motorcycle you must have, a full motorcycle licence and a motorcycle with an engine larger than 125cc. Motorcycle trailers must not exceed 1 metre (3 feet 3 inches) in width.

# 825 Mark *one* answer

**You have a sidecar fitted to your motorcycle. What effect will it have?**

- ☐ **A** Reduce stability
- ☐ **B** Make steering lighter
- ☐ **C** Increase stopping distance
- ☐ **D** Increase fuel economy

If you want to fit a sidecar to your motorcycle make sure that your motorcycle is suitable to cope with the extra load. Make sure that the sidecar is fixed correctly and properly aligned. A sidecar will alter the handling considerably. Give yourself time to adjust to the different characteristics.

## 826 Mark *three* answers
**Which THREE must a learner motorcyclist under 21 NOT do?**

- ☐ **A** Ride a motorcycle with an engine capacity greater than 125cc
- ☐ **B** Pull a trailer
- ☐ **C** Carry a pillion passenger
- ☐ **D** Ride faster than 30mph
- ☐ **E** Use the right-hand lane on dual carriageways

Learner motorcyclists are not allowed to pull a trailer or carry a pillion passenger. In addition, if you are a learner motorcyclist under 21, you may not ride a motorcycle on the road with an engine capacity of more than 125cc.

## 827 Mark *one* answer
**Carrying a heavy load in your top box may**

- ☐ **A** cause high speed-weave
- ☐ **B** cause a puncture
- ☐ **C** use less fuel
- ☐ **D** improve stability

Carrying a heavy weight high up and at the very back of the motorcycle can make it unstable, especially when travelling at high speeds.

## 828 Mark *two* answers
**You want to tow a trailer behind your motorcycle. You should**

- ☐ **A** display a 'long vehicle' sign
- ☐ **B** fit a larger battery
- ☐ **C** have a full motorcycle licence
- ☐ **D** ensure that your engine is more than 125cc
- ☐ **E** ensure that your motorcycle has shaft drive

When you tow a trailer your stopping distance will be increased. Any load on the trailer must be secure and the trailer must be fitted to the motorcycle correctly. You must obey the lower speed limit restrictions that apply to vehicles with trailers. Any trailer towed by a motorcycle must be no wider than 1 metre. The laden weight should be no greater than 150kg or two-thirds of the kerbside weight of the motorcycle, whichever is less.

## 829 Mark *two* answers
**To carry a pillion passenger your motorcycle should be fitted with**

- ☐ **A** rear footrests
- ☐ **B** an engine of 250cc or over
- ☐ **C** a top box
- ☐ **D** a grab handle
- ☐ **E** a proper pillion seat

When carrying a pillion there are certain things they should NOT do. Before carrying a pillion tell them NOT to give hand signals, lean away from the rider when cornering, fidget or move around, put their feet down to try and support the machine when you stop, or wear long, loose items that might get caught in the rear wheel or drive chain.

## 830 Mark *three* answers
**Your motorcycle is fitted with a top box. It is unwise to carry a heavy load in the top box because it may**

☐ **A** reduce stability
☐ **B** improve stability
☐ **C** make turning easier
☐ **D** cause high-speed weave
☐ **E** cause low-speed wobble
☐ **F** increase fuel economy

Carrying a heavy weight high up and at the very back of the motorcycle can cause problems in maintaining control.

## 831 Mark *one* answer
**You hold a provisional motorcycle licence. Are you allowed to carry a pillion passenger?**

☐ **A** Only if the passenger holds a full licence
☐ **B** Not at any time
☐ **C** Not unless you are undergoing training
☐ **D** Only if the passenger is under 21

You are not allowed to carry a pillion passenger until you hold a full motorcycle licence. This allows you to gain riding experience. Even when you've passed, don't carry a passenger if you are not confident of being able to do so safely. You are responsible for their safety.

## 832 Mark *one* answer
**Overloading your motorcycle can seriously affect the**

☐ **A** gearbox
☐ **B** weather protection
☐ **C** handling
☐ **D** battery life

Any load will affect the handling of your motorcycle by changing its centre of gravity. Try to keep any load as low as possible. When using panniers spread the weight evenly. Avoid carrying heavy items in a top box, as this could make your steering dangerously light.

## 833 Mark *two* answers
**You are towing a small trailer on a busy three-lane motorway. All the lanes are open. You must**

☐ **A** not exceed 60mph
☐ **B** not overtake
☐ **C** have a stabiliser fitted
☐ **D** use only the left and centre lanes

You should be aware of the motorway regulations for vehicles towing trailers. These state that a vehicle towing a trailer must not
- use the right-hand lane of a three-lane motorway unless directed to do so, for example, at roadworks or due to a lane closure
- exceed 60mph.

# Glossary

**Accelerate**

To make the motorcycle move faster.

**Advanced stop lines**

A marked area on the road at traffic lights, which permits cyclists or buses to wait in front of other traffic.

**Adverse weather**

Bad weather that makes riding difficult or dangerous.

**Alert**

A state of mind in which you are quick to notice possible hazards.

**Anticipation**

Looking out for hazards and taking action before a problem starts.

**Anti-lock brakes (ABS)**

Brakes that stop the wheels locking so that you are less likely to skid on a slippery road.

**Aquaplane**

To slide out of control on a waterlogged road surface because a film of water has built up between your tyres and the road, and your tyres are unable to grip the road.

**Articulated vehicle**

A long vehicle that is divided into two or more sections connected by joints.

**Attitude**

The way you think or feel, which affects the way you drive. Especially, whether you are patient and polite, or impatient and aggressive.

**Awareness**

Taking notice of the road and traffic conditions around you at all times when you are riding.

**Black ice**

An invisible film of ice that forms over the road surface, creating very dangerous riding conditions.

**Blind spot**

The section of road behind you which you cannot see in your mirrors. You 'cover' your blind spot by looking over your shoulder before moving off, cornering or overtaking.

**Brake fade**

Loss of power to the brakes when you have been using them for a long time. For example, when riding down a steep hill. The brakes will overheat and not work properly.

**Braking distance**

The distance you must allow to slow the motorcycle in order to come to a stop.

**Brow**

The highest point of a hill.

**Built-up area**

A town, or place with lots of buildings.

**Carriageway**

One side of a road or motorway. A 'dual carriageway' has two lanes on each side of a central reservation.

**Catalytic converter**

A piece of equipment fitted in the exhaust system that changes harmful gases into less harmful ones.

**Centre stand**

An alternative to a side stand, which gives the motorcycle more stability when parked. Also useful for carrying out maintenance checks.

**Chicane**

A road sign designed to warn road users to slow down because a sharp double bend is coming up on the road ahead.

**Choke**

Often manual on a motorcycle.

**Clearway**

A road where no stopping is allowed at any time. The sign for a clearway is a red cross in a red circle on a blue background.

**Commentary riding**

Talking to yourself about what you see on the road ahead and what action you are going to take – an aid to concentration.

**Comprehensive insurance**

A motorcycle insurance policy that pays for repairs even if you cause an accident.

**Concentration**

Keeping all your attention on your riding.

**Conditions**

How good or bad the road surface is, volume of traffic on the road, and what the weather is like.

**Congestion**

Heavy traffic that makes it difficult to get to where you want to go.

**Consideration**

Thinking about other road users and not just yourself. For example, letting another driver go first at a junction, or stopping at a zebra crossing to let pedestrians cross over.

**Compulsory Basic Training (CBT)**

A one-day training course of predominantly practical training that, when successfully completed, entitles the CBT certificate holder to ride a motorcycle up to 125cc (50cc for 16-year-olds) on the road with 'L' Plates. The certificate is valid for two years but riders are not allowed to carry pillion passengers or ride on motorways.

**Contraflow**

When traffic on a motorway follows signs to move to the opposite carriageway for a short distance because of roadworks. (During a contraflow, there is traffic driving in both directions on the same side of the motorway.)

**Defensive riding**

Riding in such a way as to create a safe zone around yourself. Anticipating hazards and the actions of other drivers and keeping yourself safe while riding.

**Disqualified**

Stopped from doing something (e.g. riding) by law, because you have broken the law.

**Distraction**

Anything that stops you concentrating on your riding and the other road users around you.

**Document**

An official paper or card, for example your motorcycle licence.

**Drive chain**

The chain between the engine and the rear wheel. A poorly adjusted drive chain can cause unpredictable acceleration, fall off or even snap causing injury to the rider or a road accident.

**Dual carriageway**

One side of a road or motorway, with two lanes on each side of a central reservation.

**Engine braking – see also gears**

Using the low gears to keep your speed down. For example, when you are riding down a steep hill and you want to stop the motorcycle running away. Using the gears instead of braking will help to prevent brake fade.

**Engine cut-out switch**

A switch, which is designed to stop the engine in an emergency, for example after a road accident, to prevent fire.

**Environment**

The world around us and the air we breathe.

**Exceed**

Go higher than an upper limit.

**Exhaust emissions**

Gases that come out of the exhaust pipe to form part of the outside air.

**Field of vision**

How far you can see in front and around you when you are riding.

**Filler cap**

Provides access to the motorcycle's fuel tank, for filling up with petrol or diesel.

**Fog lights**

Extra bright rear (and sometimes front) lights which may be switched on in conditions of very poor visibility. You must remember to switch them off when visibility improves, as they can dazzle and distract other road users.

**Ford**

A place in a stream or river which is shallow enough to ride across with care.

**Frustration**

Feeling annoyed because you cannot ride as fast as you want to because of other drivers or heavy traffic on the road.

**Fuel consumption**

The amount of fuel that your motorcycle uses. Different motorcycles have different rates of consumption. Increased fuel consumption means using more fuel. Decreased fuel consumption means using less fuel.

**Fuel gauge**

A display or dial on the instrument panel that tells you how much fuel (petrol) you have left.

**Gantry**

An overhead platform like a high narrow bridge that displays electric signs on a motorway.

**Gears**

Control the speed of the engine in relation to the motorcycle's speed. In a low gear (such as first or second) the engine runs more slowly. In a high gear (such as fourth or fifth), it runs more quickly. Putting the motorcycle into a lower gear as you drive can create the effect of engine braking – forcing the engine to run more slowly.

**Handling**

How well your motorcycle moves or responds when you steer or brake.

**Harass**

To ride in away that makes other road users afraid.

**Hard shoulder**

The single lane to the left of the inside lane on a motorway, which is for emergency use only. You should not ride on the hard shoulder except in an emergency, or when there are signs telling you to use the hard shoulder because of roadworks.

**Harsh braking (or harsh acceleration)**

Using the brake or accelerator too hard so as to cause wear on the engine.

**Hazard warning lights**

Flashing amber lights which warn you that a vehicle has broken down. Your hazard warning lights should only be used to warn other traffic that you have broken down. On a motorway you can use them to warn other road users behind of a hazard ahead.

**High-sided vehicle**

A van or truck with tall sides, or a tall trailer such as a caravan or horse-box, that is at risk of being blown off-course in strong winds.

**The Highway Code**

Essential reading for everyone, not just learners, the Highway Code sets out the rules and regulations for all road-users.

**Impatient**

Not wanting to wait for pedestrians and other road users.

**Indicator**

Often referred to as a 'signal' in motorcycling.

**Inflate**

To blow up – to put air in your tyres until they are at the right pressures.

**Instrument panel**

The motorcycle's electrical controls and gauges.

**Intimidate**

To make someone feel afraid.

**Involved**

Being part of something. For example, being one of the riders in an accident.

**Jump leads**

A pair of thick electric cables with clips at either end. You use it to charge a flat battery by connecting it to the live battery in another vehicle.

**Junction**

A place where two or more roads join.

**Liability**

Being legally responsible.

**Lifesaver**

Called a 'lifesaver' for good reason, this is the final rearward glance that a rider should give before making any manoeuvre. Forgetting to give a 'lifesaver' could cause you to lose yours.

**Manoeuvre**

Using the controls to make your motorcycle move in a particular direction. For example cornering or parking.

**Maximum**

Maximum means greatest so, the 'maximum speed' is the highest speed allowed.

**Minimum**

The smallest possible.

**Mobility**

The ability to move around easily.

**Monotonous**

Boring, for example, a long stretch of motorway with no variety and nothing interesting to see.

**MOT**

The test that proves your motorcycle is safe to drive. Your MOT certificate is one of the important documents for your motorcycle.

**Motorway**

A fast road that has two or more lanes on each side and a hard shoulder. Riders must join or leave it on the left, via a motorway junction. Many kinds of slower vehicles – such as bicycles – are not allowed on motorways.

**Multiple-choice questions**

Questions with several possible answers where you have to try to choose the right one/s.

**Observation**

The ability to notice important information, such as hazards developing ahead. The term 'observation' is often used in addition to 'lifesaver'.

**Obstruct**

To get in the way of another road user.

**Octagonal**

Having eight sides.

**Oil level**

The amount of oil that is in the engine. The oil level should be checked as part of your regular maintenance routine, and the oil topped up or replaced as necessary. The engine cannot run effectively and may be damaged if the oil level is too low.

**Pedestrian**

A person walking.

**Pegasus crossing**

An unusual kind of crossing. It has a button high up for horse riders to push. (Pegasus was a flying horse in Greek legend.)

**Pelican crossing**

A crossing with traffic lights that pedestrians can use by pushing a button. Vehicles must give way to pedestrians on the crossing while the amber light is flashing. You must give pedestrians enough time to get to the other side of the road.

**Perception**

Seeing or noticing (as in Hazard Perception).

**Peripheral vision**

The area around the edges of your field of vision in which you can see movement but not details. Wearing a motorcycle helmet diminishes a motorcyclist's peripheral vision and means that riders need to use extremely careful observation while riding.

**Positive attitude**

Being sensible and obeying the law when you ride.

**Priority**

The vehicle or other road user that is allowed by law to go first is the one that has priority.

**Protective clothing**

Essential when riding, because it protects the rider from the weather, objects thrown up from the road or in case of an accident.

**Provisional licence**

A first motorcycle or car licence. All learners must get one before they start having lessons.

**Puffin crossing**

A type of pedestrian crossing that does not have a flashing amber light phase.

**Reaction time**

The amount of time it takes you to see a hazard and decide what to do about it.

**Red route**

You see these in London and some other cities. Double red lines at the edge of the road tell you that you must not stop or park there at any time. Single red lines have notices with times when you must not stop or park. Some red routes have marked bays for either parking or loading at certain times.

**Residential areas**

Areas of housing where people live. The speed limit is 30mph or sometimes 20mph.

**Road hump**

A low bump built across the road to slow vehicles down. Also called 'sleeping policemen'.

**Road surface**

The type and quality of the road that you are riding on. Slippery road surfaces, such as loose chippings, leaves and, even road markings, can make the road surface hazardous for riders, particularly in wet weather.

**Rumble strips**

Raised strips across the road near a roundabout or junction that change the sound the tyres make on the road surface, warning riders to slow down. They are also used on motorways to separate the main carriageway from the hard shoulder.

**Safety margin**

The amount of space you need to leave between your motorcycle and the vehicle in front so that you are not in danger of crashing into it if the driver slows down suddenly or stops. Safety margins have to be longer in wet or icy conditions.

**Separation distance**

The amount of space you need to leave between your motorcycle and the vehicle in front so that you are not in danger of crashing into it if the driver slows down suddenly or stops. The separation distance must be longer in wet or icy conditions.

**Shoulder check**

A term often used instead of 'lifesaver'.

**Side stand**

A metal support that enables you to stand your motorcycle when you want, for example, leave it parked. Leaving the side stand down when riding is extremely dangerous and could cause you to have a serious accident, particularly when cornering.

**Single carriageway**

Generally, a road with one lane in each direction.

**Skid**

When the tyres fail to grip the surface of the road, the subsequent loss of control of the motorcycle's movement is called a skid. Usually caused by harsh or fierce braking, steering or acceleration.

**Slow-riding**

Riding a motorcycle in a controlled manner at a walking pace using the throttle, clutch and rear brake.

**Snaking**

Moving from side to side. This sometimes happens with trailers when they are being towed too fast, or they are not properly loaded.

**Staggered junction**

Where you drive across another road. Instead of going straight across, you have to go a bit to the right or left.

**Steering**

Control of the direction of the motorcycle. May be affected by road surface condition and the weather.

**Sterile**

Clean and free from bacteria.

**Stopping distance**

The time it takes for you to stop your motorcycle – made up of 'thinking distance' and 'braking distance'.

**Tailgating**

Riding too closely behind another vehicle – either to harass the driver in front or to help you see in thick fog.

**Tax disc**

The disc you display to show that you have taxed your vehicle (see Vehicle Excise Duty, below).

**Thinking distance**

The time it takes you to notice something and take the right action. You need to add thinking distance to your braking distance to make up your total stopping distance.

**Third party insurance**

An insurance policy that insures you against any claim by passengers or other persons for damage or injury to their person or property.

**Toucan crossing**

A type of pedestrian crossing that does not have a flashing amber light phase, and cyclists are allowed to ride across.

**Tow**

To pull something behind your motorcycle, possibly a small trailer.

**Traction Control System (TCS)**

A safety system that is fitted to some motorcycles that helps prevent rear-wheel spin on slippery road surfaces.

**Traffic-calming measures**

Speed humps, chicanes and other devices placed in roads to slow traffic down.

**Tram**

A public transport vehicle which moves along the streets on fixed rails, usually electrically powered by overhead lines.

**Tread depth**

The depth of the grooves in a motorcycle's tyres that help them grip the road surface. The grooves must all be at least 1mm deep.

**Turbulence**

Strong movement of air. For example, when a large vehicle passes a much smaller one.

**Two-second rule**

In normal riding, the ideal minimum distance between you and the vehicle in front can be timed using the 'two-second' rule. As the vehicle in front passes a fixed object (such as a signpost), say to yourself 'Only a fool breaks the two-second rule'. It takes two seconds to say it. If you have passed the same object before you finish, you are too close – pull back.

**Tyre pressures**

The amount of air which must be pumped into a tyre in order for it to be correctly inflated.

**Vehicle Excise Duty**

The tax you pay for your motorcycle so that you may drive it on public roads.

**Vehicle Registration Document**

A record of details about a vehicle and its owner.

**Vehicle watch scheme**

A system for identifying vehicles that may have been stolen.

**Vulnerable**

At risk of harm or injury.

**Waiting restrictions**

Times when you may not park or load your motorcycle in a particular area.

**Wheel alignment**

To ensure smooth rotation at all speeds, the wheels of your motorcycle need to be aligned correctly. Poor alignment can cause wheel wobble and make riding and, in particular, cornering dangerous.

**Wheel spin**

When the motorcycle's wheels spin round out of control with no grip on the road surface.

**Zebra crossing**

A pedestrian crossing without traffic lights. It has an orange light, and is marked by black and white stripes on the road. Riders must stop for pedestrians to cross.

# Answers to Questions

## Section 1 – Alertness

| | | | | | | | | |
|---|---|---|---|---|---|---|---|---|
| 1 B | 2 B | 3 D | 4 A | 5 C | 6 B | 7 C | 8 D | 9 D |
| 10 C | 11 A | 12 C | 13 D | 14 D | 15 A | 16 A | 17 B | 18 C |
| 19 AE | 20 C | 21 C | 22 D | 23 A | 24 C | 25 D | 26 D | 27 C |
| 28 C | 29 BDF | 30 D | 31 C | 32 C | 33 C | 34 C | 35 B | 36 C |
| 37 B | 38 A | | | | | | | |

## Section 2 – Attitude

| | | | | | | | | |
|---|---|---|---|---|---|---|---|---|
| 39 B | 40 D | 41 C | 42 B | 43 C | 44 BD | 45 C | 46 D | 47 A |
| 48 C | 49 D | 50 D | 51 B | 52 BCD | 53 ABE | 54 A | 55 D | 56 B |
| 57 A | 58 B | 59 A | 60 A | 61 C | 62 A | 63 D | 64 D | 65 D |
| 66 A | 67 B | 68 C | 69 B | 70 A | 71 B | | | |

## Section 3 – Safety and Your Motorcycle

| | | | | | | | | |
|---|---|---|---|---|---|---|---|---|
| 72 D | 73 C | 74 A | 75 B | 76 B | 77 C | 78 D | 79 C | 80 B |
| 81 A | 82 ABC | 83 D | 84 BE | 85 D | 86 D | 87 A | 88 B | 89 D |
| 90 B | 91 D | 92 B | 93 B | 94 BC | 95 C | 96 D | 97 C | 98 A |
| 99 A | 100 C | 101 D | 102 B | 103 A | 104 C | 105 D | 106 A | 107 C |
| 108 D | 109 C | 110 D | 111 B | 112 C | 113 C | 114 B | 115 C | 116 D |
| 117 A | 118 A | 119 A | 120 B | 121 A | 122 A | 123 ACD | 124 AE | 125 C |
| 126 A | 127 A | 128 BCDE | 129 AD | 130 CD | 131 A | 132 B | 133 B | 134 D |
| 135 D | 136 D | 137 AB | 138 AB | 139 C | 140 ACF | 141 C | 142 B | 143 D |
| 144 C | 145 D | 146 D | 147 D | 148 A | 149 AE | 150 D | 151 B | 152 B |
| 153 ABF | 154 BEF | 155 D | 156 A | 157 A | 158 B | 159 C | 160 D | 161 A |
| 162 B | 163 C | 164 D | 165 A | 166 B | 167 A | 168 B | 169 B | 170 B |

## Section 4 – Safety Margins

| | | | | | | | | |
|---|---|---|---|---|---|---|---|---|
| 171 C | 172 D | 173 B | 174 A | 175 A | 176 C | 177 BDE | 178 D | 179 BC |
| 180 D | 181 D | 182 D | 183 BD | 184 B | 185 A | 186 B | 187 AB | 188 A |
| 189 ABDF | 190 AB | 191 D | 192 D | 193 A | 194 C | 195 A | 196 CD | 197 B |
| 198 D | 199 BE | 200 D | 201 C | 202 D | 203 D | 204 D | 205 D | 206 A |
| 207 B | 208 BC | 209 B | 210 D | 211 C | 212 C | 213 B | 214 B | 215 C |
| 216 A | 217 C | 218 A | 219 D | 220 ACD | | | | |

# Answers to Questions

| | | | | | | | | |
|---|---|---|---|---|---|---|---|---|
| 221 AD | 222 D | 223 D | 224 ABC | 225 B | 226 ACE | 227 D | 228 A | 229 B |
| 230 B | 231 A | 232 D | 233 A | 234 C | 235 AB | 236 D | 237 B | 238 D |
| 239 CD | 240 C | 241 A | 242 D | 243 ACE | 244 C | 245 C | 246 D | 247 B |
| 248 A | 249 A | 250 A | 251 C | 252 C | 253 B | 254 A | 255 C | 256 D |
| 257 B | 258 B | 259 C | 260 A | 261 D | 262 D | 263 C | 264 B | 265 BF |
| 266 B | 267 A | 268 A | 269 AE | 270 C | 271 A | 272 D | 273 B | 274 CD |
| 275 ACE | 276 ABD | | | | | | | |

## Section 6 – Vulnerable Road Users

| | | | | | | | | |
|---|---|---|---|---|---|---|---|---|
| 277 D | 278 ABC | 279 A | 280 A | 281 A | 282 D | 283 B | 284 AE | 285 B |
| 286 A | 287 AD | 288 B | 289 C | 290 C | 291 D | 292 D | 293 C | 294 C |
| 295 B | 296 D | 297 D | 298 C | 299 D | 300 A | 301 D | 302 D | 303 B |
| 304 D | 305 D | 306 AC | 307 C | 308 C | 309 A | 310 D | 311 C | 312 D |
| 313 ABC | 314 C | 315 AC | 316 D | 317 A | 318 D | 319 C | 320 C | 321 D |
| 322 D | 323 B | 324 A | 325 C | 326 D | 327 C | 328 C | 329 A | 330 D |
| 331 A | 332 A | 333 B | 334 B | 335 A | 336 A | 337 C | 338 B | 339 D |
| 340 A | 341 D | 342 D | 343 D | 344 A | 345 C | 346 ABD | 347 B | 348 D |

## Section 7 – Other Types of Vehicle

| | | | | | | | | |
|---|---|---|---|---|---|---|---|---|
| 349 C | 350 AB | 351 A | 352 A | 353 B | 354 B | 355 D | 356 B | 357 BC |
| 358 A | 359 C | 360 B | 361 D | 362 B | 363 D | 364 D | 365 A | 366 D |
| 367 A | 368 A | 369 A | | | | | | |

## Section 8 – Motorcycle Handling

| | | | | | | | | |
|---|---|---|---|---|---|---|---|---|
| 370 AD | 371 AB | 372 A | 373 BDE | 374 BE | 375 A | 376 CE | 377 D | 378 C |
| 379 B | 380 C | 381 A | 382 C | 383 C | 384 A | 385 ABC | 386 C | 387 C |
| 388 D | 389 D | 390 ABD | 391 D | 392 A | 393 A | 394 D | 395 A | 396 D |
| 397 ACDE | 398 B | 399 B | 400 D | 401 D | 402 C | 403 A | 404 A | 405 C |
| 406 B | 407 D | 408 D | 409 A | 410 ACE | 411 A | 412 CD | 413 D | 414 A |
| 415 C | 416 C | 417 DE | 418 C | 419 D | 420 D | 421 C | 422 BDF | 423 C |
| 424 B | 425 B | 426 D | | | | | | |

## Section 9 – Motorway Rules

| | | | | | | | | |
|---|---|---|---|---|---|---|---|---|
| 427 A | 428 B | 429 A | 430 A | 431 A | 432 C | 433 D | 434 C | 435 D |
| 436 D | 437 D | 438 D | 439 A | 440 C | 441 C | 442 C | 443 A | 444 C |
| 445 C | 446 C | 447 C | 448 C | 449 C | 450 B | 451 B | 452 A | 453 B |
| 454 D | 455 C | 456 ADEF | 457 ADEF | 458 D | 459 B | 460 A | 461 A | 462 C |
| 463 B | 464 B | 465 D | 466 A | 467 A | 468 B | 469 D | 470 D | 471 B |
| 472 D | 473 D | 474 C | 475 D | 476 C | 477 D | 478 A | 479 CDF | 480 D |
| 481 C | 482 B | 483 D | 484 B | 485 D | 486 B | 487 D | | |

## Section 10 – Rules of the Road

| | | | | | | | | |
|---|---|---|---|---|---|---|---|---|
| 488 A | 489 DE | 490 B | 491 D | 492 D | 493 D | 494 A | 495 ACF | 496 D |
| 497 B | 498 B | 499 C | 500 ABC | 501 C | 502 D | 503 B | 504 A | 505 C |
| 506 D | 507 ADF | 508 A | 509 B | 510 A | 511 B | 512 A | 513 D | 514 A |
| 515 D | 516 C | 517 A | 518 ACE | 519 C | 520 D | 521 BD | 522 B | 523 A |
| 524 C | 525 A | 526 B | 527 CDE | 528 B | 529 AE | 530 B | 531 A | 532 ABD |
| 533 A | 534 A | 535 D | 536 A | 537 AD | 538 D | 539 B | 540 C | 541 B |
| 542 B | 543 B | 544 C | 545 D | | | | | |

## Section 11 – Road and Traffic Signs

| | | | | | | | | |
|---|---|---|---|---|---|---|---|---|
| 546 C | 547 B | 548 A | 549 D | 550 A | 551 C | 552 B | 553 A | 554 B |
| 555 D | 556 D | 557 A | 558 A | 559 B | 560 A | 561 D | 562 B | 563 D |
| 564 D | 565 D | 566 A | 567 C | 568 B | 569 D | 570 C | 571 B | 572 A |
| 573 B | 574 B | 575 C | 576 C | 577 A | 578 C | 579 B | 580 C | 581 D |
| 582 D | 583 C | 584 C | 585 D | 586 A | 587 D | 588 D | 589 B | 590 A |
| 591 A | 592 A | 593 B | 594 B | 595 A | 596 D | 597 ACEF | 598 C | 599 A |
| 600 B | 601 C | 602 B | 603 D | 604 A | 605 A | 606 C | 607 D | 608 A |
| 609 C | 610 B | 611 D | 612 B | 613 B | 614 C | 615 C | 616 D | 617 C |
| 618 B | 619 C | 620 D | 621 B | 622 A | 623 A | 624 C | 625 BDF | 626 A |
| 627 C | 628 C | 629 B | 630 A | 631 C | 632 A | 633 A | 634 D | 635 D |
| 636 B | 637 A | 638 D | 639 C | 640 D | 641 C | 642 B | 643 C | 644 C |
| 645 A | 646 B | 647 D | 648 B | 649 B | 650 A | 651 D | 652 A | 653 B |
| 654 B | 655 D | 656 C | 657 B | 658 A | 659 B | 660 C | 661 A | 662 B |
| 663 A | 664 C | 665 B | 666 B | 667 A | 668 C | 669 A | 670 B | 671 B |
| 672 B | 673 A | 674 C | 675 A | 676 C | 677 B | 678 D | 679 C | 680 B |
| 681 C | 682 A | 683 C | 684 A | 685 C | 686 B | 687 C | 688 A | 689 B |
| 690 A | 691 A | 692 C | 693 D | 694 B | 695 B | 696 B | 697 B | 698 D |
| 699 A | 700 B | | | | | | | |

# Answers to Questions

## Section 12 – Documents

| | | | | | | | | |
|---|---|---|---|---|---|---|---|---|
| 701 ADF | 702 C | 703 C | 704 B | 705 B | 706 ABF | 707 BCE | 708 BD | 709 C |
| 710 B | 711 A | 712 C | 713 ABE | 714 BE | 715 BDE | 716 A | 717 C | 718 BCE |
| 719 B | 720 C | 721 C | 722 D | 723 D | 724 C | 725 B | 726 BE | 727 A |
| 728 C | 729 C | 730 B | 731 C | 732 D | 733 A | 734 C | 735 D | 736 C |
| 737 ABD | 738 A | 739 B | 740 A | 741 B | | | | |

## Section 13 – Incidents, Accidents and Emergencies

| | | | | | | | | |
|---|---|---|---|---|---|---|---|---|
| 742 B | 743 A | 744 B | 745 ADE | 746 B | 747 D | 748 A | 749 C | 750 A |
| 751 ABCE | 752 A | 753 AB | 754 A | 755 C | 756 B | 757 D | 758 B | 759 B |
| 760 D | 761 B | 762 D | 763 B | 764 D | 765 B | 766 A | 767 C | 768 B |
| 769 BD | 770 A | 771 ABE | 772 A | 773 ACF | 774 A | 775 ABD | 776 ACE | 777 DEF |
| 778 ABE | 779 ACF | 780 C | 781 BC | 782 A | 783 B | 784 B | 785 BDE | 786 C |
| 787 D | 788 CD | 789 C | 790 B | 791 D | 792 B | 793 BDE | 794 B | 795 D |
| 796 B | 797 B | 798 AE | 799 ACDE | 800 B | | | | |

## Section 14 – Motorcycle Loading

| | | | | | | | | |
|---|---|---|---|---|---|---|---|---|
| 801 A | 802 AD | 803 ACD | 804 D | 805 A | 806 C | 807 B | 808 C | 809 D |
| 810 A | 811 B | 812 A | 813 D | 814 C | 815 A | 816 B | 817 D | 818 C |
| 819 D | 820 B | 821 C | 822 B | 823 B | 824 D | 825 C | 826 ABC | 827 A |
| 828 CD | 829 AE | 830 ADE | 831 B | 832 C | 833 AD | | | |